The Single Market Review

IMPACT ON SERVICES

INSURANCE

The Single Market Review series

Results of the business survey

EUROPEAN COMMISSION

The Single Market Review

IMPACT ON SERVICES

INSURANCE

The Single Market Review

SUBSERIES II: VOLUME 1

OFFICE FOR OFFICIAL PUBLICATIONS
OF THE EUROPEAN COMMUNITIES

KOGAN PAGE . EARTHSCAN

This report is part of a series of 39 studies commissioned from independent consultants in the context of a major review of the Single Market. The 1996 Single Market Review responds to a 1992 Council of Ministers Resolution calling on the European Commission to present an overall analysis of the effectiveness of measures taken in creating the Single Market. This review, which assesses the progress made in implementing the Single Market Programme, was coordinated by the Directorate-General 'Internal Market and Financial Services' (DG XV) and the Directorate-General 'Economic and Financial Affairs' (DG II) of the European Commission.

This document was prepared for the European Commission

by

CEGOS SA

It does not, however, express the Commission's official views. Whilst every reasonable effort has been made to provide accurate information in regard to the subject matter covered, the Consultants are not responsible for any remaining errors. All recommendations are made by the Consultants for the purpose of discussion. Neither the Commission nor the Consultants accept liability for the consequences of actions taken on the basis of the information contained herein.

The European Commission would like to express thanks to the external experts and representatives of firms and industry bodies for their contribution to the 1996 Single Market Review, and to this report in particular.

Office for Official Publications of the European Communities
2 rue Mercier, L-2985 Luxembourg
ISBN 92-827-8777-X   Catalogue number: C1-68-96-001-EN-C

Kogan Page . Earthscan
120 Pentonville Road, London N1 9JN
ISBN 0 7494 2313 7

Table of contents

List of tables

List of figures

List of abbreviations

AGF	Assurances Générales de France
BIPAR	Bureau International des Producteurs d'Assurance et de Réassurance
BNP	Banque Nationale de Paris
CAPA	Comité d'Action pour la Productivité dans l'Assurance
CEA	Comité européen des assurances
ECJ	European Court of Justice
ECU	European currency unit
EEA	European Economic Area
EMU	Economic and Monetary Union
EU	European Union
EUR-12	total of EC Member States before 1 January 1995
EUR-15	total of current Member States
FOS	free provision of services
FPS	freedom to provide services
GDP	gross domestic product
ING	Internationale Nederlanden Groep
MAT	marine, aviation and transport
OECD	Organization for Economic Cooperation and Development
PI	professional indemnity
UAP	Union des Assurances de Paris
SIM	single insurance market
SMP	single market programme

1. Summary

1.1. General aspects

The aim of this study is to examine the impact of the measures taken by the Community to create a true single insurance market (SIM) in the insurance sector. More specifically, the report seeks to:

- identify the EU measures which have had an impact on insurance business cross-border transactions;
- assess the nature and scale of the impact of these measures on this sector;
- identify the remaining obstacles to cross-border transactions;
- identify the way in which the business undertakings of the sector have adapted to this new environment; and
- assess the extent to which the completion of the single market has contributed to the performance of the sector and to making Community insurance more competitive.

The results of the study should be interpreted with some caution since they are conditioned by at least three important drawbacks: the short period since the start of the SIM on 1 July 1994, the absence of sufficiently reliable and representative data and the impact of other important factors (economic cycle, technological changes, financial innovation, increased dis-intermediation and globalization). Separating all these interacting influences from each other and identifying the sole, intrinsic impact of the SIM programme is very difficult.

Nevertheless, by way of a general conclusion it is evident from the study that neither economic operators nor consumers have yet had the full benefits and advantages of the SIM. Although there are certain signs of a more competitive insurance environment – notably in the areas of large industrial risks and driven mainly by the abolition of prior control of premiums and policy conditions – the study identifies substantial barriers to the effectiveness of SIM in the area of personal or mass risks, in particular concerning cross-border restrictions on the marketing of financial services, and points to regulatory/technical barriers with regard to conditions for sales.

1.2. Period of reference

The reference period of the study is from 1989 to 1995 (although certain sources date from 1996). It is often said that in view of the fact that Member States were allowed until 1 July 1994 to implement the single market legislation in the area of insurance, it is really too early yet to hope to be able to establish the real effects of economic integration in this area. However, this is only partly true. In fact, the main building blocks of the single market in insurance were put in place in three successive stages during the period of reference:

(a) The first stage is represented by the adoption of the Second Non-life Directive (88/357/EEC) on 22 June 1988 (to be implemented by 1 July 1990) which laid down fairly simple procedures of notification to the host country for the free provision of services cross-border under home country control. These deregulatory measures concerned only certain kinds of risk, the so-called large risks: for example marine, aviation, transport, credit and surety insurance. The size (EUR-12) is just under 20% of total non-life premiums (1992 figures) or just over ECU 42 million.

(b)   The second stage is represented by the adoption of the Motor Services Directive in November 1990 (to be implemented by December 1992) which laid down the framework for the free provision of cross-border services for the biggest non-life branch of business motor vehicle liability. The estimated worth of the *total* motor insurance branch, i.e. comprehensive cover and liability, is roughly 33% of all non-life business (1993 figure) worth about ECU 215 million.

(c)   The third stage is represented by the adoption of the Third Life (92/49/EEC)and Non-life (92/96/EEC) Directives in 1992 (to be implemented by 1 January and 1 July 1994) which introduced the concept of the single licence, home country control and abolition of prior control of premia and policy conditions for *all* insurance risks and all policyholders.

The conceptual framework of the present report is to seek to measure (evaluate and quantify) the effectiveness of the EU's insurance legislation and its impact on the single market insurance sector of the Community. The main parameters selected are the following:

(a)   changes in the market access resulting from the single market programme (SMP);
(b)   cross-border activities of EU insurance companies;
(c)   changes in modes of cross-border cooperation, identification of upstream/downstream linkages (professional reinsurance, distribution of insurance products through brokers and agents, and other points of sale);
(d)   changes in investment patterns;
(e)   changes in market concentration and competitiveness;
(f)   changes in productivity;
(g)   changes in international competitiveness;
(h)   evolution of price;
(i)   contribution to the environment;
(j)   single market impact on the cost of insurers; and
(k)   single market impact on the strategies of insurers.

1.3.   Changes in market access

Concerning the changes in the *modes of access*, the study shows that over the reference period freedom to provide services was practised by only a small number of highly targeted undertakings (life or large risks), that the number of branches has decreased but, on the other hand, that the undertakings have continued to develop through subsidiaries.

For their part, the case studies confirm the trends listed above: low levels of development of the 'new facilities' (freedom to provide services or branches) compared to the traditional means (subsidiaries). It can therefore be considered that during the reference period there has been little change in the choice of modes of access to the market, except to a limited degree for certain very precise segments: up-market life products, large risks and group contingency contracts.

The reasons why economic operators still hesitate to take advantage of the new means of accessing new markets offered by the single market legislation can be broken down into three main categories:

(a)   Regulatory obstacles pertaining to the legal framework laid down by EU single market legislation – the key obstacle stems from the introduction of the principle of the 'general good' in the single market legislation. Incorporating into the EU Framework Directives a highly complex legal concept, developed by the European Court of Justice, which is continually undergoing revisions as the Court faces new challenges and develops new case law, amounts to introducing a moving target for economic operators. The basic principle underlying the single market is that insurers should be free to market their full range of products throughout the EU, subject to limitations only in those cases where there has been no coordination at Community level and where the insurer is proven to be acting in contravention of substantial public interests. But this has been overused by certain Member States who have made the exception the rule. As a consequence, the 'general good' concept has become a legal minefield where only those with almost unlimited recourse to legal advice dare enter: the concept of 'general good' has itself become an obstacle to liberalization and a single insurance market.

(b) Regulatory obstacles pertaining to still unharmonized aspects of carrying out insurance operations within the EU – the two main obstacles are the lack of harmonization in the fields of contract law and taxation. Perversely, in the field of taxation, recent jurisprudence has effectively removed legal uncertainty as to the rights of individuals to deduct pension and insurance contributions from their taxable income, irrespective of where the providers are established, leaving the field open for increased cross-border activities. But case law cannot be a substitute for harmonized Community-wide rules. In the field of contract law, the complexity of the rules on conflict of law adopted by the single market directives to compensate for the absence of harmonization of insurance contract law makes the operation of insurance under the single licence very difficult, costly and legally intricate. This complexity acts as an effective barrier to marketing insurance across the Community on the basis of one single 'Euro-policy'.

(c) Regulatory obstacles caused by incorrect implementation of the single market legislation. A large scale project like that of the single market in insurance needs more time for Member States and the Commission to identify and remove minor problems and to agree in practical terms on how to apply the new legislation. In those areas where clear infringements have appeared, the Commission needs time to ensure the correct application, of sometimes highly complex new rules, by Member States. It is obliged to abide by the sometimes unnecessarily complex and slow procedures for dealing with recalcitrant Member States. However, the results of the Commission's efforts in this area are beginning to show: the Commission Communication on Freedom to Provide Services and the General Good in the Insurance Sector was published in 1997. This will no doubt be instrumental in clarifying some of the problems considered by the insurance industry to be obstacles to the smooth functioning of the single market in insurance, such as the right of insurance undertakings throughout the EU to carry out capital redemption operations, the language of insurance contracts and uniform bonus/malus systems.

1.4. Changes in upstream/downstream modes of cooperation

During the reference period, upstream and downstream partnership agreements between insurers have developed: in the sample of 100 undertakings, they now affect 10% of the sample and the same is true for four out of five of the case study undertakings. This movement affects large undertakings more (seven out of ten), but increasingly small undertakings are also involved. It affects the life sector more than non-life business.

Secondary sources show that the distribution of insurance products in Europe has been subject to severe competitive pressure between traditional and new channels in recent years. The

Secondary sources show that the distribution of insurance products in Europe has been subject to severe competitive pressure between traditional and new channels in recent years. The present position, measured by the gross written premium income, represents a significant change from the beginning of the decade, most notably in the rise of bancassurance, including the sale of insurance products through bank branches and, more recently, telephone sales.[1] Both channels have acted to put pressure on brokers, tied agents and other intermediaries. Direct mail and telephone sales are not expected to change significantly the predominance of 'traditional' channels of distribution-tied agents, brokers and company employees. However, insurance companies are redefining their strategies in order to meet the increased competition, and increasingly perceive their choice of distribution strategy to be the most important driver of profitability. The main factor driving this shift is the emergence of new technologies, but the implementation of EU Directives is also seen as having had a major effect, particularly on the distribution of long-term insurance products in Europe.

The above developments in the battle to maintain or increase market share explain the surge of interest within the insurance and insurance distribution community in the EU for doing away with perceived regulatory obstacles to the cross-border intermediation of insurance products and services. Such obstacles stem mainly from three sources:

(a) the diversity of national practices with regard to regulation which lays down requirements for the qualifications of intermediaries, i.e. requirements of good repute, professional competence, professional indemnity cover and other financial guarantees;

(b) the diversity of Member States' consumer guarantees in the area of cross-border intermediation, i.e. requirements on registration, sanctions and disclosure;

(c) the lack of harmonized interpretation of the demarcation between the concepts of freedom of establishment and the freedom to provide services.

1.5. Changes in investment patterns

With regard to changes in *categories* of investment, the national share of the investments of insurance undertakings remains very large, even in 1995, indicating that individual Member States have not moved closer to each other in this area. As regards changes in the *localization* of investments, 19% of the undertakings of the sample group invest beyond their frontiers and in Europe, but this does not signify a change of strategy because this number has not changed between 1989 and 1995.

Investments by these same undertakings abroad are developing slowly, rising from 2% of reserves in 1989 to 3% in 1995. Given that these figures are so low, it cannot be concluded that this is an indication of a real change in policy.

It is somewhat surprising that insurers have not to a larger degree taken advantage of the liberalization of capital movements introduced first by EU legislation and then by new provisions in the Treaty of Maastricht applicable since 1990. There are three main reasons for this caution on the part of the insurers:

---

[1]   *Source*: *The Marketing and Distribution of European Insurance*, Datamonitor 6, *Financial Times*, 1996.

(a) the currency matching requirements laid down by the EU's Framework Directives – this, however, can only be part of the reason because the vast majority of insurers do not even use their 'quota' of 20% laid down by the Directives;

(b) the degree of expertise required to manage investments in several, relatively unknown foreign markets – this, particularly for small and medium-sized enterprises, is a real reason for caution because of the difficulty of deciding when the potential gain from investing abroad is sufficiently large either to delegate the investment of assets to a specialized investment company or acquire sufficient specialized knowledge in-house;

(c) the currency risk – this reason is perceived as part of the two reasons mentioned above in that many operators indicate that they will change their policy of where to locate their investments as a consequence of the introduction of the single currency in 1999.

1.6. Changes in market concentration and competitiveness

Cecchini (1988) and many industry commentators[2] predicted that market structures would begin to change as a result of the SIM, in particular due to the deregulation of insurance prices and conditions. On balance, this expected surge in competitive conditions causing greater fragmentation, i.e. reduced market shares for the major insurance companies, has not taken place within the EU insurance market.

Rather, what has been experienced during the reference period is a consolidation by leading players of their position in their national markets. This consolidation has gone hand in hand with a weakening of smaller players. The increase in cross-border take-overs and mergers suggests that this is the preferred means of gaining EU market share of the leading companies

1.7. Changes in productivity

The results from the primary sources lead to no firm conclusions: productivity measured as premium per employee shows an increase, whereas the ratio of net profit to capital shows a general decrease. The primary results are remarkably consistent for both the panel and the case studies. However, the ratio premium per employee is somewhat unreliable because Member States define employees in different ways. Since the number of employees in general has not gone down, their productivity seemingly has indeed increased. The ratio of net profit to capital is obviously dependent on the general economic environment, so the fall in the general level of interest rates during the reference period might explain part of the fall in this ratio.

Secondary sources: the ratio of gross operating expenses to gross premiums shows a downward trend in Belgium, Denmark, Germany, Finland and Sweden but an upward trend in Italy, Spain, Luxembourg, the Netherlands and France. Results of gross claims incurred as a ratio of premium should equally be interpreted with some caution for such a short period. But it is significant that all Member States except Belgium and Sweden actually show decreasing ratios, indicating increased productivity over this reference period.

In conclusion, three out of four parameters show a degree of increased productivity throughout the reference period. However, before this trend can be validated it needs to be confirmed by more data from the period after 1 July 1994.

---

[2] See, for example, Sigma, *Deregulation and liberalization of market access: the European insurance industry on the threshold of a new era in competition*, 1996.

1.8. Changes in international competitiveness

Internationalization demands substantial resources. That is why it is the large companies and the case study undertakings which saw a substantial increase in their international turnover during the reference period although with each targeting their strategy differently.

Overall, the secondary sources for the trend in the EU's insurance flows (unfortunately incomplete) would tend to show that the EU is defending its single market effectively against insurers from the other major regions of the world and that export capacity varies depending on the EU countries. An analysis of leading European groups shows more rapid growth in their international turnover (+ 73.4%) than in Europe (+ 41.4%) or on their domestic markets (+ 23.0%).

1.9. Price changes

Few undertakings during the reference period have been concerned with harmonizing their prices and policy conditions for similar products from one Member State to another.

Nevertheless, since 1989, there has been an *increase* in undertakings introducing 'Euro' products (i.e. identical insurance products for several European countries).

Thus, half the undertakings of the sample group operating in Europe have developed one or more European products. This trend is developing particularly in the life sector or for contingency insurance programmes, but is also starting to emerge in indemnity products.

The reasons for this development are linked to *the opening up of the European market*, and more specifically the freedom to provide services. Some undertakings recently introduced such Euro-products in order to benefit from a market which is now open and more specifically relying on the freedom to provide services. Furthermore, a concern for standardization, corresponds to a will on the part of the undertaking to *simplify and cut costs*.

Another reason which is also starting to favour the Euro-product in undertakings is the demand from international customers (contingency insurance contracts or employer's liability coverage).

Overall, what is missing most would appear to be not so much a lack of ability to harmonize prices on the supply side, but the absence of a real demand-side possibility for customers to compare products with one another across the EU. In this context, the lack of true European distribution plays a contributing part. The transparency resulting from Economic and Monetary Union (EMU) and the introduction of the Euro on the other hand, should contribute considerably to overcoming the difficulties for consumers of comparing different products offered by different markets and create cross-border pressure both on economic operators to harmonize policies and prices and on regulators to adopt harmonized legislation allowing operators to do so.

1.10. Contribution to the environment

Twenty per cent of the insurers interviewed for this study have already developed products covering environmental risks. It is clearly *the demand of the policyholders* which has led insurers to offer insurance cover in the market-place against risks linked to pollution.

It can be concluded that there is in fact a trend towards the development of this type of supply, even though insurers are very prudent when dealing with a risk which they still consider today to be ill-defined and sometimes difficult to measure.

Among the undertakings interviewed, the largest proportion developing this type of policy or including specific clauses relating to pollution in their contracts comes from northern Europe. This proportion is as high as 50% of the undertakings interviewed from Germany and Denmark. The causal relationship between the increase in demand and EU insurance legislation is difficult to establish.

On the other hand, the undertakings of the south (in the sample group and case studies) are still distinctly less concerned.

1.11. Single market programme (SMP) impact on the cost of insurers

During the period of reference there has been a clear trend on the part of insurance operators towards achieving considerable reductions in overall cost. This trend tallies with the fact that during the period from 1989 to 1995, there has been a slight improvement in the productivity of European insurers.

In the majority of cases, it is clearly reasons *internal* to the undertakings interviewed, or reasons associated with their direct environment, which are the cause of the productivity gains recorded.

It is therefore difficult to establish a direct link between these measures and the SIM, but indirectly it is clear that the prospect of the creation of the single market has promoted an awareness among insurers of the threats of competition (real or to come) and of the importance of improving their level of competitiveness by taking action regarding their operating costs, on the one hand, and the quality of the way they conduct their business (claims management) and the improvement of their customer service, on the other.

Economies of scale were measured as a function of the efforts made by insurance undertakings to integrate one or more business activities at European level over the past five years.

The study shows that real progress was made towards this goal: about one-third of the undertakings operating at European level started to integrate some of their business activities at European level.

Hence, the *sharing of information* on markets and the effort made to unify advertising messages correspond to recognition on the part of the undertakings that there is a true single market, with a consumer capable of moving round and choosing, directly linked to the introduction of the freedom to provide services and the single passport.

Finally, the case studies show that, in the case of large groups, the greatest progress in the field of integration and economies of scale is first made at national level, then at the level of 'European regions'. This would tend to indicate that economies of scale at European level are limited where the national units are already large.

1.12. SMP impact on the strategies of insurers

Among the factors which influenced the strategy of insurance undertakings during the reference period, the very strong role played by the anticipation of increased competition and the ensuing investments to be made to remain competitive should be stressed.

Clearly, it is not possible to attribute this increased awareness entirely to the creation of the single market, since purely national forms of competition developed in parallel during the same period, such as those of the banks or the new distributors. Depending on the 'class' of insurance, competition will be played out at different levels: at international level for insurers selling to commercial undertakings; and at national level, though not exclusively, for insurers targeting the personal market and facing the emergence of new distribution systems, such as bancassurance, direct selling and network distributors.

2. Introduction and presentation of the study

2.1. Objectives of the study

The aim of this study is to examine the impact of the measures taken by the Community to create a true European single market in the insurance sector. More specifically, the report seeks:

(a) to identify EU measures which have had an impact on the insurance business;
(b) to assess the nature and scale of the impact of these measures on this sector;
(c) to identify the remaining obstacles to Community integration;
(d) to identify the way in which the undertakings of the sector have adapted to this new environment;
(e) and, finally, to assess the extent to which the completion of the single market has contributed to the performance of the sector and to making Community insurance more competitive.

2.2. Economic significance of the insurance sector in the EU

2.2.1. The size of the relevant market

The EU insurance sector is remarkably dynamic and of great economic significance to the Community:

(a) it groups together some 5,400 undertakings (life, non-life, composite and re-insurance companies);
(b) it provides jobs for about 1 million employees;
(c) its turnover, which reached ECU 490,246 million in 1995, grew by 34% in constant ECU in the life sector and by 27.8% in the non-life sector over the reference period;
(d) finally, the investments it makes, notably through the use of its technical reserves, represented some 30% of the gross domestic product (GDP) of the 15 Member States in 1995.

The largest life insurance market measured by gross written premiums is France, followed by Germany and the UK. Germany remains the biggest non-life market.

2.3. Regulations and administrative provisions adopted to complete the single insurance market

2.3.1. Background

On 25 May 1957, the signatory States of the Treaty of Rome set themselves the objectives of the elimination of all barriers to the free movement of persons, goods, services and capital and the harmonization of national legislation. Three decades later, the single European market became a legal reality for the insurance sector.

Some progress was made between 1957 and 1992, but it was partial. It was from 1973 for non-life insurance and from 1979 for life assurance that the European insurance market started to take shape. It was not until the White Paper of 1985 (European Commission, 1985) and its political consequence, the Single European Act of 1986 (OJ L 169, 29.6.1987, p. 1), that liberalization of the insurance market was achieved.

Finally, in 1992, the last stone of the building was laid and allowed entry into an era of almost total freedom for both insurance undertakings and policyholders. In seven years – from June 1985, the date of publication of the White Paper, to the end of 1992, when the third generation Directives were adopted, the European integration process has both developed and gathered pace considerably.

During the above-mentioned period, there were almost as many new Directives as there were between the date of signature of the Treaty of Rome and 1985. The single market in insurance was created by means of three series of basic Directives concerning non-life insurance and life assurance.

2.4. The first generation of Directives

2.4.1. Freedom of establishment

On 24 July 1973 and 9 March 1979, the European partners adopted the establishment Directives on non-life insurance (73/239/ EEC) and life assurance (79/267/EEC) respectively. These two Directives aimed to harmonize the conditions relating to the taking up and pursuit of the business of Common Market insurance undertakings and branches of third countries. They provided for administrative authorization delivered by each of the Member States concerned, under comparable legal and financial conditions and according to a uniform procedure. These Directives also harmonized prudential control, by introducing a solvency margin and a minimum guarantee fund. Certain conditions were still those provided for by the host country, such as the conditions governing technical provisions or the representation of assets.

The first generation of Directives represented considerable progress, but did not yet create a European single market. Insurance undertakings wishing to operate outside their home countries had to obtain authorization in each Member State. Branches continued to be subject to dual supervision: that of their home State and that of their host State.

2.5. The second generation of Directives

2.5.1. The transition to the freedom to provide services

Nine years passed between the last establishment Directive for life assurance and the first Directive on the freedom to provide services for non-life insurance. The building of Europe, and consequently the single market in insurance, were in abeyance. It was the recommendations of the 1985 White Paper, and their embodiment in the Single Act one year later, which promoted the new boom of the insurance sector. The White Paper gave second wind to the intentions of the signatories of the Treaty of Rome, by putting forward two main ideas: the minimum harmonization of the national regulations and, on the basis of this, the mutual recognition of the prudential control carried out by each Member State.

As an echo to this political will, a few months later, the Court of Justice handed down four important judgments. According to these decisions, it emerged that the freedom to provide services was the rule of the Treaty of Rome and that restricting it could only be an exception.

Following on directly from this political will and the decisions of the Court, the Member States adopted two new Directives on non-life insurance (80/357/EEC) and life assurance (90/619/EEC) on 22 June 1988 and 8 November 1990.

These new Directives aimed more to create a transitional technical and legal framework than to introduce a real area for ongoing economic competition. Consequently, the Directive on the freedom to provide services in relation to non-life insurance drew a distinction between two categories of risks according to size and the policyholder's status:

(a) large risks or industrial and commercial risks;
(b) mass risks or individual consumers.

The Directive on the freedom to provide services in relation to life assurance, for its part, drew a distinction between active and passive freedom to provide services. The active or passive aspect was determined by the person (policyholder or insurer) taking the initiative of the first contact:

(a) active freedom to provide services: initiative of the insurer;
(b) passive freedom to provide services: initiative of the policyholder.

For mass risks in non-life and active freedom to provide services in life, the freedom to provide services was subject to the obtention of an administrative authorization from the country of risk. Moreover, certain classes of insurance (motor third-party insurance, builder's risk insurance, nuclear liability insurance, etc.) were excluded from the scope of the Directive on the freedom to provide services in relation to non-life insurance.

These two Directives amended and supplemented those of the first generation, but only achieved partial liberalization of insurance business. Consequently, insurers could conduct operations coming under the right of establishment or the freedom to provide services simultaneously on the large risks market. On the other hand, they could not do so on the mass risks markets. On the latter, their intervention was confined to the classes of insurance for which they were authorized in their respective countries of establishment.

2.6. The single market in insurance

In insurance, as in the other financial services sectors, the construction of the European market was based on two basic premises:

(a) the opening up of the national areas by simplifying the conditions for the taking up and pursuit of cross-border insurance business in the various markets;
(b) the reduction of State interventionism and control.

The principles of the third generation are:

(a) the system of the single authorization ('European passport'), permitting any undertaking with its head office in one of the 18 Member States of the European Economic Area (EEA) and authorized in that State, to offer its products for sale, through agencies/branches or under the freedom to provide services, throughout European territory, under the initial authorization and under the technical and financial supervision (prudential supervision) of its State of origin ('home country control');

(b) the abolition of dual authorization systems under freedom of establishment in the fields of 'active' freedom to provide services (in life assurance) and freedom to provide services for 'mass risks' (non-life insurance) and general application of the procedures for the notification of the supervisory authority of the home Member State;

(c) the mutual recognition of the authorization and supervision arrangements applied by the various States of the EEA;

(d) the almost complete abolition of the prior approval of contractual conditions and scales of premiums (physical supervision)

(e) the liberalization of the rules for the investment of the technical and mathematical provisions.

These various principles evidently show the decision taken in favour of a market economy on a European scale, to a very large extent liberating the insurance business from the intervention of the public authorities with a view to creating an optimum supply of prices and products. Accordingly, the right to the widest possible choice of innovative insurance products offered at the best price by companies of all backgrounds is seen as the best guarantee of consumer protection. As everyone knows, this substantial deregulation has only been made possible through harmonization of certain essential aspects of the insurance business, in particular, the prudential standards applicable to the undertakings.

Henceforth, the consumer of insurance, while being kept in his traditional, customary linguistic and tax framework, is presented with products from the four corners of Europe. *Ex ante* control has been ended and replaced by *ex post* control. Prior communication of documents has been abolished, which enables undertakings to offer their products for sale without delay. The third generation Directives contain no provisions governing intermediaries (agents and brokers).

2.7. The single licence: the essential points

2.7.1. Authorization

Administrative authorization is granted on condition of acceptance by the supervisory authorities of the home State, which must assess:

(a) the programme of activities planned;
(b) the components of the minimum guarantee fund;
(c) the quality of the shareholders;
(d) the repute and professional experience of the managers.

For instance, a British consumer may be approached by a French insurer through three different channels:

(a) a subsidiary governed by UK law selling policies in accordance with local legislation;
(b) a branch freely established in the UK, placed under the supervision of the French authorities;
(c) an offer of insurance products under the freedom to provide services.

In addition, the single market allows more subtle distribution: the French insurer established in Italy can offer Italian policies to the British policyholder.

Companies without an establishment in the countries in which they wish to operate will not be obliged to have systematic recourse to host structures. All the same, an undertaking operating under the freedom to provide services is required to have a tax representative accredited by the supervisory authorities. Moreover, in the field of motor vehicle insurance, insurance undertakings are required to appoint an agent to guarantee claims management.

2.7.2. Financial supervision

Financial supervision lies within the exclusive competence of the Member State which has issued the administrative authorization. It is undertaken mainly through an annual inspection of the undertaking's accounting statements to check its financial situation and solvency.

An on-the-spot investigation of its business, applied for by the home country, may be conducted after informing the host country authorities. In addition, financial supervision also has the object of supervising that transfers of portfolios and acquisitions of qualified holdings have been duly carried out.

2.7.3. Price control

The third generation Directives henceforth prohibit systems of prior approval and systematic communication of the contractual conditions, whatever the nature of the insurance operation (national or cross-border) and the way in which it operates (establishment or provision of services); only communication of the contractual conditions which is not systematic and not before use can still be required to check that they conform to the law applicable to the contract.

In compulsory insurance and health insurance as an alternative to social security, the systematic communication of the contractual conditions before use – to the supervisory authority of the home country or of the branch/provision of services – nevertheless continues to be authorized. In life assurance, the home country supervisory authorities may require the systematic communication of the technical bases used, in particular to calculate the scales of premiums and technical and mathematical provisions, although this requirement may not be a prerequisite for carrying on insurance business and its sole purpose must be to verify compliance with the actuarial principles.

2.7.4. Technical provisions

According to the third generation Directives, the home State imposes the setting aside and representation of the technical provisions. On the basis of the Community provisions, the home Member State is responsible for checking that the specified categories of representative assets and their respective thresholds are respected by the insurance undertakings. The assets may be located in any Community Member State.

2.7.5. Solvency regulations and guarantee fund

These concepts enable the solvency of an insurance undertaking to be measured. These two dimensions combined give an indication of the financial health of an insurance undertaking. The calculation of the solvency margin is subject to rules specific to non-life insurance and life assurance and the amount of the guarantee fund derives from them. The majority of European insurance undertakings exceed these minimum thresholds. There are plans for the Commission to review them in 1997.

2.7.6. Undertakings in difficulties or in breach of the regulations

If an undertaking does not comply with the regulations on technical provisions, the home State may prohibit it from disposing freely of its assets, after having first alerted the host State, and even call on it to take all the necessary measures.

In the case of withdrawal of authorization, the home State informs all the States concerned of this, so that they take the appropriate measures to prevent the free disposal of assets and to protect policyholders' interests.

2.7.7. Notification

To establish a branch in another Member State, the insurance undertaking must inform its supervisory authorities, indicating to them:

(a) the State concerned;
(b) the programme of activities;
(c) the authorized agent of the branch.

The home Member State informs the State concerned of the insurance undertaking's plans. The Directives provide that if the home supervisory authorities have doubts about the quality of the administrative structures or the financial health of the undertaking, or the repute or professional qualifications of the managers of the applicant undertaking, they may decide not to notify the Member State concerned. The Member State of the branch must, in return, inform it of the conditions governing the pursuit of business deriving from the interest of the general good with which the branch will have to comply.

In the case of operations under the freedom to provide services, the insurer must inform its home Member State of the commitments it wishes to cover. The home Member State communicates to the State in which the undertaking wishes to carry on business:

(a) the solvency certificate;
(b) the classes of insurance which the insurer has been authorized to offer;
(c) the nature of the risks it wishes to cover.

Undertakings operating under either freedom to provide services or the freedom of establishment must supply the same information to the host State as that transmitted by its local competitors. In the case of irregularities concerning the insurer, it is for the home State, on the request of the host State, to take the necessary measures. This does not prevent immediate action in emergencies and the penalizing of infringements committed within its territory.

An insurance undertaking operating under the freedom of establishment or the freedom to provide services informs the State of its registered office of the amount of the premiums, claims and commissions obtained in each host State. The latter may obtain this information from the home State.

2.7.8. Liberalization of the rules for the investment of the technical and mathematical provisions

The coordination effected by the third generation Directives also covered the rules relating to the setting aside of technical and mathematical provisions and their investment in representative assets. It was first necessary to draw the lessons from the judgments of the Court of Justice of the European Communities of 4 December 1986, which had deemed it necessary to supplement the harmonization of the prudential standards started by the first Directives of 24 July 1973 (non-life insurance (73/239/EEC)) and 5 March 1979 (life assurance(79/267/EEC)), to allow the introduction of the principle of authorization and control by the insurer's State only and, consequently, the mutual recognition of the supervisory systems. Then the national regulations in the field of investment of provisions were to be adapted to the liberalization of capital movements implemented by the Directive of 24 June 1988.

These two factors provide an explanation for the fact that the Community authorities confined themselves, in this area, to harmonization based on flexible minimum conditions, on the one hand, and to the fact that the technique and principles adopted come under a liberalization approach, on the other. Thus, in the field of investments:

(a) insurance undertakings must henceforth respect the investment rules laid down by the supervisory law of their home State as regards all their business activities and no longer those of the various countries in which they operate;

(b) beyond the general principle of security, yield and liquidity of the investments, the Directives drew up a list of 'ceilings' intended to ensure diversification and an adequate spread of the investments. This list is exhaustive but very wide-ranging, in order to leave maximum flexibility not only to Member States, but also and above all to the insurance undertakings;

(c) Member States are now prohibited from requiring their insurance undertakings to invest a minimum amount of their provisions in specific assets or categories of assets;

(d) the representative assets no longer need be localized by country of operation; their localization 'in the Community' is now sufficient;

(e) insurance undertakings may henceforth hold non-matching assets (i.e. denominated or payable in a currency other than that of the commitments due) to cover an amount of up to 20% of their commitments in a particular currency.

Apart from this, the Directives contain a series of general principles, policies and recommendations essentially designed to standardize, to a certain extent, the valuation and conditions for use of the acceptable assets and to ensure that there is no excessive dependence on one category of specific assets, one investment sector or one specific investment.

2.8. Consumer protection

2.8.1. Contractual information

Like the national legal systems, the Directives turned their attention to contractual information and the law applicable to the contract. This is the cornerstone of the policyholder protection system, especially as the majority of insurance contracts have effect for a long period of time, which is particularly true of life assurance. The nature and extent of the contractual information differs between non-life insurance and life assurance.

In non-life insurance, where he or she is a natural person, the policyholder must be informed, before the contract is concluded, of the law applicable to the contract and the arrangements for handling complaints. For life assurance, the contractual details are more numerous and relate mainly to the characteristics of the insurer, its registered office, the definition of each option and benefit, the term of the contract, the means of terminating the contract, the arrangements and law applicable to the contract. In addition, the life assurance undertaking is required to inform the policyholder before the contract is concluded, but also throughout the term of the contract.

2.8.2. The law applicable to the contract

The law applicable to the contract and the freedom of choice of the parties to the insurance contract are covered by the Directives, which provide for the law applicable according to two different criteria:

1. According to the nature of the insurance contract:
    - insurance against fire and other damage to property, law of the country where the building covered is located;
    - motor vehicle insurance, the law of the country in which the vehicle is registered;
    - travel insurance, law of the country of subscription;
    - for the other classes of insurance, law of the country of residence of the policyholder.
2. According to size of risk and status of the policy-holder.

These rules apply differently according to whether the policyholder belongs to the large risks or mass risks category. For large risks, the parties can choose the law applicable to the contract. Nevertheless, this freedom is not absolute and may be limited by the interest of the general good or by the application of mandatory provisions contained in national legislation. As regards mass risks, freedom of choice is more limited. The rules for determining the law applicable to the contract are the following:

1. If the risk and the policyholder are located in the same Member State, its law applies unless this law provides for the possibility to choose another law.
2. If the risk and the policyholder are not located in the same Member State, the choice of the law applicable may be made between:
    - either the law of the State of the policyholder;
    - or the law of the State of the insurer;
    - or another law if the above so permit.

Despite this freedom of choice, in the case of compulsory insurance, the Member State may impose the application of its law. In the absence of a free choice, the law applicable is that of the country where the risk is situated.

2.8.3. The concept of the interest of the general good

The concept of the 'interest of the general good' is a pure product of case law which is mentioned, but which has not been specified in Community Directives. According to a definition commonly accepted in Community law, it earmarks all the conditions established by the Court of Justice of the European Communities to justify a national regulation constituting an obstacle to one of the freedoms enshrined in the Treaty of Rome. These conditions – which are encapsulated in recital 19 of the Third Non-life Insurance Directive (92/49/EEC) and in recital 20 of the Third Life Assurance Directive (92/96/EEC) – may be summarized as follows:

(a) the national measure may only be adopted – and invoked in relation to foreign operators – in a field which has not been the subject of harmonization at Community level;
(b) it must not lead to discrimination between EU operators;
(c) it must meet an objective in the interest of the general good enshrined by the Treaty or by the Court of Justice (in the field of insurance, this is mainly a matter, at this stage, of consumer protection and consistency of the tax arrangements);
(d) it must be objectively necessary and commensurate with the objective pursued, this requirement implying, on the one hand, that the measure is really relevant to the objective in view and does not give rise to a disproportionate impediment in relation to the objective sought and, on the other, that there is no alternative which is as effective and less restrictive for exercising the freedom concerned (test of the strict necessity and proportionality);
(e) finally, the interest it is intended to guarantee must not already be safeguarded by a rule of equivalent effect declared applicable to the insurance operation (duplication test).

2.9. Other legislative initiatives

To complement these three generations of Directives intended to ensure both the right of establishment and the freedom to provide services, the Community legislated in the following areas:

(a) motor third-party insurance;
(b) annual accounts and consolidated accounts of insurance undertakings;
(c) legal expenses insurance;
(d) credit and suretyship insurance;
(e) travel insurance; and
(f) co-insurance.

Moreover, the Community set up an Insurance Committee, responsible for assisting it in its task of cooperating with the supervisory authorities of the Member States.

Finally, the Commission presented two proposals for Council Directives on the coordination of the laws, regulations and administrative provisions concerning the compulsory liquidation of direct insurance undertakings on the one hand (COM (89)394), and insurance contracts on the other (COM (89) 641). The former proposal, presented several years ago, has little chance of adoption. The latter has been withdrawn.

2.10. Distribution

2.10.1. Distribution via insurance intermediaries

The status of insurance intermediaries has so far been the subject of a single Directive in 1976 (77/92/EEC). This Directive is based on the principle of the mutual recognition of the validity of the inspections carried out by the home Member State. To this end, the Directive calls on Member States to accept, as equivalent to their national requirements, the professional training acquired by a foreign intermediary in his home country and the proof of good repute and absence of earlier bankruptcy supplied by the home Member State.

The other aspects of the intermediary's activities, such as:

(a) financial guarantees;
(b) cover for professional liability;
(c) registration and the other business conditions;

are not covered by the Directive and continue to be subject to the national law of Member States.

This partial liberalization implies that an intermediary wishing to establish a branch in another Member State or to operate under the freedom to provide services must obtain the certificates providing evidence of his professional experience, good repute and act of bankruptcy from his home State and forward them to the host Member State. Consequently, the European authorities have not granted insurance intermediaries a system of a single licence and home country control comparable to that from which the insurance undertakings, which in certain cases are their competitors, benefit.

Each Member State is free to regulate the intermediaries' activities as it sees fit, with due regard for the provisions of the Treaty of Rome. To remedy this situation, the Commission published a recommendation in 1991 (92/48/EEC) to encourage Member States to amend their national legislation.

The points referred to concern:

(a) the distinction between dependent and independent intermediaries;
(b) the determination of a minimum level of professional competence;
(c) the fixing of cover for professional liability;
(d) the creation of a professional registration system.

Moreover, this recommendation covers all insurance intermediaries (agents, brokers, banks, travel agencies, etc.).

2.11. Competition

Ensuring that competition is not distorted is the top priority of the Community's economic approach. To this end, Articles 85 and 86 of the Treaty of Rome regulate agreements between undertakings, on the one hand, and undertakings in a dominant position, on the other. It is for the Commission, in cooperation with Member States, to have these rules respected to ensure:

(a) healthy competition; and
(b) consumer protection.

2.11.1. Cooperation between insurance undertakings

In order to establish free, healthy competition, Articles 85 and 86 of the Treaty of Rome prohibit agreements between economic operators and abuse of a dominant position.

With a view to the Third Directives, the question arose of the types of understandings, agreements and practices between undertakings which could be authorized. In fact, even competing, insurance undertakings have obvious needs for cooperation, such as, for example, statistical studies or joint participation in major risks. The Commission therefore decided in December 1992, by Regulation (EEC) No 3932/92 and based on Council Regulation (EEC) No 1534/91, to authorize cooperation agreements with the object of ensuring the smooth functioning of the insurance sector and consumer protection.

Under these two Regulations, it emerges that cooperation agreements or concerted practices between undertakings may relate to: joint calculation of net premiums and the standard conditions of insurance; joint cover of certain risks; and the verification and acceptance of security equipment.

These two Regulations prohibit cooperation agreements from defining compulsory rules which may be invoked against either insurance undertakings or policyholders. The Commission specified that the professional criteria drawn up in this way may serve only as guidance and be presented as such to policyholders.

For joint participation (in co-insurance or co-reinsurance) for risks, provision is made that the insurers signing the agreement do not abuse a dominant position and that they continue to compete regarding the other risks. Notice of the cooperation agreements does not need to be given to the Commission. If it considers they represent an infringement of free competition or constitute a threat to consumer protection, it has the direct power to pronounce them null and void.

2.11.2. Cooperation between Member States

To protect themselves against the risks of relocation or 'forum shopping' to countries with a low level of supervision, the Third Directives provided for a system of cooperation between the supervisory authorities of the Member States and the Commission. Under a single supervisory system, the activities carried out under the freedom to provide services in fact come under the supervision exercised by the authorities of the country of the insurer's registered office, pursuant to the application of the principle of mutual recognition of national legislation.

The competence of the supervisory authorities of the Member States is extended to the activities of their national undertakings carried out through branches or under the freedom to provide services within the territory of the EU. Symmetrically, they lose the supervision of Community branches operating within their territory.

The Community set up an Insurance Committee, composed of representatives of the Member States, responsible for assisting the Commission in its task of cooperating with the national supervisory authorities – Directive 91/675/EEC of 19 December 1991.

Table 2.1. Impact of European legislation

I. Structure of the profession

	Home Member State	Host Member State
1. Insurance undertaking/Single licence		
• Subsidiary	Application of the home country legislation	Application of the host country legislation
• Branch	Application of the home country legislation	Appointment of a tax representative
• Freedom to provide services		Application of the legislation of the host State
2. Intermediaries	Obtention of certificates Professional experience, good repute and no bankruptcy Forwarding of these certificates to the host State	

II. Procedures for engaging in the profession

	Home Member State	Host Member State
1. Supervision	Competence of the insurer's home country authorities	Mutual recognition of supervision Corollary: no supervision over the branches established within its territory
2. Authorization	Competence of the insurer's home country authorities	Mutual recognition
3. Prudential supervision	Competence of the insurer's home country authorities	Mutual recognition with possibility of on-the-spot investigations by or at the request of the home State
• Technical provisions	Competence of the insurer's home country authorities	...in any other Member State
• Assets	Localization in home country or...	
4. Undertaking in difficulties	If necessary, home State prohibits the free disposal of the assets within its territory	or in the host Member State On information from the home State, the host State takes the necessary measures
5. Notification		
• Freedom of establishment	Communication to the host State of the undertaking's plan, its business programme and the name of the representative	The host State informs the home State of the rules deriving from the interest of the general good
• Freedom to provide services	Communication to the host State of the undertaking's certificate of solvency, the class of insurance and the nature of the risks	
6. Interest of the general good		May prohibit the distribution of products within its territory Obligation to justify the interest of the general good
7. Taxation		According to the tax scales of the host State

2.12. Horizontal impact, taxation, capital market

The Community vision is based on the principle of European territoriality. All the operators are placed in a position of free competition within the same economic area. This is particularly true of the liberalization of capital movements in favour of the banking sector. On the other hand, insurance undertakings do not benefit equally from this same freedom because of differences in taxation between Member States.

The lack of harmonization of taxation relating to insurance contracts is the result of the Commission's choice not to open the discussion. In fact, harmonization of taxation is a subject which implies the unanimous vote of the members of the Council. In the absence of harmonization, the third generation Directives provide that any insurance contract is subject exclusively to the indirect taxes and parafiscal charges on insurance premiums in the Member State in which the risk is situated. In the field of life assurance, this is the Member State of the commitment.

An insurer operating under the freedom to provide services, depending on the Member State, will be required to appoint a tax representative within its territory or to communicate an exhaustive list of the contracts it issues locally. This rule of territoriality of the tax will not dispense Member States from harmonization of taxation since the present disparities are considerable, as shown in Tables B.1 and B.2. On the other hand, the third generation of Directives does not cover the taxes applicable to the provision of insurance. Member States are free to determine their tax scales under their sovereign rights.

The taxation question has been the subject of two major judgments handed down by the Court of Justice. In the first case (case C-204/90 [1992] ECR I-249) Mr Bachmann, a German citizen resident in Belgium and a holder of a retirement pension contract with a German company, wished to benefit from the deductibility for tax purposes provided for by the Belgian authorities. They refused, arguing that when the retirement pension contract expires, the claimant will probably no longer be in Belgium and that the indirect taxes on the payment of the capital provided for will be collected by Mr Bachman's Member State of origin.

In this case, the Court, while recognizing the discriminatory nature of the Belgian position, considered it was justified by the defence of the cohesion of its tax system. This decision was taken badly by insurance undertakings. In addition, consumers, presented as the great beneficiaries of the single market, found themselves with less freedom of choice than before.

In a second case (*Wielockx*, C-80/94 [1995] ECR 2493), which was very similar to the previous one but involved a Belgian citizen in the Netherlands, the Court of Justice modified its position. It decided that the plaintiff Wielockx was entitled to benefit from Dutch tax advantages since a tax agreement exists between Belgium and the Netherlands. The Court deemed that the existence of such an agreement ensured the cohesion of the tax system of Member States. This latter decision is very important as almost all the Member States are bound by tax agreements. Consequently, the defence of the cohesion of the tax system, as invoked by the supervisory authorities, is no longer applicable.

Table 2.2.   List of the Directives transposed into national legislation

References	Object of the Directive	Deadline for implementation
64/225	Abolition of restrictions in the field of reinsurance and retrocession	26/08/64
72/166	First Directive on motor vehicle third-party insurance	31/12/73
73/239	First Directive on non-life insurance	31/01/75
77/92	Agents and brokers	16/06/78
78/473	Co-insurance	02/12/79
79/267	First Directive on life assurance	15/09/90
84/5	Second Directive on motor vehicle third-party insurance	01/01/88 Italy : 01/01/91 Greece : 01/01/93 Ireland : 01/01/96
84/641	Travel insurance	30/06/87
87/343	Suretyship insurance	01/01/90
87/344	Legal expenses	01/01/90
88/357	Second Directive on direct non-life insurance	01/07/90
90/232	Third Directive on motor vehicle third-party insurance	31/12/92 Greece: 31/12/95 Spain: 31/12/95 Ireland: 31/12/98 Portugal: 31/12/95
90/618	Motor vehicle free	20/05/91
90/619	Second Directive on life assurance	20/11/92
91/371	Non-life insurance: application of the Swiss agreement	04/07/93
91/674	Annual accounts and consolidated accounts	01/01/94
92/49	Third Directive on non-life insurance	01/01/94 Spain: 31/12/96 Portugal: 31/12/98
92/96	Third Directive on life assurance	01/07/94

2.13. Methodological approach

The conceptual framework of the methodology of this report is to seek to measure and evaluate the effects of the EU's SIM legislation via an analysis of the impact of such measures on the economic operators – the insurance companies.

Two main types of indicators are used, namely the developments in a representative 'sample' of insurance companies (including detailed case studies) and secondary sources – basically any source of information other than the sample and case studies.

The reference period is 1989 to 1995. This period has been chosen because liberalization of the insurance sector can be said effectively to have started with the second Non-life Directive 88/357/EEC, which had to be transposed into national legislation by 30 December 1989 and implemented by 1 July 1990. This Directive deregulated part of the insurance sector by liberalizing supervisory control for particular categories of risks – the so-called large risks (aircraft, ships, and liabilities for them, etc.) – when the policyholder was engaged professionally in an industrial or commercial activity and the risks related to this activity. The final year of 1995 represents the closest to 'the present day' which was practically feasible, although certain primary and secondary sources date from 1996.

This type of inductive, indirect approach has the advantage of analysing real, concrete facts and of avoiding excessive pessimism or optimism since it does not primarily seek the *opinion* of the actors of what effect the introduction of the single market has had on their undertakings (although such indicators are occasionally used) but mainly interprets the outward signs of this effect. The main categories of indicators selected are the following: changes in the cross-border activities of EU insurance undertakings, changes in modes of cross-border cooperation, changes in investment patterns, changes in market concentration and competitiveness, and changes in productivity and price trends.

On the other hand, this approach poses the problem of establishing the *causal link* between the developments observed and the EU's single market legislation, for the motivations behind undertakings' changes in behaviour may vary considerably: developments in consumer and market needs, business management methods, trends on the financial markets, etc. all influence such changes. Consequently, support for this causal link very often has to be sought in the secondary sources.

The approach also poses the problem of the *representativeness* of the undertakings interviewed. The choice, for the *case study* of highly diversified undertakings, on the one hand, and, especially for the *sample group* of the method of sampling by quotas, on the other hand, should constitute a guarantee against distortions of information linked to the nature of the undertakings interviewed.

2.13.1. The choice of the undertakings for the case studies

To be able to analyse in greater depth how the undertakings have reacted to the creation of the single market, the decision was taken to conduct five case studies of five different undertakings, which were selected as follows:

(a) a large European group, chosen for its resolutely European policy and its leading position in this market: the UAP Group, the second largest insurance undertaking in Europe, was selected for this analysis;

(b) a medium-sized undertaking: Victoria in Germany;

(c) a large undertaking in southern Europe: the Mapfre Group in Spain;

(d) a large undertaking in northern Europe: the Fortis Group, the market leader in Belgium and among the leaders in the Netherlands;

(e) a continental European broker (Cecar) enabling the strategy of insurance intermediaries to be analysed as regards the development of Europe.

2.13.2. The sample of undertakings by size

Undertakings were divided into three categories by size:

(a) *Small undertakings*: undertakings with premium receipts of less than ECU 10 million per year;

(b) *Medium-sized undertakings*: undertakings with premium receipts between ECU 10 million and ECU 500 million per year;

(c) *Large undertakings*: undertakings with premium receipts of ECU 500 million and over per year.

The distribution within the sample of each of these size categories takes account of both the number of undertakings existing in Europe in each category and their significance in terms of turnover on the market, in order to make the sample sufficiently representative of both small and very large insurance undertakings, as shown in the table below:

Table 2.3.   Distribution of the sample by size of undertakings

Size category of undertakings (million ECU)	Distribution of undertakings in the EU by number in each category (%)		Market share held in the EU by undertakings in each category (%)		Theoretical distribution used for the survey sample (%)	Actual (number of undertakings interviewed)
	Life	Non-life	Life	Non-life		
<10	45	60	1	2	40	25
from 10 to <500	47	37	30	38	40	43
500 and over	8	3	69	60	20	32
Total	100	100	100	100	100	100

2.13.3. The sample of undertakings by country of origin

EU Member States covered by the study

Given the relatively recent accession to the EU of Austria, Sweden and Finland, it is not yet possible to measure the impact of single market Directives on the insurance business of these countries. Our study is therefore confined to the EUR-12.

The various EU Member States have been divided into three groups according to the development of their insurance markets, measured by expenditure on insurance per inhabitant.

This yields the following distribution of the undertakings interviewed, by country, respecting the following propositions:

Table 2.4.   Distribution of the sample by country groups

Country group	% of EU undertakings in each country group	Theoretical distribution of the sample (%)	Number of undertakings of each country group having replied to the survey
Group A (Luxembourg, UK, France, Netherlands)	46. 2	46	46
Group B (Germany, Denmark, Ireland, Belgium)	32.6	33	42
Group C (Italy, Spain, Greece, Portugal)	21.2	21	12
Total	100	100	100

2.13.4. The sample of undertakings by type of business activity

In order to be able to take account in the survey of the extreme diversity in the 'business activities' of insurance undertakings, it was decided to subdivide the sample into the following categories:

(a) undertakings specializing in life assurance;
(b) general non-life insurance undertakings;
(c) undertakings specializing in one of the non-life activities: health, motor vehicle, indemnity, marine/aviation/transport, liability, credit and suretyship, legal expenses. In view of the large number of their activities, we basically assumed that an undertaking could be considered as 'specialized' in one of these classes, and therefore in a 'niche', where the class of insurance in question accounted for 15% or more of its turnover. This percentage was set at 60% for specialization in 'motor vehicle insurance' in view of its particular significance in insurance undertakings' turnover in general.

The sample therefore interviewed was distributed as shown below in Table 2.5.

Table 2.5.   Distribution of the sample by business activities of the undertakings

	Sample	
	Theoretical (%)	Actual (%)
Undertakings specializing in life assurance	30	37
General non-life insurance undertakings	23	21
Undertakings specializing in a class of non-life insurance	47	42
Total number of undertakings	100	100

Representativeness of the sample

The sample thus assembled represents 2.3% of the number of insurance undertakings in the EU. Details of the methodology of this survey are set out in Appendix A.

3. Changes in access to the market due to the single market programme

3.1. Aims of the legislation

By making it easier to exercise the right of freedom of establishment and the freedom to provide services in the Union and by introducing the concept of the single administrative licence through the Third Framework Directives, the Community has set up an area without frontiers in which insurers would be able to conduct their business freely and policyholders could benefit from a wider choice by being allowed to freely call on any insurer located in the EU.

The economic rationale behind the principle of home country control stems from the White Paper on completing the internal market (COM (85) 310): by abolishing prior control of premiums and policy conditions and creating a system of a single licence for the whole of the single market, differences between national regulatory systems would no longer present obstacles to the economic operator wishing to seek new commercial opportunities abroad. In simple terms, the financial service provider would be allowed to operate within the known parameters of the legislation of his country of origin and at the same time be able to take advantage of market opportunities in the host country or countries.

The insurance provider would, *ceteris paribus*, be expected to access other new markets either by increasing the number of branches operating in other EU countries or by cross-border provision of services without establishment. Access would be likely to be increased, especially in those countries where the distribution network was *open*, i.e. multiple agents/brokers are free and ready to assure the distribution of (new) products from new providers. Home country control, however, was crucially limited to branches and operations based on the right to provide services freely across borders without establishment. This more competitive environment would imply that in particular those countries which so far had been characterized by strict product control would need to adapt. Markets were expected to be more dynamic, more innovative, with greater diversity of products, more choices offered and all-round economic benefits from improved economies of scale.

Areas of non-harmonization: the Community in its single market legislation deliberately opted for a policy of non-harmonization of contract law which, in principle, would have been the logical approach to curtail continued restrictions on the free trade of insurance products. Instead, an alternative approach was found to deal with barriers created by different provisions in national contract law across the Community: the concept of 'general good'. This doctrine developed by the European Court of Justice was inserted into the single market Life and Non-Life Directives. Its basic tenet is an acknowledgement that in the absence of harmonization, the general good *can* be invoked by Member States to maintain barriers to free trade, but only within certain limits be justified by consumer protection motivations. Furthermore, the Community did not seek to harmonize existing tax rates but accepted different tax treatment of similar insurance products, leaving tax questions to be ruled by the principle of territoriality.

The principle of home country control ought to allow for new commercial opportunities abroad, because the financial service provider can continue to operate within the known parameters of the legislation of his country of origin and at the same time take advantage of a local presence in the host country. In principle, this would argue in favour of the provider increasing the number of branches operating in other EU countries; especially in those countries where the distribution network is open, i.e. multiple agent brokers are ready to ensure the distribution of (new) products from new providers. It is equally true, however, that consumer readiness to accept new modes of distribution such as bancassurance or direct sales of insurance by telephone will render the picture less simple or transparent. Free provision of services (FOS) might be expected to increase but not dramatically if one accepts the old maxim that 'all (insurance) business is local'.

The 'modes of access' analysed here are:

(a) the establishment or acquisition of subsidiary companies;
(b) the use of branches;
(c) the freedom to provide services; or
(d) any other means of access, such as co-insurance or fronting to operate in the other Member States.

Freedom to provide services

Freedom to provide services is the latest form of market access. It corresponds to the will of the EU to promote movements within the single market. It enables an insurer, wherever he is located in one of the Member States, to sell a product, from his home country, to a policyholder located in another Member State, without having to apply for authorization in the policyholder's State (subject, however, to a certain number of operating rules).

Establishment of a subsidiary or a branch

In both cases, the insurance undertaking creates a physical establishment in the country. The subsidiary qualifies for legal personality in the country in which it is established. The branch is merely a physical representation of the insurance undertaking through employees or an independent person with a permanent mandate.

Takeover or merger

A third way of establishment is the takeover or merger. Through the capital movements liberalization provisions of the Treaty on European Union, the EU legislator has facilitated the use of this mode of access.

Other modes of access

The other modes of access are:

(a) *fronting*: in fronting operations, a company concludes an insurance contract under the cover of another company abroad. It nevertheless retains management of the contract and liability for the risk covered. This formula enables business to be conducted in closed markets or those with low financial capacity;
(b) *co-insurance*: the principle consists of sharing the cover of a given, clearly identified risk by a pool of insurers. The leading insurer manages on behalf of the co-insurers according to the terms of the agreement implemented.

3.1.1. Hypotheses to be tested

The measures taken have had a real impact on undertakings' access to the market if the following hypotheses hold:

Hypothesis 1: from the introduction of the single market, i.e. from the translation of the above texts into the legislation of the States, undertakings have changed their behaviour regarding the modes of access to the market: more subsidiaries or branches, more operations under the freedom to provide services or other modes of access (co-insurance, fronting, etc.).

Hypothesis 2: in parallel, undertakings have benefited from this opening by extending their field of operations throughout Europe (insofar, however, as the markets were not already saturated).

3.1.2. Indicators used to test the hypotheses

Over the reference period used for the analysis, the following are measured:

(a) to test hypothesis 1: the trend in the Community flow obtained both through new facilities and by traditional modes of establishment (subsidiaries);
(b) to test hypothesis 2: the extension of the geographical area of each undertaking.

3.2. The survey results

3.2.1. The development of subsidiaries and branches of the survey undertakings in the EU between 1989 and 1995

The number of undertakings

Considering the sub-sample of 'European' undertakings, it is found that from 1989 to 1994, they increased their number of subsidiaries more than their number of branches.

Table 3.1.   Change in the number of subsidiaries and branches of the sample group

	Total number of subsidiaries		Total number of branches	
	1989	1994[1]	1989	1994[1]
Total	210	232	162	161

[1] It was not possible to update these figures in 1995, since not all the undertakings interviewed replied.

Turnover

There was a very positive trend in turnover of the subsidiaries, as shown in Table 3.2.

The trend in turnover in the branches over the same period is hard to determine. In fact, very few interviewees were able to reply to this question on account of the difficulty in isolating these figures in the undertaking.

Table 3.2.   Trend in turnover of the European subsidiaries (sample group)

	Turnover ('000 ECU)		Difference 1989–94	Difference after deflation
	1989	1994[1]		
Life	2,387	3,393	+ 42%	+14.63%
Non-life	4,145	7,964	+ 92%	+54.94%

[1] It was not possible to update these figures in 1995, since not all the undertakings interviewed replied.

3.2.2. Fronting and co-insurance in the EU

In our sample, the presence of fronting and co-insurance is minimal, although it increased slightly during the period from 1989 to 1995:

(a) fronting: three undertakings stated that they engaged in fronting operations in 1989 and four in 1995;

(b) co-insurance: six undertakings stated that they engaged in co-insurance in 1989 and ten undertakings in 1995.

3.2.3. Freedom to provide services

In the sample, 14 undertakings stated that they operate under the freedom to provide services. These were:

(a) undertakings specializing in life assurance (three Luxembourg, one UK, one France, one Belgium);

(b) undertakings specializing in non-life insurance (three Germany, two UK, one France, one Belgium, one Denmark).

The turnover of these undertakings developed only recently. In 1995, the volume of business conducted by these 14 insurers varied considerably, ranging from ECU 56,000 per year to ECU 550 million per year. The average is ECU 60 million per year.

The second question is to determine whether the creation of the single market encouraged undertakings to develop a true European strategy, i.e. to seek to be present and to develop their business activities in a larger part of the European territory.

3.3. Facts and figures from the survey of 100 undertakings

In the sample questioned, the percentage of undertakings present in at least one other Member State rose from 28% in 1989 to 39% in 1995.

It is interesting to note as well that, in the sample used, it is the medium-sized undertakings (from ECU 10 million to ECU 500 million in premiums per year) and the 'specialized' undertakings (either in life or in a class of non-life) which made the most progress over the period from 1989 to 1995 towards operating in Europe.

For the 'large' undertakings, or the 'general' undertakings, it is probable, given the already high percentage of 'European' undertakings in our sample in 1989, that the move towards operating in Europe had already taken place before 1989 (see Figure 3.1).

Figure 3.1. **Presence in at least one Member State (other than the home Member State)**

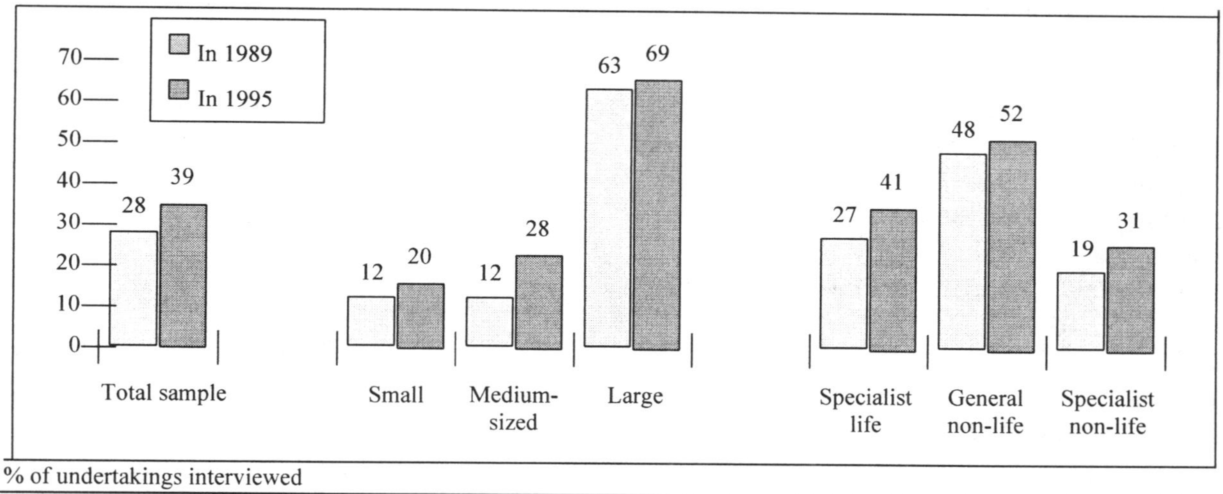

% of undertakings interviewed

3.3.1. Changes in the mean number of countries in which undertakings are present

Subsidiaries and branches

In general, undertakings extended the number of Member States in which they are present between 1989 and 1995.

Table 3.3. **Mean number of Member States in which the undertakings are present**

	Business activity	
	Life	Non-life
Through subsidiaries		
1989	2.5	2.8
1995	3.3	4.1
Through branches		
1989	2.0	2.9
1995	1.8	2.6

Co-insurance and fronting

As regards co-insurance and fronting, the very limited number of undertakings in our sample engaging in this type of operation does not allow significant averages to be calculated. Considering them individually, it can nevertheless be said that these undertakings work in two to four countries in co-insurance and in one or two countries in fronting, and that this number did not vary between 1989 and 1995.

Freedom to provide services

The 14 undertakings of the sample group having operated in 1995 under the freedom to provide services, still operate in this manner in a small number of countries:

1 country   : seven undertakings;
2 countries   : three undertakings;
5 countries   : one undertaking;
6 countries   : one undertaking;
8 countries   : one undertaking;
11 countries   : one undertaking.

3.4. Case studies

The same questions, concerning the number of countries in which they are established, were put to the following five undertakings.

A. UAP

Subsidiaries and branches

UAP increased the number of its subsidiaries between 1989 and 1994 but has very few branches.

Freedom to provide services

The group developed business under the freedom to provide services in two specific market segments:

(1) *'Up-market' life*, from a subsidiary set up specially for this purpose in 1991 in Luxembourg: Paneurolife, whose turnover grew rapidly (about ECU 300 million in 1995).

The business of this undertaking under the freedom to provide services was built up mainly in the countries bordering that of its head office (Luxembourg): Belgium, France, Germany.

UAP's reason for entering into business under the freedom to provide services, targeting the general public, is the existence of a European clientele with standard requirements, which was the case for the type of service offered by Paneurolife.

The success of Paneurolife is very closely linked to the formula and the organization set up to respond to this clientele (shareholders, product flexibility, distribution networks) which were intended to be 'European' from the start.

(2) *Large risks in non-life*: It is impossible to discover the turnover of business carried out under the freedom to provide services in the large risks sector (still low, according to UAP). Nevertheless, the Paneurorisk unit (European economic interest grouping to support the European subsidiaries for large risks) is issuing an increasing number of contracts in this form.

But it is still customer demand which is the motive force (risk manager of large risks). In fact, the risk manager finds this method makes it easier to supervise and keep track of the costs/yield of all the contracts.

The curbs (for the insurer UAP) are:

(a) the need to have a local network to handle claims;
(b) the obligation to make tax returns for each country (complicates file management).

From 1989 to 1995, the number of different Member States where UAP was present varied little (whether subsidiaries or branches are considered): in fact, the group was already present in the majority of Member States well before 1989. Nevertheless, in 1987–88, the management of UAP decided to anticipate the creation of the single market planned for 1992 and decided in favour of a certain number of large acquisitions (made from 1988 to 1992) which, without strictly speaking 'opening up' new markets, would go a long way to strengthening and intensifying the Group's presence in certain target countries: Belgium, Germany, the UK, Ireland, the Netherlands, Italy.

Similarly, the Group's main activity under the freedom to provide services (Paneurolife, in Luxembourg), with its sales mainly destined for Belgium and France, does not really open up new countries, but enables new customer segments to be reached and therefore the Group's market share to be increased there.

B. Victoria

Subsidiaries and branches

Victoria concentrated its activities within the EU in only a few countries (Portugal, Spain, Greece, the Netherlands), giving priority to the market share held in a small number of countries, as opposed to a wider geographical presence.

The strategy adopted was to develop through subsidiaries, the four branches existing in Portugal in 1989 being transformed into subsidiaries from 1992.

The reason was to have transparency in costs and yield and to make the manager of each subsidiary, considered as an autonomous profit centre, aware of his responsibilities which is not so easy to achieve with a branch.

Freedom to provide services

At present, no operations are undertaken under the freedom to provide services. Victoria gives the following reasons for this:

(a) the business philosophy, according to which proximity is the best way of serving customers. It does not seem very realistic to provide services to customers without the accompanying infrastructures in the country;

(b) the economic point of view: the necessary efforts to transcend the legal, tax and language barriers associated with exercising the freedom to provide services generate considerable costs which are not justified by the existing commercial potential.

Finally, even without the freedom to provide services, Victoria considers itself to be sufficiently represented abroad at present through its subsidiaries and its membership of insurance networks.

The European presence of the Victoria Group, subsidiaries and branches together, remained unchanged during the reference period (1989–95). The Group sought more to boost its presence in four EU countries (Portugal, Spain, Greece, the Netherlands), increasing its market shares and achieving a significant rate of return. The explanations for this lie in:

(a) the group's historical strategy, traditionally oriented more towards the countries of Central Europe (Austria, Czechoslovakia) or its neighbouring countries (the Netherlands) than towards those of Western Europe;
(b) the efforts from 1990 *to* reconquer the new *Länder,* where Victoria had its largest market in the first half of the century; the company's resources devoted to this objective were no longer available for a strategy of expansion abroad;
(c) finally, the Group's profitability objectives, which induce it to work in depth in a few countries, rather than to diversify over a larger number.

C. Mapfre

Subsidiaries and branches

Mapfre deliberately took the branch option to develop in a neighbouring country (Portugal) and the subsidiary option in Italy.

The reasons for the choice of a branch in Portugal, where Mapfre has rapidly become a major operator (leading foreign insurer), are:

(a) the simplicity of operation (management from Spain of the activities in Portugal, which is considered as an additional 'region');
(b) the possibilities available through freedom of establishment.

Freedom to provide services

However, no business is conducted through the freedom to provide services on account of the importance of proximity in the sale of mass risks insurance products in Spain and Portugal, which requires a presence (branch) in the country, both to handle claims and to manage distribution (strong influence of agents).

Mapfre's European presence has developed as follows:

The Mapfre Group's strategy concentrated as a priority on the development and profitability of its national operations (Spain) and on the development of considerable business in Latin America.

At present, the Group, which specializes in small risks (especially in private motor vehicle insurance), does not consider its priorities to lie in establishment in any of the EU markets: the reasons it gives for this are the critical size necessary, saturation and difficulties of these markets.

D. Fortis

Subsidiaries and branches

The Fortis Group has developed in the EU essentially through subsidiaries. The only branch existing in 1989 (in France) was absorbed by the French subsidiary.

The reasons for development through subsidiaries rather than branches lie in the nature of the Group's business, which focuses essentially on the personal market (70% of business) as opposed to the corporate risk market (30%).

The Fortis Group in fact considers that development on the small risks market requires:

(a) significant size and resources. The experience of Amev, which tried unsuccessfully to establish itself through branches in France, Belgium and Denmark, confirms this need for the Amev Group. For Fortis, 'success in a mass risks market is impossible if you are small'. It is therefore better to buy to reach this critical size rapidly;
(b) physical and cultural proximity to customers, which is achieved more easily by a national undertaking than by a foreign branch.

Finally, it should be noted that the reduction in the number of subsidiaries (and the disappearance of the branch) is also linked to the search for economies of scale: in England, for example, two subsidiaries were merged into one.

Freedom to provide services

The Fortis Group only operates under the freedom to provide services in one case, from its Luxembourg subsidiary, distributing life products in the neighbouring countries (mainly Belgium).

The reasons are as follows:

(a) regarding the large risk market: the low level of activity of the group in indemnity insurance for international customers,
(b) regarding life and contingency insurance: for international groups, the use of a network of partners.

Apart from Belgium and the Netherlands, the Fortis Group was present in 1990 (year of the creation of the Group from two units Amev and AG) and in 1995 in the same six EU Member States (France, Spain, UK, Ireland, Denmark, Luxembourg).

It cannot therefore be said that the SMP has broadened the Group's establishment and sales strategy in Europe.

Nevertheless, Fortis, through its creation from two national units, has endowed itself with the resources to strengthen its activities on the European markets where it was already established through the successive buy-outs of other undertakings and the creation of subsidiaries (for example: in Spain with Caixa), and even to boost its capacities on one of its national markets (buy-out of the ASLK-CGER Group in Belgium).

As far as the freedom to provide services is concerned, the only experience is the creation of a subsidiary in Luxembourg for the sale of life products to Belgian customers. This too is not an opening to new countries, but another way of strengthening its presence on one of the domestic markets.

E. Cecar

Subsidiaries and branches

Cecar opted in favour of subsidiaries to develop in Europe, for the following reasons:

(a) Cecar's development strategy: the choice of development through 'portfolio purchases' and therefore the acquisition of holdings in existing brokerage firms;
(b) the need to retain 'key people' in an influential manner in the undertakings purchased by integrating them into the capital. It is these people who ensure the continuity of customer relations;
(c) the desire of customers (large multinational undertakings) wishing for support from their broker, who is capable of providing a full service immediately, in the various European countries, has led to Cecar forming partnerships by buying into existing firms.

Freedom to provide services

Cecar considers freedom to provide services to be well suited to handling large risks, provided: it has a network at its disposal in each country to provide local or customer service; and it is directed at multinational customers managed by a risk manager. In fact, this gives the latter the advantage of being able to supervise the risks of its establishments in the various countries through a single policy.

On the other hand, Cecar considers that freedom to provide services is not at all suited to liability type contracts, on account of the non-harmonization of contract law in the various countries.

The Cecar Group was formed through subsidiaries from 1983 until 1993, the year in which the subsidiary was set up in Germany. The Group was therefore essentially formed before 1989, for two reasons:

(a) Cecar's clientele, which essentially comprises large undertakings, led the broker to ensure its growth by supporting them in their international business on the markets where they were present. With six European countries, Cecar considers today that it has not finished its establishment;

(b) the general restructuring of the large brokerage firms, during the same period, forced Cecar to enter into alliances with other firms, through financial holdings (subsidiaries) or partnership agreements.

Freedom to provide services, under this strategy, aims to provide better service to the customer who so wishes through the facility (offered to him) of a single policy or, for the broker, to manage a large account more rigorously.

3.5. Secondary sources

3.5.1 Changes in patterns of access

Statistical information from the supervisory authorities of the Member States on changes in cross-border trade within the EU[3] shows that during the period of reference the business written abroad via branches was of only relatively limited importance. Above average international activities via branches are observed for Belgium, Ireland and Italy. More non-life business seems to be carried out via branches abroad than life business. This is probably to be explained by the international character of trade in large risks.

Business written via branches in the host country mirrors this picture. In some Member States, penetration of national insurance markets via foreign EU branches is quite advanced. An exceptionally high share is recorded in Ireland, where foreign branches (often those from the UK) take a market share of more than 38%. In other countries, like France or Greece, the market share was well over 10% in 1993. On the other hand, in Austria, Finland and Sweden, foreign branches do not yet play an important role.

3.5.2. Changes in patterns of access: breakdown by country

Belgium

As regards business written abroad, it is mainly Belgian non-life insurance enterprises which achieve a significant turnover. The share of total gross premiums written attributable to foreign business was 17.8% for non-life insurance enterprises (out of total non-life insurance business), compared with 1.4% for life insurance enterprises and 0.7% for composite insurance enterprises (1993). Moreover, only a small number of the larger enterprises, which

---

[3]   Eurostat, *Insurance in Europe,* 1996.

have started to operate throughout Europe from their Belgian headquarters, are responsible for these activities.

The market share of foreign branches in Belgium in 1993 accounts for a relatively small share (6.5%) of total gross premiums written (1993). In life insurance, 1.4% of premiums were written by EU branches and 6.9% by non-EU branches. In non-life insurance, more premiums are written by EU branches (3.8%) than non-EU branches (1.1%).

Denmark

Danish insurance enterprises have not been very active abroad. The number of foreign branches active in Denmark has been fairly stable for many years. In all, 51 branches of foreign firms operate in the non-life market and two in the life market. Those branches achieved market shares of between 5 and 6% in non-life insurance and about 2% in life insurance (1993).

Germany

In all classes, direct business written abroad (whether via the freedom of providing services or via branches) was of secondary importance. This applies especially to life and health insurance, in which only three insurance enterprises were operating abroad in 1993. A far greater number of non-life enterprises (48) operated abroad in 1993, but nearly 50% of foreign business was generated by a single firm. However, this does not mean that German insurance firms are not active internationally; they generally prefer to set up a subsidiary in countries in which they do business.

Greece

The market share of branches of foreign enterprises varies from product to product. In accident insurance, foreign branches wrote 48.6% of gross direct premiums written. In legal expenses and capital redemption, they have an even more dominant position (79.4 and 89.2% respectively) (1992). The activities of Greek enterprises in markets other than the domestic one are still of little economic importance.

Spain

Considering the opportunities created by the opening up of the single market, Spanish enterprises appear to be only just starting to make inroads into other EU markets. The proximity of the Principality of Andorra makes it a particularly attractive location for branches of Spanish firms, especially those based in the neighbouring autonomous community of Catalonia, where most of the Spanish enterprises active in the Principality have their head offices. Andorra was also the location of most of the foreign branches of composite insurance enterprises.

Gross premiums written by such 'foreign' branches generally accounted for only a small share of total business, 0.7% in non-life enterprises and 0.1% in composite insurance enterprises (1993).

France

French non-life insurance firms had branches in nearly all the EU Member States, with an emphasis on the UK and Germany, which generated 28 and 12% respectively of gross premiums written by such branches (1993).

French insurance enterprises had a total of 91 branches abroad. Gross premiums written abroad by French life enterprises via branches and the freedom to provide services (FPS) totalled FF 667 million or 0.2% of total gross life insurance premiums written. In non-life insurance premiums written abroad totalled FF 9,041 million or 3.6% of total gross non-life premiums written (1993).

Ireland

In contrast to the high market share enjoyed by branches of foreign firms in Ireland, Irish insurance enterprises have only seven branches abroad, two of which are operated by life enterprises and five by non-life enterprises. They are all located in the EU. Turnover written via branches abroad totalled 7.4% of total gross life premiums written and 4.8% of total gross non-life premiums written (1993).

In addition to branch business, Irish enterprises also write business FPS. Business written in Ireland covering risks situated in other EU countries represented an aggregate 8% of gross premiums written (1993). This business is expected to grow at a steady rate owing to the establishment of a number of captive insurance enterprises in the International Financial Services Centre in Dublin.

Italy

Branches of foreign enterprises operating in Italy, in non-life accounted for 4.2% of direct Italian premiums, and 1.8% of premiums in life (1993). In 1994, the number of foreign branches active in Italy went down.

As regards the activities of Italian enterprises abroad, their foreign business, direct premiums and reinsurance premiums accepted (life and non-life) saw a 17.1% rise in 1993 in comparison with 1992. About half of this total business written abroad was written via branches while the other half was written under the freedom to provide services. The highest degree of internationalization was shown by specialist reinsurers. Composite enterprises had the highest number of branches abroad.

Luxembourg

In recent years, there has been a drop in the number of foreign branches, owing to changes in legal form and the fact that some branches have given up their authorization in preference to carrying on business under FPS from their head offices. The market share of branches of foreign firms in 1993 was only 7.8% of total life and non-life premiums written. They are generally branches of firms based in neighbouring countries and in Switzerland.

In contrast, few Luxembourg-registered firms are established outside the country: only two non-life enterprises have branches in the UK and one in the Netherlands. As regards FPS, more than 40 Luxembourg-registered firms operate outside the country, two-thirds of which are in life insurance.

Netherlands

The activities of Dutch insurance enterprises abroad (via branches or the freedom of providing services), are rather limited both in life insurance (5.2% of total gross premiums) and in non-life insurance (0.6%). In life insurance, the business written by branches abroad amounts to HFL 1,337 million, which is a share of 5.2% of the total gross premiums written. In non-life business, activities via branches abroad are even more limited (HFL 155 million or 0.6% of the total of gross premiums written). This is because most of the business of Dutch insurance groups abroad is done by subsidiaries and affiliates.

Looking at the activity of foreign enterprises in the Netherlands, the market share of these branches remains low – 6.4% in life insurance and 5.8% in non-life insurance. Enterprises with their headquarters in Switzerland constitute a large part thereof.

Austria

Hitherto, the activities of Austrian insurance enterprises abroad have been very limited in scope, the proportion of foreign business in non-life insurance being 0.1%.

In both life and non-life business, the market share of foreign branches is limited: 1% of the gross premiums earned in non-life and only 0.5% in life (1993). Most Austrian branches of foreign firms were established by German or Swiss insurance enterprises.

Portugal

Total gross premiums written abroad represented only 0.4% of total direct premiums written by Portuguese enterprises and branches registered in Portugal.

At the same time, the market share of branches of foreign enterprises operating in Portugal was 9% of total gross premiums written. Spanish enterprises had the largest number of branches, but French-registered firms had the largest market share (1993).

Finland

Branches of Finnish non-life insurance enterprises accounted for only 1.3% of total direct non-life business (1993). No Finnish life insurance enterprises had branches abroad.

Due to certain legal restrictions in the past, the market share of foreign enterprises, which operate two non-life branches in Finland, accounts for only 0.3% of total gross premiums. At the end of 1993, there were no insurance subsidiaries of foreign enterprises in Finland. The country's reinsurance enterprises accept mainly Finnish risks.

Sweden

Swedish insurers have become more active in the international market since the beginning of the 1980s, mostly by acquiring foreign firms and setting up branches abroad. This development is largely a by-product of the growing internationalization of major Swedish non-financial enterprises. The types of business carried out abroad – mostly in Europe and the USA – are large risks and reinsurance, as well as some classes of mass risks.

In 1993, Swedish enterprises had 16 foreign subsidiaries, most of them in neighbouring countries and in the UK. No information is yet available on the foreign branches of Swedish life and non-life enterprises, but the number is thought to be very small.

In the past, owing to the saturation of the market, the Swedish government has been reluctant to license captives,[4] and Swedish companies have occasionally gone abroad to countries like Luxembourg to set up such specialized enterprises.

In 1993, 15 foreign enterprises were registered in Sweden, 13 of which were branches engaging in non-life business and the remaining two, non-life subsidiaries (one operated by a Danish and one by a Norwegian firm). The share held by foreign enterprises of the non-life market is 2% (1993). Firms from EU countries accounted for the largest share.

Cross-border business (contracted under freedom to provide services) has always existed in Sweden. Since the mid-1980s, premiums earned on certain savings products in direct life insurance have increased owing to differences in the taxation of such products depending on whether they are sold by Swedish or non-resident firms. Policies sold under the freedom to provide services are almost exclusively marketed by brokers, which are often Swedish insurance enterprises or Swedish banks.

UK

The UK insurance industry has always been inherently international. Nearly 27% of non-life net premiums written and 17% of life net premiums written were earned overseas in local subsidiaries and branches (1993), in addition to international business placed in the London international market. In Europe only Switzerland has a higher overseas proportion of premium. The UK accounts for 33% of the world market for MAT business.

UK insurers' international business tends to be concentrated in the USA and Commonwealth countries.

3.5.3. Country analysis of the declarations of intent to operate under the freedom to provide services

According to the Community Directives, an undertaking intending to carry out operations under the freedom to provide services for the first time in a Member State must notify the competent authorities of the home country. The analysis below was conducted on the basis of the reports of the supervisory bodies (where the information exists) or on the basis of a survey of supervisory bodies.

Table 3.4 illustrates the intentions of economic operators to operate under the freedom to provide services. This table, which gives the number of undertakings having declared their intention to operate in one or more other Member States, can only be interpreted as a declaration of intent, since the undertakings do not always follow up this plan.

---

[4]   Second Non-life Insurance Directive, impact study, unpublished, November 1994. Captives are generally not set up specifically to gain cross-border involvement but as part of a move to 'self insurance'. Operation of captives has been facilitated by the Directive. Captives have been set up in the 'home' country to retain part of the risk or as alternatives to fronting but data suggests that few European based captives are in home countries. Most are based in, and have become much easier to operate in Luxembourg and the International Financial Services Centre in Dublin. There has been a significant move to the use of captives which is continuing (there are now over 250 in these two centres).

Table 3.4.   Number of European undertakings having declared their intention to come to each country to operate under the freedom to provide services

Country	Total number of undertakings in each country	(a)				(b)
		Life	Non-life + composite	Total	(4) / (1) (%)	
	(1)	(2)	(3)	(4)	(5)	(6)
France	599	14	49	63	10.5	n.a.
Belgium	255	6	19	25	9.8	278
Ireland	108	n.a.	n.a.	n.a.	n.a.	192
Luxembourg	73	28	10	38	52	211
UK	828	16	168	184	22	172
Italy	274	3	34	37	13.5	233
Portugal	86	0	0	0	0	8
Netherlands	491	6	80	86	17.5	n.a.
Germany	798	n.a.	n.a.	n.a.	n.a.	n.a.
Denmark	250	-	13	13	5.2	70

(a) Number of national undertakings having declared their intention to operate in Europe under the freedom to provide services.

(b) Number of European undertakings having declared their intention to come to each country to operate under the freedom to provide services.

Source: Reports and questionnaires of supervisory bodies.

Belgium

The number of European undertakings having declared their intention to operate under the freedom to provide services in Belgium doubled between 1991 (159 authorizations) and 1994 (278 authorizations). To give an idea of scale, there are 255 insurance undertakings in this country. It is also found that movement is very concentrated, since 83% of the declarations concern companies originating from the UK, France, Luxembourg, Germany and the Netherlands.

Conversely, the number of Belgian companies having declared that they wish to operate under the freedom to provide services is far lower (9.8%).

France

Belgium and Germany are the main targets of French undertakings using the freedom to provide services and operating mainly in non-life. Belgium is the exception to this rule as there are almost as many declarations in life as in non-life.

Luxembourg

This is the country which has seen the strongest growth in the number of undertakings set up (+ 85%). The development of the freedom to provide services is not lagging behind. The number of non-Luxembourg undertakings authorized to operate under the FPS is even higher than that of the national undertakings. The number of foreign branches is falling and replaced by the freedom to provide services, especially in non-life. To engage in life business, undertakings visibly opt in favour of establishing a subsidiary.

The non-Luxembourg undertakings having declared their intention to operate under the freedom to provide services come mainly from Germany, the Netherlands and Belgium. They essentially deal with large risks. According to the 1994 report of the Luxembourg supervisory authorities, the business of these companies has not really started, since the appointment of a tax representative responsible for collecting and paying the tax on insurance premiums is not effective in the majority of cases, whereas it is a prerequisite to be able to operate. Luxembourg undertakings mainly target the Belgian, German, Dutch and French markets and operate in the life sector.

Denmark

In life, half the European undertakings having declared their intention to operate under the freedom to provide services in Denmark are of Luxembourg origin. In non-life, there are more participants. The Belgian, British and Italian undertakings account for 33% of the declarations. The use of the freedom to provide services by countries which have recently joined the EU or neighbouring countries, such as Sweden, Norway, Iceland and Austria, which account for 18% of the declarations, should be noted.

Ireland

European undertakings give preference to development through the freedom to provide services in Ireland. Whereas the number of undertakings having declared that they wish to operate under non-life is starting to stabilize, declarations concerning life are getting under way. However, non-life remains far more developed.

The statistics available do not include declarations made by Irish undertakings.

UK

The number of British companies which have declared that they wish to operate under the freedom to provide services increased considerably during the reference period. Until 1993, the companies made broad declarations covering several countries. Since 1994, they have been more selective and refer to a single country.

According to the Association of British Insurers, this is attributable to experience and a real commercial development policy after the observation period of the early years.

Italy

Italian undertakings use the freedom to provide services essentially in non-life.

Undertakings of the other Member States have filed a large number of declarations of intent to operate under the freedom to provide services. There is a very great disparity between the two sectors. The number of declarations in life only amounted to 10% of those in non-life in 1994. In non-life, undertakings from the UK account for half the declarations. Belgian, German and French undertakings account for a further third. In life, Luxembourg undertakings account for half the declarations.

Portugal

No declaration in any form whatsoever was made by a Portuguese company to operate in another European country.

Conversely, eight companies from the EU declared that they wished to operate in Portugal under the freedom to provide services.

Netherlands

Dutch companies made declarations essentially in the non-life sector. As in the neighbouring countries, the number of declarations is high compared to the number of undertakings. There are two distinct types of applications: those for a specific country and those for all the Member States of the EU.

3.5.4. Supply-side obstacles to access

Primary sources and statistical information show relatively modest use by market operators of the new modes of access offered by the single market directives.

The main reasons can be broken down into the following main categories.[5]

The absence of a transparent legal framework – the difficulty of drawing a precise frontier between freedom of establishment and freedom to provide services

Although the effect of the Third Directive was to harmonize, to a large degree, supervisory regulations and the conditions of exercise of insurance by way of establishment and free provision of services (FOS) – prudential control, rules on conflict of law with regard to the law applicable, indirect premium taxes, winding-up – differences remain. These include notific-ation procedures, designation of a general agent under establishment, designation of a representative for handling claims under motor FOS, less strict terms and conditions of exercise under FOS than by way of establishment, direct premium taxes, company taxation and accounts, means of supervision and sanctions by the host country, which explain and justify why a clear distinction between the two systems should be maintained.

Articles 59 et seq. of the EC Treaty contain the principle of free provision of services. It should be noted that, according to the jurisprudence of the European Court of Justice (ECJ), the free provision of services can involve a movement of the provider of the service, as envisaged in Article 60(3) of the EC Treaty, and/or a movement of the recipient of the service to the Member State of the provider; but it may also involve a situation in which neither moves.[6]

If an activity is exercised through the free provision of services with the presence of the provider on the territory of the host country, the distinction between services and establishment will derive from the extent to which the former has a temporary character, while

---

[5]   *Sources*: CEA Contribution to the Discussions on the Barriers to the functioning of the Single Insurance Market, Paris 19/02/1996. KPMG study, Second Non-life Directive, November 1994. Marketing Non-life Insurance in Europe, Cameron Markby Hewitt, April 1996.

[6]   Joined Cases 286/82 and 26/83 *Luisi and Carbone* [1984] ECR 377. Case 76/90 *Säger* [1991] ECR I-195

the right of establishment presupposes a durable presence in the host country. The distinction stems from the Treaty itself, Article 60 of which stipulates that a person providing a service may, in order to do so, 'temporarily' pursue his activity in the State where the service is provided.

According to the most recent case-law of the ECJ, the temporary nature of the provision of services is to be determined in the light of its duration, regularity, periodicity and continuity.[7]

If an activity is carried on temporarily, but frequently, the question arises whether there might not be, on the part of the company, an intention to side-step the rules on establishment by invoking the freedom to provide services. The ECJ has acknowledged that a Member State is entitled to take steps to prevent a service provider whose activity is entirely or mainly directed towards its territory from exercising the freedom enshrined in Article 59 of the EC Treaty in order to circumvent the rules of professional conduct which would be applicable to him if he were established in that State.[8] It adds that such a situation may fall within the ambit of the chapter on the right of establishment and not of that on the freedom to provide services.[9]

The criterion of frequency is important in order to determine whether there may be an abuse of the right conferred under Article 59; it is therefore not sufficient to define the service provided (an establishment may also operate on an occasional basis). However, this reasoning is valid only for those forms of provision of services which involve movement by the service provider towards the Member State of provision considered in Article 60(3) of the Treaty.

Thus, a situation where an insurance undertaking is constantly being approached within its territory by consumers residing in other Member States is not held to constitute an abuse. In such a case there would be no intention to abuse the right recognized by the Treaty.

However, it is not always easy to draw the line between the two concepts of provision of services and establishment. Some situations are difficult to classify. This is particularly true of an instance in which the insurer has recourse to a certain permanent presence of the undertaking's own staff in the State in which it provides services. Such an arrangement is commonly referred to as a 'representative office', a flexible structure traditionally regarded simply as a means of reconnoitring the market, establishing contacts and examining to what extent establishment in the country concerned might prove viable.

The Court has therefore acknowledged that, in principle, an enterprise which has recourse to an intermediary in another Member State on a permanent basis to carry on activities in that Member State may lose its benefits as a cross-border service provider and fall within the scope of the provisions on the right of establishment. The Court seeks to prevent the abuse of the freedom to provide services in order to circumvent the rules that would apply if the undertaking were established in the host Member State.[10]

---

[7]   Judgment of 3 December 1974, Case 33/74 *Van Binsbergen* [1974] ECR 1299; Joined Cases 286/82 and 26/83 *Luisi and Carbone* [1984] ECR 377; judgment of 3 February 1993, Case 148/91 *Veronica* [1993] ECR I-487; judgment of 5 October 1994, Case 23/93 *TV10* [1994] ECR I-4795; Case 55/94 *Gebhard* [1995] ECR I-4195.

[8]   Case 205/84 *Commission* v *Germany* [1986] ECR 3755; Case 33/74 *Van Binsbergen* [1974] ECR 1299; Case 148/91 *Veronica* [1993] ECR I-487; judgment of 5 October 1994, Case 23/93 *TV 10* [1994] ECR I-4795.

[9]   Case 205/84 *Commission* v *Germany,* paragraph 22; Case 33/74 *Van Binsbergen,* paragraph 13.

[10] Case 205/84 *Commission* v *Germany* [1986] ECR 3755, paragraphs 21 and 22; Case C-148/91 *Veronica,* paragraph 13.

This possible risk of abusing the freedom to provide services has nevertheless been eliminated in the insurance sector as a result of the harmonization achieved by the Community Directives concerning the conditions for taking up and carrying on insurance activities. In effect, the prudential rules for insurance undertakings are equivalent, whichever way insurance activities are carried out: by way of establishment or through the provision of cross-border services.

Furthermore, noting the recent jurisprudence of the Court of Justice, the Commission considers that the Member State in receipt of the provision of services may not treat any permanent presence on its territory of a provider of services in the same way as an establishment and, therefore, it may not subject it to the rules relating to the right of establishment.

In fact, the Court of Justice recently acknowledged that freedom to provide services does not mean that the provider may not equip himself with some form of infrastructure (chambers, office, etc.) in the host Member State in so far as it is necessary for the purposes of performing the services in question.[11] The Court takes the view that in such cases the temporary character of the services provided should be determined by their duration, frequency, periodicity and continuity.[12]

If the staff do not carry out insurance activities, it is clear that such offices cannot, of course, be regarded as branches although the host State may always require to be informed about the opening of such an office and could also subject it to a light form of non-systematic control to verify that the office is not undertaking insurance activities.

If the permanent staff engage in insurance activities, the situation is quite clear. The insurance undertaking is regarded as having a branch. The problem, however, is where to draw the line between 'temporary' and 'permanent' and when a permanent presence can be considered to be 'acting like an agency'. The insurance industry hopes that clear criteria for a distinction can be established in this area − if the various European supervisory authorities are not to develop widely differing 'case-law'. The question remains whether anything short of harmonized regulations (as opposed to interpretative Commission Communications explaining the position of the Community) is enough to remedy the double difficulty of ensuring that (a) Member States apply the Court's jurisprudence as interpreted by the Commission the same way, and (b) Member States interpret new ECJ developments correctly and in the same manner.

Diverging interpretations of the 'general good'

The concept of general good introduced by the Third Insurance Directive is a key element in the system. It stems directly from the case law of the Court of Justice providing that an insurance undertaking operating under a single licence must comply with host-country rules adopted in the interest of the general good. In particular, it applies:

(a)   as part of the procedure for opening a branch: the host Member State may inform the insurance company of the conditions under which, in the interest of the general good,

---

11   Case 55/94 *Gebhard* [1995] ECR 1-4195. It should be pointed out that, in his opinion on Case 205/84 *Commission* v *Germany*, the Advocate-General stated that the appointment of an agent or representative (in the host Member State) did not in itself necessarily constitute establishment.

12   Case 55/94 *Gebhard*. It should also be noted that in Case 205/84 *Commission* v *Germany*, the Advocate-General indicated that the use of an agent or permanent representative (in the host State) would not in itself imply establishment.

business must be carried on in that Member State. The host Member State has two months in which to do so;

(b) as regards the marketing of insurance contracts;

(c) in connection with health insurance taken out as an alternative to health cover provided by a statutory social security system: the Third Non-life Directive stipulates that any Member State may require that the contract comply with the specific legal provisions adopted by that Member State to protect the general good in that class of insurance. It may also require that the insurance conditions applicable be notified before the insurance is marketed;

(d) last, an insurance company authorized in its home Member State may advertise its services, through all available means of communication, subject to compliance with any rules governing the form and content of such advertising adopted in the interest of the general good.

Restrictive measures justified by reference to the general good must: come within a field which has not been harmonized; pursue the interest of the general good; be non-discriminatory; be objectively necessary; and be proportionate to the objective pursued.

Finally, it is also necessary for the interest of the general good not to be safeguarded by rules to which the provider of services is already subject in the Member State in which he is established.

The Commission has been confronted with a number of issues and complaints concerning Member States' interpretation of the general good. It will shortly publish a Communication setting out its interpretation of key issues. The following are examples of measures which the Commission is likely to hold as not complying with the general good tests:

(a) the prior notification of contractual terms (control only allowed *ex post*);

(b) capital redemption operations of insurance undertakings (no reason to prohibit the marketing of capitalization products);

(c) mandatory uniform no claims rebate systems (not permissible);

(d) the local language requirement of insurance contracts (not always justified);

(e) professional codes of conduct (may not always be applied to foreign operators);

(f) maximum technical interest rates for life assurance (may not be imposed on foreign operators).

Notification procedures and the concept of the general good

The Third Insurance Directive provides that the supervisory authority of the country of the branch or service (depending on whether it is establishment of FOS) inform, where appropriate, the supervisory authority of the foreign insurer's home State of the conditions of the general good with which he must comply when he operates in that country.

On some markets, it can be seen that the supervisory authorities of the host country, rather than indicating, with reasons, provisions whose compliance they intend to impose on foreign operators under general good, merely provide – more often than not in their own language – a list of the legislation applicable on their market either stating that they are all general good or leaving to the foreign operator the task of determining which provisions must be considered, in his own specific case, to come under general good.

This effectively transfers to operators an obligation which devolves on the supervisory authorities and thus, given the legal insecurity it causes, is a substantial obstacle to the functioning of the single market.

Differences in tax arrangements

A particular problem in life assurance was raised by the ECJ's decision of *Bachmann* v *Belgium* (Case C-204/90 [1992] ECR 249)which represented a major setback for those companies hoping to market their savings in other Member States. Although the Court confirmed that rules allowing only tax reliefs on contributions to pension policies sold by nationally established companies were discriminatory, it decided that this discrimination was justified for reasons of 'fiscal cohesion'.

In a more recent decision (*Wielockx* (Case C-80/94 [1995] ECR 2493)*)*, the Court has all but reversed its position and practically removed the ability of Member States to use 'fiscal cohesion' as a defence. Because although the ECJ agreed in the Wielockx case that certain practices were discriminatory but could nevertheless be justified for reasons of 'fiscal cohesion', it pointed out that if there was a double taxation convention in force between the countries concerned, this convention ensured that there was fiscal cohesion between the two countries. Since double taxation conventions, based on the OECD model, exist between nearly all Member States, the impact of this decision is enormous.

Comparative studies on fiscal regimes governing insurance show significant differences in tax levels and bases. In addition, there are on some markets differences in the way in which contracts concluded with local and foreign insurers (life insurance in Sweden, for example) are treated or between the different categories of insurance operators (tax distortions in favour of mutuals in supplementary health insurance in France; in favour of banks for pension funds in Spain; in favour of benefit funds for doctors in Belgium, for example). These fiscal differences may have a negative effect on competition, even on markets where established and non-established insurers are treated equally in other respects.

The applicable law and conflicts of law

In a cross-border context, an insurance policy will have connections with at least two different Member States. There is a conflict of laws: one has to decide which law is applicable. There is also a conflict of jurisdictions: which national court would have jurisdiction if a dispute were to arise?

An EU insurer who intends to exercise his EU rights will need to look at the legal environment of the policy to ensure, as much as possible, that the policy will be enforceable before whatever judge may have jurisdiction under whatever law (and rules) may be applicable. He cannot assume that his policy drafted in the light of his home country law would be fully valid when sold abroad for two main reasons:

(a) The EU rules on conflicts of laws and jurisdictions are very complex. Parties to an insurance contract are not always free to choose the law applicable to the policy. Even when the parties are free to choose, they cannot be sure that only this law will govern their policy. The rules of another EU country may also apply.

(b) Although the parties may choose any law as the law applicable to their policy, their freedom is not without limit. Their choice may be overridden in certain circumstances by the application of 'mandatory rules'. For example, where the policy is connected with one country only (e.g. insurer, insured and risk are in England), the parties cannot derogate from the mandatory rules (e.g. rules on unfair contact terms) of that country by subjecting their contract to the law of another country.

In relation to insurance risk, the EU law is in the Second and Third Non-life Directives. The parties' freedom of choice depends on the nature of the risk involved and is wider in relation to 'large risks' than 'mass risks'. The Second Non-life Directive has introduced four different tests to determine where the risk is located. The risk is located in the Member State: where the property is situated in relation to building insurance; of registration in relation to vehicle insurance; where the insured took out his policy in relation to travel insurance; or where the insured has his habitual residence or establishment in all other cases.

The Third Non-life Directive has extended freedom of choice to all large risks. Under the Third Non-life Directive, the parties may choose any law. This agreement simplicity is, however, deceptive. 'Mandatory rules' and 'general good' provisions may override the parties' choice. The parties cannot be guaranteed that only the provisions of the law they have chosen will apply to their policy. They need to look at the wider legal environment in which the policy is being issued to identify the rules which may interfere with their initial choice.

Mass risks are all risks other than large risks. The parties' freedom of choice is limited to specific laws designated by the Second Non-life Directive unless those laws allow a wider freedom. The rules are based upon the situation of the risk and/or the insured's residence. Where the insured normally resides or has its central administration in the same EU State where the risk is located, the law of that State applies. Where the insured and the risk are not in the same EU State, the parties may choose to apply: the law of the country of the insured; or the law of the country of the risk; or any other law, if the foregoing laws allow greater freedom of choice.

An EU State may, by way of derogation from the rules above, require that the law applicable to a compulsory insurance contract is the law of the State which imposes the obligation to take out insurance. This difference may lead to serious practical difficulties. For example, an English insurer sells a policy to a French company (France has exercised the above option) in relation to a large risk. As there is freedom of choice, the English insurer chooses English law. Two situations may arise in case of a dispute. If the English judge has jurisdiction, he will enforce the parties' choice of English law as the law governing the policy. If the French judge has jurisdiction, he will disregard the parties' choice and apply French law instead whenever French law imposes the obligation to take out insurance upon the French company.

In the absence of an express choice (or a choice demonstrated with reasonable certainty), the policy will be governed by the law of the country with which it is most closely connected. This country is presumed to be the country where the risk is located.

Whenever there is freedom of choice, its exercise may be limited by two major obstacles: mandatory rules and the concept of general good. The EU Directives give no precise definition of mandatory rules. Indeed, the term 'mandatory rules' may have a different meaning in different provisions of the Second Non-life Directive. Mandatory rules may override the choice of law made by the parties in the following circumstances:

(a) Under Article 7(1)(g) of the Second Non-life Directive, the mandatory rules (referred to as the rules which cannot be derogated from by contract) of that State may apply irrespective of the law chosen by the parties. For example, although insurer, insured and risk are located in England, the parties choose French law as the law applicable to the policy. English mandatory rules may still apply.

(b) Under Article 7(2) of the Second Non-life Directive, the judge who has jurisdiction (who under the Brussels and Lugano Conventions is very likely to be the judge of the insurer's domicile) may apply the mandatory rules of his country irrespective of the law otherwise applicable to the policy.

(c) On certain markets, use of the policyholder's language in insurance documents is compulsory even when this requirement does not seem justified by consumer protection consideration or is not in line with the wishes of the consumer.

(d) Non-compliance on certain markets with provisions in the Third Directives relating to the abolition of material and prior control of contractual and rating conditions.

On certain markets, forms of *a priori* control of contractual and rating conditions still exist which are incompatible with the provisions in the Third Insurance Directives. For example, on some markets, operators must – in order to inform the supervisory authorities which impose this condition – communicate product particulars on new types of contract before they are used. On other markets, supervisory authorities recommend or impose on operators compliance with specific contractual conditions in the form of instructions which, if not complied with, may result in a binding intervention. And last, on yet other markets, the supervisors prohibit, under the general regulations on unfair terms, the use of contractual conditions which are in line with insurance contract legislation but whose validity has never been tested to date in civil courts.

Free reserves

The strictness of rules on the spread of assets linked to own funds. The Third Insurance Directives prohibit States from establishing rules with regard to the choice of assets which do not represent technical reserves.

However, legislation in certain Member States controls the investment not only of the assets representing technical reserves but also those which correspond to the undertaking's own funds, which creates distortion of competition (reserve discrimination) to the detriment of local companies.

Cross-border management of pension funds

National and foreign life insurers are sometimes prohibited from managing group pension funds. In certain States, local or foreign life insurers may not manage group pension funds (with or without guarantee), and yet these activities come under the scope of the Life Insurance Directives (class 7 in the annex to the first Establishment Directive). This provision unjustifiably restricts the exercise of life insurance activities on the market.

Classification of insurance

The definition and classification of life insurance products (distinction between pension insurance products (savings) and insurance products covering death risks; definition and classification of life insurance products linked to investment funds) is not the same on all markets. On the other hand, over the past few years, new forms of insurance cover (e.g. contracts for the provision of services and cover for funeral expenses in death insurance) or new insurance risks (e.g. computer risk insurance in non-life insurance) have emerged.

In the face of this uncertainty and these developments, the need to preserve the transparency of classifications in the context of mutual recognition of agreements calls for consideration to be given to: the equivalence of insurance classes (life and non-life) in Europe; and/or the desirability of periodically adapting the classification of risks per class in the first Insurance Directives.

Motor insurance complexity

The terms and conditions of membership of Motor Guarantee Funds and the national Bureau cause difficulties in a minority of States.

An advance payment of future premiums calculated in accordance with Article 12 of the Non-life FOS Directive (92/49/EEC) may seem acceptable – in so far as it is only required when joining these bodies. However, the way in which Bureaux and Motor Guarantee Funds in some Member States oblige motor liability insurers operating under FOS on their market to pay minimum fixed and non-returnable contributions annually is, on the other hand, not in line with the above provision.

Maximum technical interest rates

Compulsory compliance is required in life insurance with maximum technical interest rates laid down by the legislation of the country of activity. This prudential measure is justified (by those States which apply it) to protect consumers against possible unfair practices (circulation of misleading information on guaranteed interest rates). It is also linked to bonus sharing conditions: the adoption of a prudent interest rate often goes hand-in-hand with bonus sharing.

Compulsory mortality tables

Compulsory compliance in life insurance with the mortality tables of country of commitment. Some delegations consider that this obligation – which means rating is based on the (local) risk covered by the contract – is compatible with the principles of the Third Life Directive. In addition, on some markets, insurance companies are allowed to use their own mortality tables (experience tables) if they have been certified by an independent authorized actuary.

Demand-side obstacles – the consumer

Since 1 July 1994 it has been theoretically possible for the European consumer to take out insurance in any Member State of the EU by contacting directly a company or broker in another Member State, without the need for the foreign insurance company providing the cover to be established in his country. This theory has been put to the test in several consumer surveys.[13]

To the European consumer freedom of movement does not mean 'harmonization'. In other words, the lack of 'Euro-policies' means that insurance taken out in another country will not

---

[13]   One recent example is 'Verzekering in Europa' (Insurance in Europe), Euroconsument, January 1995.

necessarily cover the same risks as the 'same' insurance taken out in the consumer's own country. To the consumer, the legal confusion surrounding the principles of applicable law is a considerable initial obstacle to freedom of movement for insurance services.

When the consumer seizes the initiative, obstacles are also encountered. In one study, a number of insurance companies in various Member States were asked whether they would be prepared to insure a Belgian. Two out of three British companies said 'No' and one said 'Yes' (but not for car insurance); three out of four Luxembourg companies said 'No' and one 'Yes' (but not car insurance), four out of six Dutch companies said 'No' and two 'Yes' (but not car insurance); and five French companies said 'No'. Only two of the companies which gave a positive reply were prepared to offer their Belgian clients contracts governed by Belgian law.

The reason put forward by these companies to justify their refusal included: poor knowledge of the market, little interest in the market, excessive cost, poor understanding of legal differences, and above all the presence in Belgium of a subsidiary of their company to which Belgian policyholders could turn. This final point in the opinion of consumer organizations runs contrary to the interest of consumers. Applying to a national subsidiary of a foreign company does not give free rein to competition, as the rates between one company and another in the same country generally vary considerably less than from one country to another. True competition would consist of being able to compare rates between companies established in different countries in order to highlight their (frequent) distortions so as to be able to buy the policy in the cheapest country.

3.5.5. Report on two Non-life Directives

The Commission, under Article 29 of the Second Non-life Directive (88/357/EEC) commissioned a report[14] on the developments in insurance transacted under the conditions of freedom to provide services for large risks as laid down by the Directive.

For the purposes of this study and under Article 5 of the Directive, large risks were broadly identified as those where either of two qualifying criteria – risk type or policyholder size – is satisfied: if the risk written was a marine aviation and transport or a credit or suretyship risk, then by definition it was viewed as a 'large risk'. Fire and property, general liability and sundry financial loss risks were also classified as large risks where the policyholder concerned met specified size criteria in at least two out of three measures, i.e. balance sheet total, net turnover and average employee count.

The study confirms that while there has not been evidence of a substantial increase in the use of cross-border insurance since the Directive was implemented, it has facilitated the development of the market for multinational companies and large risks. It has legitimized cross-border business, some of which has historically taken place. There has been movement from fronting to direct placement, for example, on marine business from Spain into the London market. In recognizing the trend by larger companies to consider cross-border cover and use of global/European cover, some insurance companies have reacted by clarifying their strategy and forming stronger international networks either internally, through formation of separate 'global' operations or by cross-border acquisition.

---

14   Second Non-life Insurance Directive, impact study, unpublished, November 1994.

There is evidence of a separation of the large risk market for multinationals and the largest corporations which expect to use the international insurance market from the medium-sized and smaller local companies which invariably use local insurance markets. This is starting to be reflected in insurance companies' strategies and approaches. Research was focused on major companies which would clearly fall within the 'large risk' definition. These companies were almost invariably aware of the broad provisions of the Second Non-life Directive and of the availability of the broader European insurance market for their needs. Where companies were not aware of the broad provisions of the Directive, they were 'local' companies or subsidiaries of a foreign parent which arranged their insurance.

The majority of these large risk companies use brokers to advise on their insurance requirements and for placing their needs. The facilities used by the companies included:

(a)   captive insurance companies;
(b)   fronting insurers,[15] plus reinsurers – *fronting* is still used by a number of policyholders. This had been used before the Directive in those countries where freedom to provide services did not exist, particularly by multinationals;
(c)   lead underwriters, plus reinsurers;
(d)   co-insurance with a panel – *co-insurance*.[16] Council Directive 78/473/EEC enabled cross-border activity to take place on a co-insurance basis provided that certain provisos (single contract, Community-based risk, duly authorized leader) were satisfied. There was evidence of some co-insurance activities in all Member States. The major exception was where no use was yet made of placement in foreign markets related to motor insurance which was still provided locally.

Cover for major multinationals is invariably arranged on a multinational basis not restricted to EU countries – hence when there was awareness of pan-European policies as such, they were only seen as particularly relevant where operations were confined to EU countries. To the extent that FPS is now available across the EU, it has facilitated arranging cover for these companies.

Policyholders able to gain the greatest benefit are those located in previously heavily regulated markets, such as the German insurance market, where the impact of deregulation of policy terms and conditions and premium rates combines with the ability to take advantage of the Directive and place the business outside the local market. Policyholders see themselves as drivers of the need for international coverage and new products, in particular companies with risk or insurance managers who understand risks better. The Directive has helped such managers in more cost effective placement of their business.

All the following routes to gaining more cost effective insurance coverage have been frequently indicated as being used by respondents. Captive numbers continue to increase. A significant number of the Luxembourg captives are insurance subsidiaries of Swedish business companies, and France appears to be a major source of parent companies for Luxembourg

---

[15]   Fronting 'hides' the extent to which cross-border activity takes place since the business then placed as reinsurance is even less easily measured, and is thus outside the scope of the Directive. It continues to be used in some cases rather than direct placement since the fronting company can handle claims on behalf of the reinsurers.

[16]   Coverage of a risk by more than one insurer for a proportionate share of an overall premium is the classic form of co-insurance: this has, for example, been an accepted form of risk acceptance in the London market for generations.

captives. These captives are both direct writing and reinsurers, single owners or joint. An example of a joint reinsurance captive covers three major German chemical companies for environmental impairment liability.

Major brokers play a significant role in the placement of business for the large risk market and multinational client. They have knowledge of risk management, insurance company and London market strengths and local insurance markets. For example, the largest broker in Europe has European insurance commission and fee revenues in excess of ECU 450 million and has offices in all EU countries.

All international brokers were aware of the Directive, had considered placing business with foreign insurers and most had done so. Most had handled business on behalf of foreign policyholders – generally subsidiaries of client companies. The Directive has made placing business easier for brokers, especially in handling multinational accounts, which is recognized by the major brokers as key to their success and retention of clients. Intermediaries take the lead in placing business cross-border in order to gain lower price or other benefits for clients. An example of this activity beyond major/large cases is 'local' cross-border activity such as Luxembourg to Belgium. A further reason for placing business with foreign insurers was difficulty of placing risks locally.

In smaller countries, such as Portugal, not all were aware of the Directive and had not considered placing business elsewhere. No evidence in this case was found of 'in' or 'out' FPS activity.

The Directive was seen to have enabled brokers to have increased the scale of competition among insurers to enable the broker to negotiate more broadly on behalf of clients. However, for there to be greater use of FPS, insurers will need to promote themselves better to intermediaries in other countries. Currently, lack of such activity deters local brokers from placing business on an FPS basis. The main areas of FPS activity which have continued from before the Directive or developed since, have been in respect of: marine aviation and transport insurance – which has always been 'international' by nature; coverage of multinational companies or major companies seeking better rates, capacity or cover; and 'near neighbour' activity, in particular between the Netherlands, Belgium, Luxembourg and Germany or from Portugal into Spain or potentially Spain to Portugal, for example on a pooling participation.

One of the key reasons for lack of strong marketing activity by insurers to generate FPS business is the existence of subsidiary and branch operations for most of the leading European insurers in the other major EU countries. This is particularly true for the largest UK companies, the major Dutch companies, increasingly the French companies, the largest German, and indeed the Swiss companies which are perhaps the strongest 'multinational' oriented operations. This situation is increasingly important. In some cases, subsidiaries or branches must be consulted before business is taken direct by a parent or co-subsidiary. If they do not have a subsidiary or branch, they do not actively market, since it is considered necessary to have a local organization to deal with clients, even for large risks. In addition, for commercial lines business, most of the major companies depend upon brokers for their business. They market to the brokers in their 'home' country and locally as their prime source of business. Their business structure is designed to support this.

Co-insurance has always been the underlying basis of operation in the London market and has been used, but to a much lesser extent, in the Dutch market. Some continuing co-insurance activity was referred to in each of the other countries. In London, the operation of the marine and non-marine company markets and of Lloyds is clearly structured, with a lead underwriter agreeing rates with the broker, supported by the market bureau and organizations. All provide central policy signing, premium and claims settlement services to support the operation on a co-insurance basis. London market co-insurance is thus facilitated by the processing bureau and support functions in contrast to, for example, the German co-insurance business which has to be handled by the client, policyholder, or broker with the co-insuring companies.

Generally pools were confined to local requirements and local insurers (and locally registered foreign owned insurers). As an example, the German Pharmapool set up in 1978 to provide liability coverage for medicines was extended to include re-insurers and recently to include foreign insurers. The German aviation pool has cross-border revenue of over 20%, but this has not changed since 1989.

As an example of cross-border business, the 'Strike Club' provides world-wide cover which claims to cover 80% of ship operators world-wide against the risk of operating crews of the ship going on strike. This has operated for many years for shipping companies in most EU countries. P&I (protection and indemnity) clubs have similarly operated cross-border for many years. There are at least six UK clubs and three Luxembourg clubs with revenue of approximately ECU 500 million. The areas where barriers to FOS were seen by policyholders were:

(a) fiscal – uncertainty exists over a lack of clarity of responsibility for payment and understanding of the basis of premium taxes. Particular issues over tax and complexity were repeated with regard to Spain, Italy, France – causing delays and higher costs; lack of common tax laws was seen as a barrier in most cases;

(b) regulatory – the wide range of different regulatory environments is seen as a barrier. For example relating to Italy on aviation policies;

(c) intermediaries were not seen by some policyholders to have sufficient knowledge of foreign insurers;

(d) fronting is a barrier to FPS. It is cited as: being more flexible; quicker to arrange; able to circumvent local management of a foreign insurer; easing claims since the fronting insurer handles; and bringing in major reinsurers to a panel;

(e) concern over understanding the financial strength of foreign insurers was cited. It was suggested that access to understandable data on financial strength was not facilitated by regulators, but should be.

Insurers

(a) Regulatory issues – appointment of fiscal representatives – precisely what is required and who is responsible for what, is unclear to some companies who have registered for FOS.

(b) Different contract law and concern over interpretation was frequently seen as a barrier to development; in particular the need to produce contracts in local languages was seen to be essential in France following a court case which determined an exclusion to be invalid because the contract was not in French.

(c) A further problem was determined in particular in accident and health business – police and local authorities are not aware of the legislation which implements the Directive and permits coverage by a foreign insurer.

(d) As a general issue, little evidence was found of regulators publicizing the impact and effects of the Directives.

(e) Differences in definition of risks were seen as causing problems on claims settlement.

The key classes where issues and activity have emerged are as listed below.

Accident and health

In this class, the prime cross-border activity highlighted has been coverage of nationals working in foreign countries, in particular in Spain, also in Belgium and France.

There is an example of active planned marketing from Dutch and British companies to their nationals in other countries. A major Dutch insurer wrote 30% of its revenue in this class in other EU countries.

Property and liability

Apart from marine aviation and transport, these classes were seen to be the most commonly covered. A major part of multinationals' and major businesses' insurance requirements relate to property insurance and a variety of needs for liability coverage. Compulsory liability cover, for example for employees liabilities, was still generally placed in home markets. Additional cover, for example for loss of profits, is placed in the most effective manner – by FPS where that is effective.

Motor

This was not specifically included as a class placed cross-border in any cases of policyholder, intermediary or insurer. Reasons for not including (lack of regulatory change to enable FPS on this class – for example, Germany) related to differing requirements for coverage in different countries' legislation; regulated markets where prices were held low and unprofitable, e.g. Greece. The need to meet each State's requirements for compulsory coverage was seen as a major barrier.

Marine aviation and transit

The largest class for use of cross-border provision. Marine business has always been seen as being international, a significant proportion of world-wide and thus EU business having been placed in the London market. Even in countries not fully deregulated such as Greece, significant amounts of business has been placed cross-border, e.g. one major UK marine insurer wrote direct marine business from Greece in excess of ECU 13 million in 1993. In Denmark, a major shipping company has moved 25% of its insurance costs to foreign insurers over the past five years.

An example of the impact of the Directive in this class of business has been an apparent significant move from 'fronted' reinsurance business to 'direct' placement of business. A London market company's marine account business from other EU countries in 1989 was 38%

direct, 62% reinsurance, but in 1993 it was 56% direct and 44% reinsurance. This represented 119% growth in direct business. This marine account was less than 50% EU business.

Aviation business is considered still to be more traditional – historically a tariff market – with much of the international cover appearing still to be on a reinsurance basis, with the lead insurer being from the country of origin. The market tends to be international rather than European. There was some response that the satellite insurance field ('new' as opposed to 'traditional') had the scope perhaps to benefit from FPS placing, but there was no evidence that this had occurred.

Credit and suretyship

In this business segment, there seemed to be a good awareness of the possibilities offered by the Directive and larger credit insurers are considered to be acquiring a more multinational focus. There was scepticism, however, whether this would ever be reflected in FPS cross-border activity as it was considered that – despite analysing and advising on a policyholder's global risk – close contact was required with the client to achieve a complete understanding of the client's operating climate: it was suggested that such a *service de proximité* did not lend itself easily to FPS.

Member State differentiation

The state of development and deregulation of the insurance markets in each of the different countries has had a key influence on the extent to which the Directive has impacted each market. The key differences and issues arising are as follows.

Broadly the UK, Dutch, Belgian, Irish and Luxembourg markets have all been international with policyholders having the ability to place their insurance internationally for many years. The major UK and Dutch insurers have had subsidiaries or branches in a number of EU countries and operated in those countries. The major intermediaries have become multinational – many as part of the major US brokers and have a network of subsidiaries/fellow subsidiaries across Europe. The major impact in these countries seen by the Directive has been the easier provision of a centralized insurance package to multinationals.

UK insurers and Lloyds have accepted business from EU countries almost exclusively through brokers and have not regarded themselves as responsible for ensuring that the policyholders were free according to local regulation to place business in the UK. The Benelux countries in addition and in some respects the neighbouring countries of Denmark and France, in particular, and latterly Germany, have seen increasing amounts of cross-border business under FPS and also acquisitions of insurers cross-border.

In Luxembourg, 37% of the non-life business relates to the maritime register and the FPS activity is dominated by the 225 captives. However, many of these are for entities established outside the EU. Significant numbers from Sweden were noted in a search. In Greece, de-regulation of premium has only been partially introduced and FPS is not permitted. Despite this, there is substantial direct placement of hull (for the larger shipping lines), and most cargo is placed internationally and, in particular, in London. Fronting remains in existence; for example, the State-owned airline through a government owned insurer and thence to the international reinsurance market. Belgium is one of the countries where FPS data is available:

48% of the business is to neighbouring countries of the Netherlands and Luxembourg. Twenty-five per cent of the FPS data collected by the regulator is to a US-owned company arising from the Netherlands where it had applied in the mid-1980s for a branch status, but where it was suggested by the Dutch regulator to operate under FPS. In Italy, co-insurance dominates cross-border activity. Difficulties in relation to tax and regulatory approval have been encountered by many foreign insurers.

3.6. General conclusion on the changes in market access and interpretation of the results

The single market in insurance has been in existence for some classes of insurance – large risks – since 1990, for others – motor vehicle third party liability insurance – partly since 1992 and for all classes of insurance since July 1994. It is therefore too early to assess with certainty to what degree economic operators have taken advantage of the benefits of improved and facilitated procedures of access to other EU countries as was expected when the single market legislation in insurance was passed. One thing is certain, however, the measures aimed at the enabling and the taking-up and pursuing the business of insurance, a major building block for constructing the single market, has not had a 'big bang effect'. The large majority of European insurers continue to favour the policy of establishment through subsidiaries; freedom of services is most prevalent in the field of large risks, which traditionally have benefited from a large degree of contractual freedom, and it has not taken off to the extent expected in life assurance, a product for which it was expected to be ideally suited.

Concerning the analysis of primary sources, the survey of 100 undertakings shows that, over the reference period and for this sample:

(a) freedom to provide services is practised by only a small number of highly targeted undertakings (life or large risks);
(b) the number of branches of this sample has not increased;
(c) on the other hand, the undertakings continue to develop through subsidiaries.

For their part, the case studies confirm the trends listed above: low level of development of the 'new facilities' (freedom to provide services or branches) compared to the traditional means (subsidiaries).

It can therefore be considered that it is obvious that up to 1995 there was little change in the choice of modes of access to the market, except to a limited degree for certain very precise segments: up-market life products, large risks and group contingency contracts.

Interviewees' replies to the question concerning the choice of subsidiaries rather than branches, together with the more detailed examination of this same question with the managers of the case study undertakings, enabled a certain number of reasons to be defined for them preferring development through subsidiaries rather than through branches. These are:

(a) the clarity of the results and managers being made more aware of their responsibilities;
(b) better adaptation of resources to the size of the target markets;
(c) the preference of local consumers for a 'national' undertaking;
(d) the tax aspects, especially the fear of double taxation in the case of branches.

The following comments should be added to the reasons given by the undertakings:

(a) a large number of insurance markets may today be considered to be close to saturation, which is the case of certain markets in Northern Europe for certain products intended for the personal insurance market (for example, personal motor insurance). In such cases, the undertakings choose to buy market shares (subsidiaries), rather than to create them through branches;

(b) a branch is less 'visible' than a subsidiary. To make a new establishment, the presence of a company or a trade mark known, a subsidiary is more visible for customers and more prestigious for its local managers.

The interviewees of the sample group gave the following reasons for companies not making more use of the freedom to provide services to develop in the EU:

(a) freedom to provide services does not fit in with their development strategy (61% of the replies);

(b) legal uncertainties still associated with this operating method (29%);

(c) regulatory problems or administrative requirements of the host country (25%);

(d) extra costs associated with the functioning of the freedom to provide services: translations, tax representative, etc. (21%).

These obstacles seem to be sufficiently serious for a majority (61%) of the interviewees to believe that their company's strategy will not change in the coming years regarding the freedom to provide services. These reasons are largely consistent with those put forward by the case study undertakings, which specified the practical difficulties of exercising the freedom to provide services:

(a) it requires legal experts within the undertaking who are capable of interpreting the rule of the interest of the general good in force in the target country(ies) and the law of contract of these same countries;

(b) it presupposes that, to be used in an efficient manner for the undertakings, the products sold are similar, if not identical, in the various countries of sale;

(c) the insurance business still requires proximity in many cases in order to sell, advise, study the risk, or manage claims. The solution adopted by the undertaking to obtain this proximity must not, however, be open to assimilation with a permanent establishment, or tax difficulties will be incurred.

Conversely, the examples of start-up or success under the freedom to provide services analysed in the case studies generally involve highly targeted 'niches':

(a) the undertakings specializing in large risks are more open to the freedom to provide services, in particular on account of pressure from customers, who find many advantages in managing a single policy. The stakes in question (size of contracts) allow the extra costs of the contracts to be absorbed more easily. Nevertheless, even in the case of group contracts, in life and contingency insurance, some undertakings, rather than operating under the freedom to provide services, prefer to support their customers by entering into cross-partnership agreements in the other countries with groups of the same size and dealing in the same class of insurance, which enables them to secure customer loyalty while providing a reliable service, tailored to the customer, in the various countries.

(b) Finally, mention must be made of the undertakings specializing in up-market life, which, with the specific characteristics of banking in Luxembourg (notably secrecy), found an opportunity to serve the more well-to-do customers through the freedom to provide services. This positioning does not require a local service (term of contract, amount of payments), but it is developing on the basis of an organization and a product which are intended to be 'European' from the start and not vice versa.

On account of all these difficulties, and until the uncertainties they create are cleared up, it can be concluded that, as regards the freedom to provide services, a certain number of undertakings are currently in a preparatory or examination phase. This conclusion is supported by the many declarations of intent recorded, but also by the large number of competing new establishments which followed the pioneering work of Paneurolife in Luxembourg, whose 'formula', i.e. the way in which the freedom to provide services is interpreted in a specific niche, was then widely copied by others.

Concerning the question of whether the undertakings extended the European area within which they conduct their business, the trend in the sample group and the case studies seem to show that the Europeanization of undertakings is gaining ground and is now reaching medium-sized undertakings. Whereas a large percentage (63%) of the large undertakings were present in at least one other Member State as early as 1989, it is among the medium-sized undertakings that this proportion has grown the most in the past five years, rising from 12% to 28%.

Likewise, during the same period, the number of different Member States in which the undertakings extended their insurance business rose, mainly in the case of the medium-sized undertakings and especially through subsidiaries. For all the undertakings which are not present in at least one other Member State, the main reasons lie in the fact that they are too small (80%), or in the level of investments required to develop in another country (40%), which boils down to the same idea, or in the idea that their product, which is too specific, only suits their home country (50%).

Examining the same subject in greater depth with the case study undertakings, nuances emerge depending on the size of the undertakings or the nature of their business:

(a) the largest undertakings had already established themselves in Europe well before 1989. The following years for them were far more a period of consolidation and reinforcement (through new acquisitions) of their already established presence than a period of opening up to new territories in the EU;

(b) the undertakings operating in small risks have in common that they consider it was necessary for their profitability and their survival in another country both to hold a significant market share and to reach a sufficient size there. Their strategy therefore essentially consisted more in strengthening their presence in the countries where they had established than in dispersing their presence over a larger number of Member States.

The reasons why economic operators still hesitate to take advantage of the new means of accessing new markets offered by single market legislation can be broken down in three main categories:

(a) Regulatory obstacles pertaining to the legal framework laid down by the single market legislation – the key obstacle stems from the introduction of the principle of the 'general good' in the EU's single market legislation. Introducing a highly complex legal concept, developed by the European Court of Justice, which perhaps even more importantly is continually undergoing revisions as the Court faces new challenges and develops new case law, amounts to introducing a moving target for the economic operators. The basic principle underlying the single market is that insurers should be free to market their full range of products throughout the EU, subject to limitations in only those cases where there has been no coordination at Community level and where the insurer is proven to be acting in contravention of substantial public interests. But this has been turned on its head by the 'general good' concept being made into a legal minefield. The concept of 'general good' has itself become an obstacle to deregulation and a single insurance market.

(b) Regulatory obstacles pertaining to still unharmonized aspects of carrying out insurance operations within the EU – the two main obstacles are the lack of harmonization in the fields of contract law and taxation. Perversely, in the field of taxation, recent jurisprudence has effectively done away with legal uncertainty as to the rights of individuals to deduct pension and insurance contributions from their taxable income irrespective of where the providers are established, leaving the field open for increased cross-border activities. But case law cannot be a substitute for harmonized Community-wide rules. In the field of contract law, the complexity of the rules on conflict of law adopted by the single market directives to compensate for the absence of harmonization of insurance contract law makes the operation of insurance under the single licence very difficult, costly and legally intricate. This complexity acts as an effective barrier to marketing insurance across the Community on the basis of one single policy.

(c) Regulatory obstacles caused by incorrect implementation of the single market legislation. A large scale project like that of the single market in insurance needs more time for Member States and the Commission to identify and remove minor problems and to agree in practical terms on how to apply the new legislation. In those areas where clear infringements have appeared, the Commission needs time to ensure the correct application by Member States of sometimes highly complex new rules and to follow the established procedures for dealing with recalcitrant Member States. The Commission Communication on Freedom to Provide Services and the General Good in the Insurance Sector was expected to be published in 1997. This will no doubt be instrumental in clarifying some of the problems considered by the insurance industry to be obstacles to the smooth functioning of the single market in insurance, such as the right of insurance undertakings throughout the EU to carry out capital redemption operations, the language of insurance contracts and uniform bonus/malus systems.

4. Development of upstream and downstream partnership links

4.1. Aims of the legislation

Article 59 of the EU Treaty grants insurance intermediaries the right to transact their business via freedom of services and Article 52 stipulates that intermediaries are free to take up their activities in another Member State. Intermediaries according to EU definition are either brokers, who act with complete freedom as to their choice of undertaking, agents, who under one or more contracts act in the name of or on behalf of one or more insurance undertakings, or sub-agents, who carry out introductory work or collect premiums provided no insurance commitment towards the public is given. In 1976, the EU adopted a Directive on Intermediaries (77/92/EEC) which provided for mutual recognition between Member States of the professional experience of intermediaries. The impact of this Directive has been limited because professional qualifications constitute only one aspect of the regulation of intermediaries.

In 1991, it was clear that prior approval of insurance premiums and policy conditions were about to be abolished in the context of the single market for insurance. This would in turn lead to greater need for qualified advice for consumers in those Member States where such prior approval had existed. The insurance intermediary is still by far the most important source of information for customers, notwithstanding trends towards 'direct writing'. An increase in the responsibilities of intermediaries was therefore expected to occur.

The Commission adopted a Recommendation on Insurance Intermediaries (92/48/EEC), on 18 December 1991. Insurance intermediaries were recommended to: be of good repute (Article 4(4)); be professionally competent (Article 4(2)); possess professional indemnity insurance (Article 4(3)); and be registered (Article 5). Insurance brokers in particular should furthermore: have sufficient financial capacity if necessary (Article 4(5)); and disclose the state of their independence (Article 3).

Given the non-binding nature of a Recommendation, a review clause was included by which the Commission maintained the right to propose a binding Directive in future, if such coordination measures became necessary to remove any remaining barriers to market access or to introduce further guarantees for the protection of the consumer.

In the field of reinsurance, Directive 64/225/EEC of 25 February 1964 abolished the last remaining restrictions on the freedom of establishment and the freedom to provide services for reinsurance. This Directive definitively adopted the freedom of establishment and the freedom to provide services in the European Community in respect of reinsurance. Since reinsurance is overwhelmingly conducted as a service, the latter of the two freedoms was particularly important. Although the Directive was not confined to the measures explicitly listed in Article 3, it was never applied to those measures which represented only an indirect restriction on reinsurance, e.g. to the gross system for calculating reserves with the lodging of a deposit practised in various countries.

Another text directly applicable to reinsurance is the Directive on the annual accounts and consolidated accounts of insurance undertakings (91/674/EEC), as can be seen from Article

2(1)(c). An attempt was made, within this measure, to take account of the special features of reinsurance. Article 33(4) gives Member States the option of permitting reinsurance undertakings whose activities consist of life assurance as well as non-life insurance to use the profit and loss technical account normally reserved for non-life insurance business for both branches.

In the area of reinsurance, more than 30 years have elapsed since this last evaluation of the situation and the signs are increasing that today the conclusion could be different. It was therefore no surprise that participants at the 1993 13th Conference of European Supervisory Authorities in Copenhagen agreed that reinsurance undertakings should be put under 'some' financial supervision, i.e. thereby speaking out in favour of direct supervision of reinsurance. This trend can also be seen within the OECD. Whereas even ten years ago the OECD dealt with reinsurance predominantly from the point of view of 'freedom of reinsurance', recently 'regulatory aspects' have certainly also been discussed and 'internationally valid ratios' for the solvency of reinsurance undertakings were on the agenda.

At the present time, particularly in the USA, due to experiences in this field in recent years, intense effort is being devoted to introducing a new system of insurance regulation, which would extend direct supervision to domestic and foreign professional reinsurers and thus be likely to have an effect on Community undertakings. So far, however, no new regulatory initiatives have appeared. The origin of this development lies in the overcapacity of the reinsurance market which began in the mid-1970s. According to information from a Swiss reinsurance company, in the period 1975 to 1988 the number of professional reinsurers in Western Europe rose from 120 to over 160 firms. In the period 1987 to 1990, the capital of existing firms increased by 50% and that of American firms by as much as 63%. This development went hand-in-hand with an increase in retention levels by ceding companies. This had the effect of depressing premium income more severely from one year to the next.

Increasingly the trans-border activities of consumers, whether private individuals purchasing holiday homes abroad or companies opening branches in other Member States, lead them to approach their intermediaries with requests for insurance cover abroad. But the benefits of opening up markets for insurance companies are lost if intermediaries are hampered in their cross-border activities or if insurance companies run into difficulties selling their products abroad because they have no access to developing upstream and downstream partnership links and/or distribution networks.

4.1.1. Hypothesis to be tested

It is a matter of analysing here:

(a) the extent to which the SMP has encouraged European insurers to develop partnership links with other undertakings in the sector;
(b) the business strategy followed here;
(c) whether this trend has intensified during the reference period.

The single market has led to changes in the way in which insurers, reinsurers and intermediaries co-operate, if it is really possible to record development in the partnership links over the reference period.

4.1.2. Indicators

(a) the trend in the number of such agreements over the reference period;
(b) analysis of the 'type' of agreements formed.

4.2. The survey results

In the sample interviewed, the number of undertakings which set up partnership agreements in another Member State rose over the reference period. The characteristics of these undertakings were the following.

Table 4.1.   Trend in the number and characteristics of the undertakings having developed upstream/downstream partnership agreements

	1989	1995
Total	4	10
(a) Size		
• Small undertakings	–	1
• Medium-sized undertakings	–	2
• Large undertakings	4	7
(b) Business activity		
• Specialist life	2	4
• Specialist non-life	–	2
• General non-life	2	4
(c) Home country of undertakings		
• France	3	4
• Germany	1	3
• Spain	–	1
• Luxembourg	–	1
• Netherlands	–	1

It can be seen that:

(a) one-third of undertakings had no establishment (branches, subsidiaries) in Europe apart from this partnership. This is particularly important for the smallest undertakings to have access to the market;
(b) six cases out of ten relate to life products and another two cases involve offering moving customers continuity of service in indemnity insurance;
(c) seven cases out of ten come from two countries: Germany and France.

Table 4.2.   Ten examples of European partnership in 1995

Case no	Home country	Length of partnership Old (89)	New (94)	Business of undertaking Specialist life	Specialist non-life	General non-life	Country of partnership	Type of partner(s)	Product sold	Existence of a structure in the EU
1	Spain		X			X	• Greece	Insurance company		None
2	Luxembourg		X	X			• Germany	(1) Bank (2) Fronting with reinsurance	Life	No structure - all business is conducted in Germany and UK by freedom to provide services or partnership
3	Germany	X				X	• Belgium • France • Netherlands • UK		Pension fund	
4	Germany		X	X			• UK	Fronting: - Insurance company - Reinsurance	Life	Existence of a structure in the EU
5	Germany		X		Motor vehicle specialist		• Belgium • France • Luxembourg • Spain • Italy – Portugal	Fronting with insurance companies	Life and accident	No structure in the EU
6	France		X		Motor vehicle specialist		• Sweden • Belgium • Italy • Luxembourg	European economic interest grouping (mutual society)	- Exchange of experience - Customer support for certain products in common	None
7	France	X		X			• Germany • Belgium • Netherlands • UK		Life	
8	France	X		X			• Belgium • Spain • Italy • Luxembourg • UK	Banks		Yes
9	France	X				X	• Portugal	Bank	Life	Yes
10	Netherlands		X			X	• Spain	Bank	Life	Yes (subsidiaries)

(Results of the sample of 100 undertakings)

4.3. Case studies

A. UAP

There is no cross-border partnership agreement, strictly speaking, in the group. Such agreements do exist, however, within Member States.

(a) In 1989, only three countries were concerned:

Belgium: Royale Belge and BBL agreements;
Spain: sale of life products in the banks;
Netherlands: sale of life products in the banks.

(b) In 1995, this trend has gathered pace with new agreements:

Belgium: agreement with La Poste;
France: agreement with BNP (non-life);
Italy: agreement with small banks.

In almost all cases, these are agreements signed between the local subsidiary and banks, for the purpose of stepping up distribution in the country in question.

Mention should be made, within UAP and between its European subsidiaries, of the Paneurorisk European economic interest grouping, which allows exchange of experience and joint reinsurance, for large risks. The main object of this structure is to enable the smallest structures to handle large risks which they could not otherwise have done.

B. Victoria

The Victoria Group participates in two major partnership agreements:

(a) INI (International Network of Insurance);
(b) IGP (International Group Program).

In both cases, these are groups whose business is not confined to Europe, but concerns the whole world.

IGP is a network of insurers selling life contingency contracts and pension funds to companies (group contracts). The customers are large multinational undertakings wishing to offer continuity of their contingency contracts to expatriate employees. The network is represented in 50 countries through 38 member undertakings.

INI is a network of insurers represented in 60 countries, which offers international industrial undertakings fire and liability insurance services. It allows an international customer either to be dealt with globally ('master' policy) or just locally. Victoria is represented in this network for Germany and Austria. For Victoria, which limited its establishment (subsidiaries or branches) to a small number of European countries (see Section 3.4), the two agreements were chosen because they provide:

(a) the basis for international development (within and outside the EU), without establishment;
(b) the means to secure the loyalty of major national customers (by supporting them abroad);
(c) supplementary national turnover, through the business contributed by the foreign network.

C. Mapfre

Mapfre does not at present have any partnership agreement in Europe concerning direct insurance.

D. Fortis

The Group embarked upon a partnership agreement in 1992 with Caixa in Spain to sell life products.

Through this partnership, Fortis is targeting the small risk product market in Spain. As early as 1994, Vida Caixa had become the 'Number 1' in the sale of life products in Spain and Segur Caixa had made a good start with 40,000 contracts signed.

For Fortis, the reasons for this agreement were the following:

(a) Caixa provides a network, i.e. immediate access to the market with resources on a scale corresponding to the requirements of the mass markets;
(b) Caixa provides know-how and, in particular, the 'knowledge' of the target country: product marketing, regulatory and administrative aspects.

E. Cecar

Cecar drew up a partnership agreement with Bain Hogg, a British broker.

The object of this partnership agreement is to exchange business contributed by customers where it relates to the countries in which one of the two partners is established:

(a) the seven EU countries for Cecar (France plus subsidiaries in: Spain, Portugal, Italy, Belgium, Germany, Luxembourg);
(b) UK, South-East Asia, USA (mainly) for Bain Hogg and its international network Excelnet.

The priority objective of this agreement is to be able to support customers in their international business, without additional investments.

4.4. Secondary sources

The situations of the (approximately) 30,000 brokers in the EU obviously vary considerably with regard to size and market, which essentially correspond to the customer segments they deal with.

(a) *Large-scale brokerage*, with business focusing on multinationals, is traditionally dominated in Europe by American and British firms. On this market, the past five years have been characterized by the efforts made by the Anglo-American brokers to penetrate the European area more effectively and to derive benefit from the prospects offered by the single market (freedom to provide services and co-insurance). They have engaged in an impressive series of buy-outs of brokers during 1990 to 1994 in order to form European networks (Sedgwick, Willis Coroon, Johnson & Higgins, etc.).
In parallel and/or as a reaction, the European brokers have organized themselves, with a twofold objective: on the one hand, to react to the pressure created in this way by the Anglo-American brokers and, on the other, to retain or conquer an increasingly international clientele. This reaction takes the form of the buy-out of or merger with other brokers, the purchase of portfolios, the creation of associations with each retaining its individuality, for example: the Unison network (Johnson & Higgins – USA; Gras & Savoye – France; Jauch & Hübener – Germany; etc.) and, more recently, the Excelnet network (Bain Hogg – UK; Boels & Begault – Belgium; Cecar – France; etc.).
However, since the prime objective is still customer service, retaining (and developing) very large customers, these networks are quite naturally seen to develop beyond Europe to reach the strongly developing regions of the world (USA, Canada, South-East Asia).
(b) *Small and medium-sized brokerage* is facing a different situation, its customers being either highly specialized (niches) or operating on a more regional scale. Their problem is both to achieve better control of their operating costs and enlarge their clientele and to support their customers in their international development. Certain professional syndicates assist them in various ways: availability of 'business fairs' to assist them to find foreign correspondents to mount cross-border operations, preparation of quality charters, training programmes. The following facts dominate the development of insurance distribution in Europe during the reference period:

The progress of bancassurance

The appearance of banks on the insurance market and their rapid progress certainly constitute the most profound change experienced by the insurance distribution sector in recent years.

Banks have taken an important place in the life products market in almost all the EU Member States (with the exception of Germany), since they have become the leading distributor of life products in France and the second largest in Belgium, the Netherlands and Spain.

In the non-life sector, the market shares of bancassurance are still small (with the exception of the Netherlands), but the majority of large banks have set up an organization to sell non-life products during the past four or five years. This organization may take the form of the creation of a direct insurance company (example: Crédit Agricole and Pacifica), or involve a brokerage company or a partnership agreement.

The recent development of direct selling (telemarketing and mailing)

Direct selling may be defined as selling where the entire negotiation of the contract takes place directly between the policyholder and the company, without any intermediary other than the telephone (even though it must then be confirmed by a written agreement on the part of the policyholder). Direct selling is most widely used as a sales technique in the personal motor vehicle insurance sector, followed, to a lesser extent, by housing and health insurance products. This sales technique has developed considerably in the UK, followed by the Netherlands. It is currently developing far more slowly in the other European countries. According to a Datamonitor survey, the market share of direct selling in 1994 was:

Personal non-life:	Netherlands:	25% of the market
	UK:	14% of the market
Personal life:	Netherlands:	16% of the market
	France:	5% of the market
	UK:	2% of the market

The appearance on the market of insurance offered by retail distributors

Department stores and hypermarkets have recently appeared on the insurance market. Among them, mention should first be made of El Corte Inglés (Spain), which has been offering life and non-life products to its customers since 1982. This initiative was followed later by Carrefour (France) in 1993, Cofinoga (France), then Marks & Spencer (UK) in 1995. These distributors generally take care of the logistics by setting up a partnership with insurers, for example: Marks & Spencer and Equitable Life Assurance, Carrefour and Alpha Assurances (AXA Group).

In 1995 Datamonitor ('Marketing and Distribution of European Insurance') calculated the following market shares for the various distribution methods for the personal market only (see Table 4.3).

Table 4.3.   Market share of the various personal insurance distribution methods in Europe in 1994 in seven Member States (%)

Country	Agents		Brokers		Sales offices and salaried salesmen		Banc-assurance		Telephone sales		Other	
	life	non - life	life	non-life	life	non-life	life	non-life	life	non-life	life	non-life
Belgium	9	11	57	72	15	13	19	3	0	1	–	0
Germany	61	81	30	5	2	11	7	2	–	–	–	1
Spain	48	64	12	17	16	15	23	3	1	0	–	1
France	13	43	7	4	20	45	55	5	5	1	–	2
Italy	43	91	11	3	26	5	20	–	–	–	–	1
Netherlands	7	3	45	40	14	5	18	15	16	25	–	12
UK	7	15	45	54	33	8	13	1	2	15	–	7

Source: Extract from Datamonitor 'Marketing and Distribution of European Insurance', 1995.

It is clear that by looking at individual markets, Belgium, the Netherlands and the UK have traditionally had a strong independent intermediary sector, often brokers. Other major markets, most notably Germany, Spain and Italy, have maintained a bias towards tied agents as a distribution channel.

This has been the case in both long-term and general insurance, with the exception of the Spanish market, where agents have traditionally been dominant in general lines but have shared the distribution of long-term insurance with brokers and now banks.

Telephone sales, more active in general insurance than in long-term markets, have a limited share of the overall market, and have made significant headway only in Sweden, the Netherlands and, to a lesser extent, France.

Across Europe, however, present distribution figures presented above demonstrate the degree to which the intermediary is under threat. Compared to the late 1980s, the rise of bancassurance and telephone sales as channels for insurance distribution represents a significant and dramatic alteration in the market. Both bank branches and telesales are forecast to increase their share of product distribution in personal general and individual long-term markets, so that intermediaries will remain under pressure and must emphasize what advantages remain to them in order not merely to compete, but also to survive. This applies to both independent intermediaries and brokers. In the past decade, these channels have lost market share, to arrive at the present position, where their dominance is under serious threat.

Taking the point of view of the insurance companies, the CEA deplores the fact that the absence of harmonization of the status of intermediaries at European level (with the exception of the Directive of limited scope of 1976 (77/92/EEC) and the Recommendation of 1991 (92/48/EEC)) in practice prevents the companies from using their own distribution channels to market their products throughout Europe. Indeed, unlike insurance undertakings, intermediaries are not eligible for either the provisions of the establishment regime or those of the freedom to provide services or the facilities of the single licence.

This prohibits insurance undertakings from using their own distribution networks to market their products in other Community countries. In some cases, such as Belgium, this restriction requires the local intermediaries to guarantee that contracts drawn up by non-authorized undertakings comply with the provisions in the interest of the general good. This obligation, which seems discriminatory, constitutes an obstacle to the free distribution of insurance products. Since insurance business has been liberalized, it is appropriate, according to the CEA, for the status of the intermediaries to be reviewed and placed on the same footing as that of the insurance undertakings.

For its part, BIPAR (Bureau International de Producteurs d'Assurance et de Réassurance - the EU lobby for intermediaries), in a paper of July 1995 addressed to the Commission, clearly describes the obstacles which prevent intermediaries from catering for the cross-border requirements of their customers, especially where private individuals are concerned. According to BIPAR, these obstacles are of four types:

(a) uncertainties regarding the European regulations governing insurance intermediaries (especially when operating under the freedom to provide services);
(b) requirement to comply with several sets of national legislation simultaneously, when transacting cross-border business;
(c) lack of specifications concerning intermediaries' obligations when operating in another Member State;
(d) lack of application (or incorrect application) by Member States of the 1991 Recommendation.

BIPAR is of the opinion that although the single market for insurance companies is by now in force in nearly all the EU Member States, insurance intermediaries do not benefit at all from any meaningful system of mutual recognition. They are thus still confronted with a number of serious obstacles when transacting cross-border business. The (virtual) absence of any compulsory and harmonized Community legislation for insurance intermediaries in their opinion has led to a confusing and chaotic regulatory situation for the profession.

In particular, it is the lack of any clear-cut definition of the element which triggers the application of the legislation on insurance intermediaries of the host Member State and the application of two, or even more, sets of national legislation on insurance intermediaries which effectively deprives customers of the benefits of the increased range of insurance products theoretically on offer in the single market.

4.5. Changes in patterns of distribution

4.5.1. Life insurance and pensions

The period 1990 to 1995 saw profound change in the importance of distribution channels, which, in many cases, had changed little for decades. For example, in agent and broker dominated markets, the primary distribution channel found bancassurers eroding their market share substantially. Nevertheless, most European life insurance and pensions markets remain dominated by a single distribution channel.[17] In most EU countries, either agents, brokers or company employees remain the clear dominant channel.

Intermediaries such as tied agents and brokers are historically the most dominant channel of distribution in many European countries. For example, in Germany, tied agents took over 65% of new annualized premiums in 1995 for total life insurance and pensions, while in the Netherlands, Belgium and Ireland, brokers dominate the distribution of life and pensions insurance, accounting for over 50% of new business written in 1995.

Company employees are the primary distribution channel in most of the European countries in which intermediaries play a minor role. For example, in Greece and Finland, company employees accounted for over 80% of new annualized business, while in Sweden and Denmark they have a market share of well over 50%. In contrast, French life and pensions products are distributed primarily by bancassurers, while the UK is characterized by multiple distribution channels. Bancassurance is making a huge impact in several markets as banks take advantage of often inefficient and undeveloped markets. Banks have capitalized on their large customer base and an extensive branch network which provides not only large geographic coverage but strong links and frequent contact with customers.

Tied agents and company employees have lost out the most to alternative distribution channels, partly because of the high costs associated with these channels. Tied agents and company employees lost market share between 1990 and 1995 in nearly every European life and pensions market where they had a significant presence. Moreover, this is predicted to continue in the latter half of the 1990s as in many cases these channels appear ill equipped to meet changing customer requirements. Brokers have also lost substantial market share, principally to bancassurers, in the broker dominated markets of the Netherlands, Belgium and Ireland. However, they are now fighting back, particularly in the Netherlands, where they have improved their service levels considerably, notably through the development of IT and telephone support.

However, despite the widespread concern over alternative distribution channels, many insurance companies have demonstrated a clear and ongoing commitment to their traditional intermediary channels. Even those companies which have invested heavily in new telephone operations to supplement their existing business appear to have no intention of fully substituting direct for intermediary distribution. More typically, where alternative channels are being used, it is very much peripheral to the principal challenge which insurers are perceived to be facing: improving business through intermediary channels.

A number of insurers are committed to retaining their intermediaries in order to cope better with the demands of a changing market, most notably where tied agents or company employees are used as the principal distribution channel. However, insurers are even keener to improve intermediary productivity aligned to a perception that closer intermediary management will become a crucial element in the insurance culture of the future. Direct mail and telephone sales have gained in prominence as a means of cutting costs and attracting new customers. However, in most European countries, direct channels have not proved as

---

[17]   European Life Insurance and Pensions Distribution 1996, Datamonitor.

successful in the individual life insurance and pensions markets as they have in some personal motor and property insurance markets.

In general, across Europe life and pensions insurance companies perceived the choice of distribution channels to be the single most important driver of profitability. This is essentially the result of three recent developments in European markets: deregulation of European markets; the emergence of bancassurance and the effects of increasing levels of competition which is forcing insurance companies to look for new competitive advantages and for new means of reducing costs.

Insurance companies across the EU are redefining their strategies in order to meet the challenges of the modern insurance market. Distribution strategy is central to this. According to the study quoted above, implementation of the EU insurance directives has had a major effect on the distribution of long-term insurance products in Europe, increasing levels of competition and forcing insurers to consider lower cost distribution channels.

4.5.2. Non-life insurance

European non-life insurance markets are characterized by a shift towards multichannel distribution systems as new channels, most notably bancassurance and telesales, are eroding the share of traditional channels. The facts driving this shift include the emergence of new technologies and alternative marketing and selling processes, the pressure on insurance companies to cut costs and the increasing willingness of consumers to buy general insurance from non-traditional sources.

As for life assurance, non-life insurance companies across Europe also perceived the choice of distribution channels to be the single most important driver of profitability and this development is again perceived to be the result of three recent developments in European markets: deregulation of European markets; the emergence of bancassurance and telesales; and the effects of increasing levels of competition which is forcing insurance companies to look for new competitive advantages and for new means of reducing costs.

While the rise of alternative distribution channels in Europe, most notably bancassurance and telephone sales seems to have dominated the headlines, this ignores the fact that 'traditional' channels, namely tied agents, brokers and company employees, continued to account for virtually all general insurance distribution in most markets in 1995. In 1995, 'traditional' channels accounted for more than 90% of total general insurance gross written premiums in eight of the EU markets. Of the remaining seven, only in four have the new channels really made an impact: Ireland, the Netherlands, Sweden and the UK. In Denmark and Greece, the relatively low share of 'traditional' channels is due to the substantial ownership of ordinary insurance companies by local banks, thereby boosting the share of bancassurance.

However, it would be erroneous to say that distribution is less of an issue to insurers in the markets still adhering to 'traditional' channels than to those in the remainder. The truth is rather that the majority of companies are striving to rationalize, energize and renovate these existing distribution networks, fearful of increasing competition from other intermediary-focused insurers as well as alternative channels.

Despite all of the hype surrounding the move to more cost-efficient distribution channels, the superior efficiency of telephone sales, the inherent advantages of bancassurance and the untapped potential of the Internet, 'traditional' channels are still forecast to account for

US$ 316.0 billion out of a total of US$ 384.5 billion in total general insurance premiums by the year 2000. It is telling that these figures are derived from forecasts which are generally quite 'bullish' as regards the likely penetration of new channels in the future. Moreover, even if only personal general insurance is used to calculate these values, 'traditional' channels would still account for far more business than either direct channels or banking channels. The value of direct distribution channels by the beginning of the 21st century is forecast to be US$ 35.4 billion, most of it attributable to telephone sales. The value of banking channels, on the other hand, is expected to be in the region of US$ 33.1 billion.

At a general level, the conclusion must be that for many companies, the need to develop alternative distribution structures is perhaps less pressing than has been suggested. Although this need clearly varies from market to market, from company to company and from product to product, many insurers, especially those not endowed with limitless resources, concentrate on their existing distribution infrastructure, seeking to modernize and develop in such a way that it remains competitive in an increasingly tough operating environment. Indeed, companies which have diversified boldly into alternative distribution systems, such as the myriad telesellers in the UK, have often failed to acquire the business volume and generate the level of profit which they had initially envisaged. Hence, reinforcing tried and tested distribution strategies may prove, for many insurers, to be not only the safer but also the wiser option.

Table 4.4.   Distribution channels as a % of total life insurance and pensions: 1995

1995	A	B	DK	FIN	F	D	GR	IRL	I	NL*	P	E	S	UK
Intermediary channels	**4**	**72**	**10**	**12**	**23**	**94**	**10**	**68**	**52**	**79**	**47**	**51**	**23**	**42**
Tied agents	0	10	1	10	14	67	9	17	45	6	36	32	3	4
Brokers	3	59	6	0	7	15	0	51	3	63	8	17	19	34
Banks as intermediaries	1	3	3	2	2	1	1	0	4	10	3	2	1	4
Direct channels	**47**	**18**	**57**	**88**	**25**	**4**	**90**	**21**	**17**	**13**	**12**	**11**	**72**	**47**
Company employees	46	17	57	87	21	2	90	18	17	6	12	11	68	45
Telephone sales	0	0	0	0	0	0	0	0	0	6	0	0	1	0
Direct mail	1	1	0	0	4	2	0	3	0	1	0	0	3	2
Other (e.g. Internet)	0	0	0	<1	0	0	0	0	0	0	0	0	0	0
Bancassurance channels	**49**	**10**	**33**	**<1**	**52**	**2**	**0**	**11**	**31**	**8**	**41**	**38**	**5**	**11**
Bank branch networks	49	10	28	0	52	1	0	11	31	7	40	20	5	9
Other (e.g. sales forces)	0	0	5	0	0	1	0	0	0	1	1	18	0	2

NB: Percentages are rounded to the nearest whole percentage point.
* ING is not defined as a bancassurer for the purpose of this report.
Source: Datamonitor European Insurance Distribution Database 1996.

Table 4.5. Distribution channels as a % of total general insurance: 1995

1995	A	B	DK	FIN	F	D	GR	IRL	I	NL	P	E	S	UK
Intermediary channels	**13**	**83**	**14**	**30**	**66**	**83**	**10**	**83**	**93**	**66**	**82**	**81**	**19**	**77**
Tied agents	0	5	2	28	45	60	1	2	81	3	64	58	6	2
Brokers	13	77	9	1	19	19	6	64	11	61	17	22	13	69
Banks as intermediaries	0	1	3	1	2	4	3	17	1	2	1	1	0	6
Direct channels	**87**	**14**	**71**	**68**	**33**	**16**	**48**	**17**	**7**	**22**	**16**	**16**	**81**	**22**
Company employees	87	13	69	67	31	14	48	12	7	7	14	15	63	11
Telephone sales	0	1	2	0	1	0	0	4	0	13	2	1	10	9
Direct mail	0	0	0	0	1	2	0	1	0	2	0	0	8	2
Other (e.g. Internet)	0	0	0	1	0	0	0	0	0	0	0	0	0	0
Bancassurance channels	**0**	**3**	**15**	**2**	**1**	**1**	**42**	**1**	**0**	**12**	**2**	**4**	**0**	**1**
Bank branch networks	0	3	1	1	1	1	0	1	0	7	2	3	0	1
Other (e.g. sales forces)	0	0	14	1	0	0	42	0	0	5	0	1	0	0

Source: Datamonitor European Insurance Distribution Database 1996.
NB: Percentages are rounded to the nearest whole percentage point.

4.6. Regulatory obstacles to cross-border insurance distribution

The developments and dynamic changes in insurance distribution have led to increased interest in initiatives at EU-level to facilitate the cross-border intermediation of insurance services, whether as life, non-life or pension products. It is particularly significant in this context to note that not only the EU-wide organization of intermediaries – BIPAR,[18] but also insurers – CEA[19] are now lobbying for an EU initiative in this area, no doubt as a result of the increased perception among insurers of the prime necessity of improvements in the area of distribution in order to improve profitability.

Under current EU legislation, insurance intermediaries are facing major obstacles to carrying out their activities across the borders. The basic problem is lack of harmonization: the situation of intermediaries is comparable to that of insurance companies before the Insurance Framework Directives. The divergence of national legislation and the divergent way the provisions of the Treaty are interpreted by Member States mean that their Treaty given right of freedom to provide services into another EU State is limited in practice. Divergencies between Member States can be broken down as follows: countries with no legislation on intermediaries versus countries with legislation; and countries with legislation which differs between Member States (for example, between those countries which have no financial guarantees and those who do).

Countries which do have financial requirements differ between each other, for example in terms of the amount, ranging from ± ECU 51,000 in Portugal to ± ECU 1.5 million in France; and the conditions which surround these financial guarantees, i.e. to deposit guarantees in protected bank accounts where residence address is sometimes required (Ireland/UK), membership of Guarantee Funds, investment in approved assets (for example in Greece: government bonds, etc.).

Tables 4.6 and 4.7, broken down by country and by agent and broker, indicate whether Member States have adopted measures in the areas defined by the Commission's Intermediaries Recommendation (92/48/EEC), i.e. registration, professional competence, good repute, professional indemnity insurance, financial requirements, disclosures and sanctions.

Tables 4.8 and 4.9 indicate if and how these Member States have implemented the provisions of the EU Recommendation on professional indemnity insurance and financial guarantees.

---

[18] BIPAR – Memorandum on Practical Obstacles for the Provision of Services by Insurance Intermediaries in the European Single Market of Insurance, Brussels, 20 July 1995.

[19] CEA – Contribution to the Discusssion on the Barriers to the Functioning of the Single Insurance Market, Paris, 19 February 1996

Table 4.6. Broker*

	Article	A	B	D	DK	E	F	FIN	GR	I	IRL	L	NL	P	S	UK	Total Yes	Total No
Registration	(5)	No[1]	Yes	No	No	Yes	Yes	Yes	Z	Yes	No	Yes	Yes	Yes	Yes	Yes	10	4
Professional competence	(4)	Yes	Yes	No	No	Yes	Yes	Yes	Yes	Yes	Yes	Yes	Yes	Yes	Yes	Yes[2]	13	2
Good repute	(4(4))	Yes	Yes	No	No	Yes	Yes	Yes	Z	Yes	Yes	Yes	Yes	X	Yes	Yes[3]	11	2
Professional liability insurance	(4(3))	No	Yes	No	No	Yes	Yes	Yes	Z	Yes	Yes[4]	Yes	No[5]	Yes	Yes	Yes	10	4
Financial requirements	(4(5))	No	Yes	No	No	Yes	Yes	X	Z	Yes	Yes	No	No	Yes	No	Yes	8	6
Disclosure	(3)	No	Yes	No	No	Yes	Yes	Yes	Z	Yes[6]	Yes[7]	Yes	No	X	No	Yes	8	5
Sanctions	(6)	Yes	Yes	No	No	Yes	Yes	Yes	Z	Yes	Yes	Yes	Yes	Yes	Yes	Yes	12	2

* Definition: Directive 77/92/EEC. Article 2(1) (a).

X = no information.

Z = no legislation yet.

[1] No special register in the sense of Article (5/3) but announcement of the activity.

[2] In process.

[3] Are there regulations concerning bankruptcy and properness?

[4] Minister has power to prescribe.

[5] Requirements exist for members of professional organizations.

[6] Are there any disclosure duties vis-à-vis the client?

[7] Are there any disclosure duties vis-à-vis the authorities?

Table 4.7. **Agent***

	Article	A	B	D	DK	E	F	FIN	GR	I	IRL	L	NL	P	S	UK	Total Yes	Total No
Registration	(5)	No[1]	Yes	No	No	Yes	Yes	No	X	Yes	No	Yes	Yes	Yes	No	Yes	8	6
Professional competence	(4)	No	Yes	No	No	Yes[2]	Yes	No	X	Yes	No[3]	Yes	Yes	Yes	No	Yes[1]	8	6
Good repute	(4(4))	Yes	Yes	No	No	?	Yes	No	X	Yes[4]	Yes	X	Yes	X	No	Yes[5]	7	4
Professional liability insurance	(4(3))	No	No	No	No	No	No	No	X	X	X	No[6]	No[7]	Yes	No	No	1	11
Sanctions	(6)	?	Yes	No	No	Yes	Yes	No	X	Yes	Yes	Yes	Yes	Yes	No	Yes	9	4

* Definition: Directive 77/92/EEC, Article 2 (1) (b).

X = no information.

Z = no legislation yet.

? = not clear.

[1] In process.

[2] Without examinations.

[3] Only recommendations.

[4] Are there any indications concerning bankruptcy?

[5] Are there regulations concerning bankruptcy and properness?

[6] Made by the insurance company.

[7] Requirements exist for membersof professional organizations.

Table 4.8.   Professional indemnity insurance

Country	Is professional liability insurance compulsory...			If yes, minimum sum required (ECU)
	...by law?	...by the association?	...no obligation	
Denmark (FMB)		Yes		1,369,295
Ireland (IBA)	Yes			307,239 in the aggregate
Portugal	Yes			509,962
United Kingdom (BIIBA)	Yes	Yes		296,247
Sweden (SFMS)	Yes			Life: 779,116 per claim Non-life: 2,337,348 per claim
Finland	Yes			518,862 per claim
Austria			Yes	452,291 per insurance period
Germany (BVK)			Yes	1,542,165
France (FCA)	Yes	Yes		1,288,670
Belgium (UPCA)		Yes		1,251,917 per claim and year
Spain (CONSEJO)		Yes		No minimum required but member associations impose certain financial requirements
Netherlands (NVA)		Yes		Between a minimum of 492,965 and a maximum of 1,478,896
Italy (FIBRAS)	Yes			1,288,670
Luxembourg	Yes			

Table 4.9.   Financial guarantees

Country	Brokers	Agents	Details
France	Yes	No	Minimum ECU 115,662.
Italy	Yes	No	0.5 % of annual gross premium to a Guarantee Fund.
UK			(a) Minimum working capital (IBRC) of ECU 1,185. Lloyd's in practice ECU 592,495. (b) Separate bank account in UK (approved banks). Brokers must invest IBA funds in certain approved assets. (c) All registered brokers are to be members of Protection Fund and contributions are based on number of employees (50 employees = ECU 5,925).
Portugal			No formal requirement - insurance intermediaries must possess an appropriate financial and economic structure.
Germany	No	No	n.a.
Denmark	No	No	n.a.
Spain	Yes	No	Minimum guarantee before activity: ECU 62,596 (in the form of bank guarantee).
Belgium	Yes	No	Minimum ECU 12,887 (not yet adopted).
Luxembourg	No	No	n.a.
Greece	Yes	?	Minimum working capital in approved bank account or long term government bonds of ECU 84,000.
Ireland	Yes	?	(a) Requirement to maintain a protected client bank account. (b) Bonding requirements; Non-life: ECU 30,724, Life: ECU 30,724.
Netherlands	No	No	n.a.
Sweden	No	No	n.a.
Finland	Yes	No	Minimum guarantee ECU 34,591.
Austria	No	No	n.a.

? = not clear

To the problem of wide divergencies between Member States' regulations should be added the supplementary difficulty of lack of a harmonized interpretation of the demarcation between the concept of freedom of provision of services, which is crucial to the non-permanent cross-border intermediation of insurance services, and the concept of freedom of establishment. It is not easy to draw the line between the two concepts of free provision of services and establishment. This is particularly true when the insurer has recourse to intermediaries. The European Court of Justice has acknowledged that, in principle, an enterprise which has recourse to an intermediary in another Member State on a permanent basis to carry on activities in that Member State may lose its benefits as a cross-border service provider and fall within the scope of the provisions on the right of establishment.

The issues at stake are to define the arrangements applicable to intermediaries established in Member State A, to whom insurance undertakings in Member State B have recourse in order to do business in Member State B; the conditions under which intermediaries might be regarded as permanent establishments, rather than as activities carried on under the freedom to provide services; and the resulting legal implications.

It follows from the Court's jurisprudence that for the links between an (independent) intermediary and an insurance undertaking to be regarded as meaning that the insurance undertaking falls within the scope of the arrangements governing a branch, the intermediary must meet the following three cumulative conditions. The intermediary must have received an exclusive brief from the insurance undertaking it represents; it must be able to negotiate on behalf of the insurance undertaking and commit the latter; and it must operate on a permanent basis. It is therefore only where the intermediary acts as a genuine extension of the insurance undertaking that the insurance undertaking falls within the scope of the arrangements applicable to the establishment of a branch.

The Commission will shortly publish a Communication on the freedom to provide services and the general good in the insurance sector in parallel to its Communication on the banking sector (OJ C 320, 30.11.1995). This Communication will contribute to clarifying the position of the Community on how to interpret the jurisprudence of the Court of Justice. It cannot, however, be a substitute for binding harmonized legislation, nor will it be able to deal with the fact that the constantly changing jurisdiction of the Court presents a moving target for economic operators.

4.7. Conclusion

During the reference period, the upstream and downstream partnership agreements between insurers have developed:

(a) in the sample of 100 undertakings, they now affect 10% of the sample;
(b) the same is true for four out of five of the case study undertakings, which developed partnership projects.

This movement affects large undertakings more (seven out of ten), but now the small undertakings are also involved. It affects the life/contingency sector more than non-life business. Two major types of partnership stand out:

(a) agreements with other insurers (of the fronting type);

(b) agreements with non-insurers distributing financial products through networks: banks, post office, etc.

However, in all cases, these agreements refer to very specific activities, the target potentially being a customer segment, a country or a type of product.

In this development of partnerships, there are as many formulas to create a strong bilateral relationship (Fortis/Caixa) as to create true multinational networks (Victoria). There are multifarious reasons for these changes. They are linked to the market situations of the various countries and to the aspirations of the various operators:

(a) For the companies, it is a matter of becoming increasingly competitive, while cutting their cost of access to customers as much as possible.

(b) Recourse to these new distribution channels enables companies to conquer new markets. In conquering the markets, the banks provide insurers with strength and the cover of extremely powerful distribution systems; it should be recalled that in Germany there are nearly 50,000 outlets (including banks and post office), 22,000 in Italy, 32,000 in Spain (including the savings banks), 43,000 in France (including the post office). The same is true of the flow of customers passing daily through the hypermarkets.

(c) In addition to these considerations on the part of the insurers, there is also the interest of the new insurance distributors. For instance, the banks are seeking to improve the very small margins they have elsewhere. Finally, for some major distributors, this sale corresponds to the search for fuller exploitation of the potential of their dossiers (or their customer flows).

(d) Confronting these trends, for traditional distribution channels, the search for defence strategies has been largely oriented towards growth in size, internationalization, economies of scale or greater professionalism.

As regards insurers' explanations concerning the questions put to the sample of undertakings on whether or not they use national brokers to reach the other European markets and on the partnership agreements, the descriptions given (and grouped together in Table 4.2) show that their prime objective is access to a market segment (or to the world market) which they could not have achieved otherwise or only in a far more costly manner.

The replies given by the case study undertakings provide more details on this aspect of market access. In the cases encountered, setting up the partnership, without having to make a heavy investment (purchase or establishment in a country), allowed immediate access to the target customers, whether they were:

(a) corporate customers (especially through network partnerships at Victoria, the Paneurorisk European economic interest grouping at UAP, Cecar and its Bain Hogg network); or

(b) personal customers (especially through partnerships with banks or between insurers: case of Fortis/Caixa).

In all cases, the logic involved is that of the optimization of business resources (access and cost of this access to customers) and of the more rapid acquisition of the necessary know-how and market experience.

The disadvantages of the absence of a 'single licence' for the insurance intermediaries were presented and argued by the professionals of the sector (CEA and BIPAR) (see above). From the consumer's point of view, recourse to partnership only offers a partial service, since it is a formula which is often exclusive and the broker offers the consumer more possibilities to make comparisons and choices among products and insurers. Consequently, the development of partnership agreements is doubtless partly linked to the lack of cross-border access of the traditional intermediaries.

The lever for the movement towards the development of partnership agreements is quite obviously the internationalization of the markets (development of the undertakings towards other countries or internationalization of customers). However, this internationalization except possibly for the small risk products, is not confined to Europe, as shown by the creation of networks which are directed just as much towards the markets of the North American undertakings as the European markets (e.g. Victoria).

The reasons for the insurers' choice of a partnership formula are also often as much the choice of a distribution channel as the choice of a means of access to the markets. The comparative advantages of the various types of distribution possible (for example, traditional intermediaries versus bancassurance) are weighed up taking account of the target. To reach a market of private individuals when supplying a relatively commonplace product, it is clear that bancassurance, for example, offers more advantages than a network of brokers of often very unequal size or skills, sometimes little specialized in the personal market, with fewer points of sale than a bank.

The distribution of insurance products in Europe has been subject to severe competitive pressures between traditional and new channels in recent years. The present position, measured by the gross written premium income, represents a significant change from the beginning of the decade, most notably in the rise of bancassurance, including the sale of insurance products through bank branches and, more recently, telephone sales. Both channels have acted to put pressure on brokers, tied agents and other intermediaries. As yet, however, telesales have had a limited impact in European markets, except in the UK and the Netherlands, where they have met the most success in the sale of motor insurance.

It is in the personal segments of the overall insurance market that changes in distribution strategies are being felt most profoundly. In group business, traditional distribution channels have retained their advantage against direct channels, and the greater influence of the needs of the customer have already made the market competitive and reduced margins. As a result, it is in the personal sector that distribution has become the key to the winning of market share and to enhancing profitability.

In practice, the majority of insurance companies utilize more than one distribution strategy. Many of the larger insurance groups not only have multi-distribution strategies in their main market, perhaps for different product ranges, or different types of product within the same range, but also pursue different strategies in their pan-European operations. The insurance industry sees single-focused distribution strategies as inherently risky unless they are carefully consumer-focused, like telesellers, or bring a potential customer base with them, like bancassurers.

However, the cost of establishing a multi-distribution strategy can be considerable. Insurance companies require a certain critical mass to justify the investment in administration and systems which is needed to run multiple distribution channels. There is also a danger of conflict between channels. Consumer focus will be the key to pursuing any distribution strategy. This focus itself depends on the application of clear thought to all elements of the marketing mix. Ultimately, the distribution channel exists to link provider with consumer and to facilitate the profitable selling of insurance. There is clear evidence that many European markets are witnessing a drift away from intermediary-based channels, although the exact nature of this differs from market to market.

Secondary sources show that the distribution of insurance products in Europe has been subject to severe competitive pressures between traditional and new channels in recent years. The present position, measured by the gross written premium income, represents a significant change from the beginning of the decade, most notably in the rise of bancassurance, including the sale of insurance products through bank branches and, more recently, telephone sales.[20]

However, insurance companies are redefining their strategies in order to meet the increased competition, and increasingly perceive their choice of distribution strategy to be the most important driver of profitability. The main factor driving this shift is the emergence of new technologies, but the implementation of the EU Directives is also seen as having had a major effect, particularly on the distribution of long-term insurance products in Europe. It is the above developments in the battle to maintain or increase market share that explain the surge in interest within the insurance and insurance distribution community in the EU for doing away with perceived national and other regulatory obstacles to the cross-border intermediation of insurance products and services.

Any solution to the above mentioned regulatory obstacles would have to overcome at least three obstacles:

(a) the diversity of national practices with regards to regulations laying down requirements for the qualifications of intermediaries, i.e. requirements of good repute, professional competence, PI cover and other financial guarantees;

(b) the challenge of establishing sufficient consumer guarantees for cross-border intermediation, i.e. mutually compatible rules on registration, sanctions and disclosure, to allow Member States to mutually recognize one another's systems; and

(c) the lack of a harmonized interpretation of the demarcation between the concepts of freedom of establishment and the freedom to provide services is as big a problem in the field of cross-border insurance intermediation as it is for the cross-border provision of the service itself.

---

[20]   *The Marketing and Distribution of European Insurance*, Datamonitor 6, *Financial Times* 1996.

5. Changes in the pattern of investments

5.1. Aims of the legislation

The Third Generation Directives (92/49/EEC and 92/96/EEC) and the Insurance Companies Accounts Directive (91/674/EEC) lay down common rules dealing with the valuation of assets and their investment, technical provisions (provisions for unearned premiums, unexpired risks and outstanding claims) and admissible assets covered by the technical provisions as well as the diversification, matching and localization of such assets. Taken together, these measures paved the way for the mutual recognition of the different systems of control in the various Member States and thus for the single licence and home State control.

The harmonization introduced by the Third Directive reconciles the prudential demands which are necessary to ensure the financial stability of insurers with the principles of Community law in terms of the free movement of capital laid down by the Treaty on European Union. The objective pursued is to ensure the financial stability of insurers so as to protect policyholders but also to ensure that these rules are not used for other purposes, which cannot be prudentially justified, i.e. motivated by consumer protection concerns. For example, some EU States traditionally require insurers to invest in particular types of assets with a view to facilitate the funding of public finances or State housing programmes. Such obligations are clearly a severe restriction to insurers' freedom to invest and thus to the freedom of capital movement.

Turning to the rules themselves, the Directive first lays down a general principle of prudence on the investment of the assets representing technical provisions which is similar to principles set up in the majority of the legislations of Member States. The Directive then lays down an exhaustive list of categories of assets in which insurers are allowed to invest as well as principles to ensure a sufficient spread and level of prudence. The relevant provisions allow the home State to lay down stricter rules for the undertakings it supervises and, for instance, to reduce the list of permissible assets.

The spreading rules contain maximum percentages for some categories of investments. For example, an insurer may not invest more than 10% of its total gross technical provisions in any one piece of land or building. In addition, an insurer may not invest more than 5% of its total gross technical provisions in shares and other negotiable securities treated as shares, bonds, debt securities and other money and capital market instruments from the same undertaking. A similar 5% limit is laid down for guaranteed loans. As is the case with permissible assets, these rules set up a minimum level required to permit mutual recognition between Member States' supervisory regimes. Hence, each Member State may impose stricter limits than those of the Directive on its 'own' insurers whom it supervises under the single licence regime.

As regards the localization of assets covering technical provisions, and taking into account the free movement of capital as provided for in Council Directive 88/361/EEC, the Third Directive provides that, in respect of risks situated within the European Community, Member States may not insist that assets be invested in their own Member State but only that they be localized within the Community. For the same reason, the Directive prohibits Member States from insisting that insurers invest in particular categories of assets (for example: equities, bonds and debt securities issued by a particular State or regional or local authorities).

Directive 88/361/EEC on the liberalization of capital movements (before 1 January 1994 and Articles 73(b) et seq. of the Treaty on European Union) introduced the freedom for residents to invest abroad. This freedom is unconditional for households and undertakings of the non-financial sector, but subject to prudential rules for financial institutions (as established in Article 4 of the Directive and Article 73(d) of the Treaty).

According to the case law of the Court of Justice of the European Communities, these restrictive rules must be based on prudential reasons and pass the proportionality test to be compatible with Article 73(b) of the Treaty. Nevertheless, in order to secure the policyholder against exchange risks, the legislator introduced limitations on what could have been 'perfect' freedom of capital movements through the introduction of minimum matching. According to Annex I on matching rules to the Third Life Directive, life assurance undertakings are authorized not to hold matching assets to cover an amount not exceeding 20% of their commitments in a particular currency.

5.1.1. Hypotheses to be tested

The following hypotheses are to be tested:

Hypothesis 1: if the Directive has had an impact, there was a change in the categories in which investments are made in national currency (beyond changes strictly linked to interest rate and exchange rate variations).

Hypothesis 2: if the Directive has had an impact, insurers have increased the percentage of their investments in other Member States from 1988.

5.2. Facts and figures from the survey of 100 undertakings

In our sample:

(a) 23% of undertakings state that they invested a proportion of their technical reserves outside their country in 1989; this proportion tends to increase over the reference period (29% in 1995);

(b) only 19% made investments in the EU and this number has not increased over the reference period.

In Table 5.1, undertakings have been grouped according to various criteria:

(a) home country: the countries of the EU have been grouped according to the 'maturity' of their insurance markets, the maturity indicator being annual expenditure on insurance per inhabitant;

(b) size of undertakings, expressed in volume of their annual premium receipts in ECU;

(c) business activity: three categories of undertakings were created: undertakings specializing in life; undertakings specializing in one type of non-life product; and general non-life undertakings. The details of this classification are set out in Appendix A 'Methodology'.

Table 5.1. **Changes in the geographical distribution of the investments of insurance undertakings between 1989 and 1994 (%)**

	% of investments made in 1989 in the following countries			% of investments made in 1994 in the following countries		
	Home country	Other European countries	Other non-European countries	Home country	Other European countries	Other non-European countries
General mean (all undertakings together)	98.2	1.4	0.6	95.5	2.3	0.7
Variation by country group A (France, Luxembourg, Netherlands, UK)	97.4	1.9	1.2	93.5	4.1	1.4
B (Germany, Belgium, Denmark, Ireland)	98.7	1.2	0.2	96.6	1.2	0.2
C (Spain, Greece, Italy, Portugal)	100	–	–	99.5	–	–
Variation by size of undertaking Large (> ECU 500 million per year)	96.3	2.6	1.4	92.6	4.6	1.3
Medium–sized (from ECU 10 million to less than ECU 500 million per year)	98.8	1.0	0.3	97.7	1.6	0.4
Small (< ECU 10 million per year)	99.7	0.4	–	95.5	0.9	0.5
Variation by business activity of undertakings Life specialists	99.8	0.2	–	93.5	2.4	0.1
Non-life/general	94.7	3.7	2.2	93.4	4.7	2.5
Non-life/specialists	98.6	1.2	0.3	98.3	1.2	0.3

NB: Percentages may not total 100%, on account of the variable number of 'Don't know' replies. These figures could not be updated in 1995 since not all the undertakings interviewed had replied.

Table 5.1 shows that:

(a) the share of investments made in the home country remains predominant, even though it tends to decrease slightly;
(b) the volume of investments made in Europe increases slightly;
(c) the investments in the rest of the world remain stable.

Undertakings with the greatest tendency to increase their investment in other EU countries are large undertakings and life assurance undertakings.

5.2.1. Types of investment and their localization in other EU Member States

Geographical spread of investments

The countries in which the interviewees make their investments also remain the same in 1995 as in 1989. Six recipient countries take the lead (UK, France, Germany, Netherlands, Spain). The other destinations are less significant (see Table 5.2).

The mean number of different Member States where investments were made has not changed:

(a) in 1989, it was 3.6 countries (for 8 undertakings);

(b) in 1995, it was 3.1 countries (for 11 undertakings).

Table 5.2.   Member States in which the technical reserves were invested (number of replies by beneficiary country)

Beneficiary country	1989	1995
UK	5	7
France	4	7
Germany	3	5
Netherlands	3	4
Spain	3	5
Italy	2	4
Belgium	2	4
Denmark	2	2
Luxembourg	2	2
Greece	1	1
Ireland	1	2
Portugal	1	1
Total number of replies	**29**	**44**
Total number of interviewees replying	**8**	**14**
Mean number of countries per interviewee (spread)	**3.6**	**3.1**

Types of investment

When they invest their technical reserves in another Member State, the undertakings interviewed choose the following types of investment (several replies possible for the same undertaking).

Table 5.3.   Types of investment chosen by insurers to invest in another European country

Type of investment [1]	1989	1995
Debt securities, bonds and other money and capital market instruments	11	14
Loans	2	2
Shares and other variable yield participations	4	9
Units in undertakings for collective investment in transferable securities and other investment funds	1	3
Land, buildings and immovable property rights	3	1
Other	0	7
Total number of interviewees having replied	**8**	**14**

[1]   To classify the possible investment, it was agreed to use the investment terminology appearing in the CEA's publication *Codification CEA des Directives européennes de l'assurance*, pp. 70 and 71.

Investment in shares was therefore the 'European' type of investment which progressed the most during the reference period.

5.3. Case studies

A. UAP

In the UAP Group, each European subsidiary (Sun Life, Royale Belge, etc.) manages its own investments. Although there are exchanges of information and experience is shared among the various managers, each country remains in charge of its strategy.

In general, the various companies make almost all their investments in their home country, with the exception of the UK which turns slightly more to the outside world.

The reasons are the following:

(a) investment outside national frontiers requires sound knowledge of the market in which the investment is made. However, the switch to the single currency will change the situation radically and is already giving rise to consideration of the future investment strategy at UAP;

(b) the exchange risks: not to increase the policyholder's risk through an investment in a foreign currency.

B. Victoria

Victoria's insurance payments are secured by matching cash investments. During the period 1989–94, investments in foreign currencies were strictly limited to the cover value of the contracts concluded in foreign currency. Consequently, the proportion of foreign shares gradually rose to 30% in the share portfolios.

After the amendment of the Investment Directives, Victoria continued the internationalization of its investments.

C. Mapfre

Mapfre makes all its investments in the country in which its companies operate and this strategy remained unchanged between 1989 and 1995. The main reason given is the refusal to expose itself to any exchange risk.

D. Fortis

The Fortis Group invested as follows:

(a) for the Belgian company, in 1994 as in 1989, 100% of its reserves in Belgium;
(b) as regards the Dutch company (Amev Nederland), the policy was already the following in 1989:
  • investments in bonds and shares in eight other Member States;
  • property investments in two other Member States.

In 1994, the spread (country, type of investment) was the same. The amounts invested nevertheless fell over the period 1989–94 by about 25%.

The foreign currency investments are linked to two reasons:

(a) either they correspond to specific products, denominated in a non-national currency (this was the case in particular of the products in pesetas sold to Dutch customers);
(b) or they were pension funds set up by multinational customers (e.g. IBM) requiring multinational investments.
The fall (see above) in the amounts invested in foreign currency in fact corresponds to the fall in sales of these products.

5.4. Secondary sources

According to the CEA[21] (see Tables 5.4 and 5.5) which have tracked the investment of insurance companies from 1990 to 1994 broken down by main categories, the global amount invested by insurance companies in Europe was ECU 2,299 billion at the beginning of 1995, up by 8.5% compared with 1993.

As previously, the UK market was by far the largest, with a global amount of ECU 692.8 billion invested, representing more than 30% of the European total (CEA members). This figure must be compared with the 21% of global premium income.

On the other hand, the French market had a much smaller share: 15.4% against a 22% share of premium income, a situation which expresses the different structures of activities between the two markets, particularly regarding the importance of pension funds – implying long-term savings – largely developed in the UK and almost non-existent in France.

Meanwhile, the German market had almost the same proportion of investments and of premium volume (23.2% and 23.5%).

Not surprisingly, 'debt securities and other fixed-income securities' represented the main part of global investments (34.6%), followed closely by 'shares and other variable yield securities' (25.3%).

---

[21]   CEA, *European Insurance in Figures*, 1995.

With the 'loans' category, these three categories of investment account for nearly 81% of the total.

Nevertheless, some figures are still lacking and the real proportion may be slightly different from the proportions indicated.

Finally, it is important to note that the breakdown per category differs significantly from one country to another: Portugal, Greece, and Finland having a higher level of 'land and buildings' while the UK has a higher proportion of 'shares and same type of securities' (according to the data provided).

Table 5.4.   Investments 1994: breakdown per category

Member State	Total 1994	(a)	(b)	(c)	(d)	(e)	(f)	(g)
					(%)			
Austria	30,476	9	4	45	–	37	4	1
Belgium	53,170	5	11	7	54	17	3	3
Germany	532,895	6	6	14	17	55	1	1
Denmark	55,710	2	13	11	63	2	2	7
Spain	34,802	10	4	2	52	3	11	18
Finland	27,443	14	–	12	26	43	–	5
France	354,069	9	17	–	70	2	1	1
UK	692,811	8	–	48	32	3	2	6
Greece	1,881	16	4	14	61	2	3	–
Ireland	19,358	9	–	82	–	–	–	10
Italy	88,295	14	15	66	–	2	3	0
Netherlands	139,142	6	–	14	23	48	2	7
Portugal	6,412	18	72	–	–	1	9	–
Sweden	81,341	8	5	28	50	8	1	–

(a) land and buildings
(b) investments in affiliated undertakings and participating interests
(c) shares and other variable yield securities and units in unit trusts
(d) debt securities and other fixed-income securities
(e) loans, including loans guaranteed by mortgages
(f) deposits with credit institutions
(g) other

Table 5.5.   Investments 1994: breakdown per category (million ECU)

Member State	Total 1994	(a)	(b)	(c)	(d)	(e)	(f)	(g)	Real evolution 94/90 (%)
Austria	30,476	2,880	1,242	13,763	n.a.	11,266	1,141	184	25.8
Belgium	53,170	2,552	5,767	3,871	28,486	9,192	1,530	1,773	26.1
Germany	532,895	29,926	32,446	76,180	90,933	292,804	6,878	3,728	22.4
Denmark	55,710	1,056	7,283	6,248	35,056	1,205	891	3,971	26.3
Spain	34,802	3,561	1,255	803	17,931	1,046	3,823	6,383	75.4
Finland	27,443	3,820	n.a.	3,255	7,209	11,817	n.a.	1,342	27.7
France	354,069	32,916	59,118	n.a.	246,724	6,288	4,101	4,921	72.6
UK	692,811	55,505	n.a.	334,531	224,684	20,329	17,046	40,716	53.9
Greece	1,881	304	79	270	1,144	37	49	−2	104.4
Ireland	19,358	1,647	n.a.	15,820	n.a.	n.a.	n.a.	1,892	23.0
Italy	88,295	12,020	13,476	58,272	n.a.	1,777	2,753	6	65.1
Netherlands	139,142	8,087	n.a.	19,496	32,654	66,690	2,753	9,462	31.4
Portugal	6,412	1,160	4,616	*	*	58	578	n.a.	104.5
Sweden	81,341	6,367	3,879	22,981	40,478	6,434	1,203	n.a.	18.7

(a) land and buildings
(b) investments in affiliated undertakings and participating interests
(c) shares and other variable yield securities and units in unit trusts
(d) debt securities and other fixed-income securities
(e) loans, including loans guaranteed by mortgages
(f) deposits with credit institutions
(g) other
* (b) includes (c) and (d)

5.4.1. Investments according to the OECD

The changes in the nature of the investments are detailed in Tables 5.6 and 5.7.

The various EU countries all have their specific investment strategy, with some countries having a tradition where land and buildings are strongly represented (Portugal, UK, Spain, France), and others traditionally investing more in the securities market: Germany (mortgage loans and bonds), Belgium (bonds), etc. Moreover, these strategies differ considerably within the same country according to the business sector of the insurers (life or non-life). Over the past five years, there have been considerable changes in the investment strategies of the various countries:

(a) in the 'life' sector, there has been a strong breakthrough by bonds in Belgium, France, Italy, the UK, while land and buildings (Portugal, France) and mortgage loans (Belgium, Netherlands) are tending to become less significant in the traditional strongholds of these forms of investment;

(b) in the 'non-life' sector, there is generally more stability, although bonds have become more important in Denmark, Ireland and the Netherlands.

Table 5.6. Type of investments in life (%)

	Total[1] (100%)		Property		Mortgage loans		Shares		Bonds		Other loans		Other investments	
	1989	1994	1989	1994	1989	1994	1989	1994	1989	1994	1989	1994	1989	1994
B	779	1,195	7.6	4.7	23.3	17.2	13.6	15.0	46.5	55.3	2.1	1.7	6.8	6.0
D	492	739	6	5.3	15	14.6	3.6	4.6	24.2	14.3	48.3	46.8	2.9	14.4
DK	214	307	3.4	1.7	1.9	1.4	10.6	25.8	77.9	64.3	1.61	1.0	4.6	5.7
E	109	n.a.	6.8	n.a.	4.0	n.a.	11.5	n.a.	53.3	n.a.	0.4	n.a.	23.9	n.a.
GR	66	n.a.	30.3	n.a.	1.6	n.a.	7	n.a.	57.9	n.a.	3.2	n.a.	0	n.a.
F	759	2,002	11.4	7.7	0.0	0.0	22	18.6	55.7	66.6	10.6	2.8	0.3	4.2
I	35,822	107,799	12.9	11.5	7.4	1.6	12.4	11.8	64.9	72.8	0.0	0.0	2.3	2.2
IRL	10	8	4.2	8.1	0.0	0.0	14.2	9.0	19.3	34.4	0.1	5.0	62.1	43.5
L	n.a.	n.a.	n.a.	4.7	n.a.	0.0	n.a.	12.0	n.a.	63.3	n.a.	0.0	n.a.	20.0
NL	155	267	8.8	5.6	21.9	14.7	11.1	13.6	9.2	25.3	44.4	35.1	4.7	5.8
P	90	574	15.6	3.2	0.1	0.2	80.8	87.6	0.0	0.0	2.3	0.1	1.1	8.8
UK	234	386	16.7	9.3	1.3	0.4	58.7	60.6	19.6	25.0	1.5	1.6	2.2	3.0

[1] In billion national currency.
Source: OECD.

Table 5.7. Type of investments in non-life (%)

	Total[1] (100%)		Land and buildings		Mortgage loans		Shares		Bonds		Other loans		Other investments	
	1989	1994	1989	1994	1989	1994	1989	1994	1989	1994	1989	1994	1989	1994
B	329	497	7.8	11.5	7.6	4.5	14.2	15.6	55.7	53.2	0.5	0.1	14.3	15.1
D	123	190	7.7	6.5	3.3	3.1	9.5	10.8	33.4	20.4	43.5	42.3	2.6	16.8
DK	88	87	4.5	4.0	2.6	2.0	28.2	26.1	40.3	45.1	1.4	2.7	23.0	20.1
E	994	n.a.	26.5	n.a.	1.8	n.a.	15.8	n.a.	45.5	n.a.	0.6	n.a.	9.9	n.a.
EL	38	n.a.	35.2	n.a.	2.2	n.a.	22.1	n.a.	40.0	n.a.	0.5	n.a.	0.0	n.a.
F	337	493	15.7	16.5	0.0	0.0	32.5	31.1	42.8	38.9	5.8	2.2	3.2	11.3
I	35,930	68,400	18.0	17.0	2.4	2.6	20.3	20.7	52.9	55.2	0.0	0.0	6.4	4.5
IRL	2	2.2	2.9	2.4	0.0	0.0	9.8	15.3	43.4	59.4	0.0	0.0	44.0	22.8
L	n.a.	37	n.a.	3.8	n.a.	0.0	n.a.	10.3	n.a.	72.1	n.a.	0.0	n.a.	13.8
NL	27	30	4.7	2.4	3.9	3.0	12.6	17.3	32.1	42.4	37.4	34.3	9.3	0.5
P	188	477	34.5	35.1	0.3	0.8	65.1	58.7	0.0	0.0	0.0	0.0	0.1	5.4
UK	30	39	11.7	5.6	3.6	2.1	40.6	32.0	40.6	56.9	1.3	1.3	2.2	2.1

[1] In billion national currency.
Source: OECD.

There are no official statistics keeping track of the geographical diversification of the investments corresponding to the insurance undertakings' reserves. Some supervisory authorities mention it in their reports, but this information is not at all frequent. The prevailing trend in the EU, especially in life, where savings products have gradually taken the lion's share of the market, is moreover similar in the USA, where investments have evolved as follows:

Table 5.8.   Changes in the distribution of the investments of American insurers (% of total investments)

Category of assets	Life (a)		Non-life (b)	
	1985	1993	1985	1992
Government borrowing	15	20	62	59.5
Private bonds	36	40.6	12.6	17.8
Shares	9.4	13.7	23	19.6
Mortgage loans	20.8	12.8	2.3	2.5
Land and buildings	3.5	3.1	2.3	2.5
Loans to policyholders	6.6	4.6	2.3	2.5
Other	8.7	5.7	2.3	2.5

Sources: (a) Acti, published in Risques No. 22 – April/June 1995. (b) Insurance Information Institute, published in Risques No. 22 – April/June 1995.

It can therefore be said that the changes in the types of investment by European undertakings have been very similar to the movements observed on the other side of the Atlantic.

5.4.2.   Changes in investment patterns in the EU broken down by country[22]

Belgium

In most of the period under review, Belgian legislation set minimum and maximum percentages for investment in each category. This meant that undertakings' investment policies had to be conducted within the narrow boundaries set by legislation.

Denmark

In Denmark, life assurance undertakings are commonly owned by non-life undertakings, and, for tax reasons, life assurers generally transfer part of their business to subsidiaries. These factors go a long way towards explaining the high share of investments in affiliated undertakings and participating interests.

Investments, particularly by life undertakings, have traditionally concentrated on mortgage bonds. The Danish system of property finance has led to the creation of a large bond market trading securities that are suitable for insurers. Insurers have traditionally invested their money in Denmark. However, in recent years there has been a tendency for a higher proportion of funds to be invested abroad, particularly in foreign shares. Investment in foreign assets still accounts for a very small, but fast growing, share.

Germany

For all insurance undertakings, attention should be paid to the growing percentage of investments in investment funds. Undertakings take advantage of the opportunities that shares in investment funds offer to avoid restrictions on equity investment.

Attention should also be drawn to the share of mortgage loans in the investments of life assurance undertakings. Such mortgage loans are generally linked to a life assurance policy whereby repayment of the mortgage is deferred until the maturity of the insurance policy (endowment mortgages). Many insurance groups are headed by a reinsurance undertaking, not

---

[22]   *Source*: Eurostat, *Insurance in Europe*, 1996.

least because reinsurers are less tightly regulated than direct insurers (e.g. missing solvency guidelines). This accounts for the high proportion of investments in affiliates and participating interests of reinsurance undertakings.

Greece

Investments totalled DR 411,467 million at the end of 1993, an increase of 21.7% on the 1992 figure. Investments in bonds (short, medium and long-term bonds issued by the Greek State or by State-owned banks) accounted for the majority of total investments (62.3%). Shares and land and buildings also represent significant shares of total investments (16.2% and 19.6% respectively).

Spain

The largest share of investments was in debt securities and other fixed-income securities and in participations in investment pools. In non-life undertakings, land and buildings claimed a relatively large share of total investments.

As regards investment policy, undertakings strove, on the one hand, to reduce tangible investments and variable-yield securities (shares) and, on the other, to maintain the share of investment in affiliated undertakings and participating interests. A considerable proportion of investment was also devoted to fixed-income securities. This situation is essentially determined by the particular suitability of fixed-income securities for investing technical provisions and by the situation on the financial markets, which was largely marked by high interest rates.

France

In life assurance, investments (1988 = 100%, 1993 = 279%) grew much faster than premiums (1988 = 100%, 1993 = 208%) over the period in question. This is the result of the large number of new single-premium and endowment policies written in this period.

The breakdown of investments follows different patterns for life and non-life undertakings. Among non-life insurers over the period in question, loans and deposits lost ground to investments in affiliated undertakings and participating interests and shares and other variable-yield securities; among life assurers this item lost ground to debt securities and other fixed-income securities. This trend is due partly to the appearance of new operators in the market (subsidiaries of banks) and partly to the type of products most commonly sold (single or periodic premiums, eight-year term).

Foreign assets accounted for only a small proportion of total investments: as little as 0.3% of the total investments of life undertakings and 2.8% of those of non-life undertakings in 1993. Nevertheless, the trend in foreign investments between 1988 and 1993 was steadily upward in both absolute and relative terms owing to the increasing business.

Ireland

Non-life insurers invest substantially in Irish and EU government securities. Indeed, in 1993, 61% of investment was in government securities. Cash held in banks and other financial institutions made up 18% of total investments.

In life assurance, shares and securities (bonds and variable-interest securities) accounted for a lower percentage than in non-life insurance. A larger part of the investment of life undertakings was in unit trusts.

Italy

For all categories of direct undertakings, investments concentrate on debt securities and other fixed-income securities. However, for specialist reinsurance undertakings, shares and other variable-yield securities and units in unit trusts predominate.

Life assurance investments in land and buildings declined from 38.5% of total investments in 1983 to 16.2% in 1993, while investments in securities rose from 36.2% in 1983 to 70.5% in 1993. In the non-life sector, the structure and development of investments were rather similar.

Luxembourg

Of the investment holdings of insurance companies in 1993, 70.7% was in the form of debt securities (of which 16.8% was composed of Luxembourg public debt or equivalent issues and 17.5% debt securities by Luxembourg companies), 11.1% was in shares (of which 3.3% was composed of shares in open-end funds) and 13.9% was in other assets, including sight and term bank deposits in particular.

As regards the Luxembourg portfolio, there is no significant difference between the investment structures of life and non-life business, as the investment policies of all insurance companies are determined by the same legal framework.

To date, cover for liabilities denominated in currencies other than Luxembourg francs has been decided case by case. On the whole, debt securities and units in unit trusts are the main assets used to cover such liabilities, with property and mortgage loans playing a minor role.

Netherlands

Historically, the major investments have been in fixed-interest assets, especially loans to local government agencies, hospitals, social housing and other types of semi-government institutions and bonds. Since about 1985, investments have been increasingly directed towards shares and real estate, partly as investment abroad. Investments with the Dutch government and investments in loans are becoming less important.

Austria

As composite undertakings have traditionally dominated the Austrian insurance market, they naturally have the largest amounts of investments. A substantial proportion of these assets comprise loans made by insurance undertakings to the State. In December 1993, the total value of these loans was ATS 83,346 million, which represents 21.7% of total investments.

Portugal

Owing to the market dominance of composite insurance undertakings, their total investments were greater than those of all the specialist life and non-life insurance undertakings put together.

The structure of investments varied between the different categories of undertakings. Non-life insurance undertakings invested more in land and buildings, while composite and life assurance undertakings invested less in property and considerably more in other financial assets. One reason for this is the need of such undertakings to obtain better short-term yields, which is not always possible when investing in land and buildings.

Finland

Land and buildings and debt securities and other fixed-income securities are the two highest categories for both life and non-life insurance companies, with share and unit trust investments gaining in importance.

Sweden

In Swedish insurance undertakings, only certain types of assets were acceptable as cover for technical provisions. The translation of EU regulations will allow other types of assets (e.g. shares) to be used. The investment policies of life undertakings will therefore become more liberal, and there will be a greater emphasis on risk management. On the other hand, it will mean more regulation for non-life undertakings. The new rules prescribe a ceiling on the percentage invested in any given type of assets (e.g. to prevent excessive exposure to mortgage bonds issued by housing finance institutions) and place a limit on the size of holdings in any one organization or of a given asset. Sweden has been granted a transitional period up to 1 January 2000, because some undertakings currently exceed such limits.

In life assurance, investment has to some extent been confined to bonds and loans, but a larger part of the surplus (bonus fund) has been invested in shares and buildings. Since the abolition of exchange controls in 1989, Swedish life assurance undertakings have invested abroad in order to diversify their portfolios. They have mainly acquired foreign shares but have also, at least up to the financial crisis, invested in foreign property. After a temporary increase around 1989, investment in property has fallen back.

UK

The investment portfolios of life and non-life insurance undertakings are clearly different, reflecting the short versus long-term liabilities each takes on. (Non-life insurers do take on some long-term obligations, but liabilities are primarily short-term.) One of the strengths of the UK's life assurance industry is its relative freedom to invest in ordinary stocks and shares. Guaranteed surrender values are not a legal requirement in the UK, and at present few 'with profits' policies offer these. As a consequence, undertakings' investment does not have to be concentrated in fixed-rate securities and mortgages, bonds and deposits, whose value is predictable for matching purposes, and UK insurers usually have a high (by international standards) proportion of their portfolios in shares which have historically given higher long-term rates of return.

5.4.3. Insurers' opinions of the impact of the single market on their investments (Eurostat survey)

In reply to the question on this subject, i.e. *Has the liberalization of capital had a positive or a negative effect on your undertaking?*, the majority of the insurers interviewed, i.e. 61.6%, replied that this measure has had no effect. Nevertheless, 23.4% thought that this measure has had a positive effect.

5.5. Conclusion

Generally, one should be very careful when drawing conclusions from the primary and secondary sources presented in this chapter because of the very short time span between 1 July 1994, when the relevant provisions of the Third Generation Directives entered into force, and the date of this report. The investment strategies of insurance undertakings have to be closely linked to their portfolios and are not likely to change overnight. Primary sources are the most up-to-date.

The survey of 100 European undertakings on the trend in their investments shows that the national share remains very large, even in 1995.

Nineteen per cent of the undertakings of the sample group invest beyond their frontiers and in Europe, but this is an old strategy as their number has not changed between 1989 and 1995. Investments by these same undertakings abroad are developing slowly, as seen above, rising from 2% of reserves in 1989 to 3% in 1995. Given that these figures are so low, it can hardly be stated that this is a real change in policy.

It is somewhat surprising that insurers have not to a larger degree taken advantage of the liberalization of capital movements introduced first by EU legislation and then by new provisions in the Treaty on European Union applicable since 1990. There are three main reasons for this caution on the part of the insurers. The first is the currency matching requirements laid down by the EU's Framework Directives but this can only be part of the reason, because the vast majority of insurers do not even use their 'quota' of 20% laid down by the Directives. The second is the degree of expertise required to manage investments in several, relatively unknown foreign markets. This, particularly for medium-sized and small enterprises, is a real reason for caution because of the difficulty of deciding when the potential gain of investing abroad is sufficiently large either to delegate the investment of its assets to a specialized investment company or to acquire sufficient specialized knowledge in-house. Finally, the currency fluctuation risk is perceived as part of the two reasons mentioned above in that many operators indicate that changes in the localization of their investments are sure to come about as a consequence of the introduction of the single currency in 1999.

6. Changes in market concentration and competition

6.1. Aims of the legislation

The removal of barriers to competition within financial services and insurance in the EU was seen by the research on 'The Cost of Non-Europe'[23] as having three interlocking effects.[24]

The first was a surge in competition within the financial services sectors themselves as a result of what has been termed 'X-inefficiencies'. This covers a poor internal allocation of resources – human, physical and financial. Conditions of weak competition cause such 'X-inefficiencies'. In general terms it was estimated[25] that the total effect of moving to a competitive integrated market with fuller achievement of potential economies of scale and reduction of 'X-inefficiencies' might be twice to three times the direct cost of identified barriers. Second, a knock-on boost to all sectors using financial services; and finally a deregulated financial services sector would exert a positive influence on the conduct of macroeconomic policy within the EU.

Furthermore, the harmonization of conditions governing the take-up and pursuit of insurance implemented by the Framework Directives on insurance involved an important measure of deregulation for certain national markets by abolishing the possibility of Member States to require the prior approval or systematic notification of premiums (i.e. prices) and general and special policy conditions.

6.1.1. Hypothesis to be tested

The hypothesis we put forward is that these effects have already started to be felt in the insurance business if changes could be observed during the reference period concerning:

(a) concentration in the sector (at national or European level), and
(b) changes in the structure of the sector: new entrants, closures, mergers or the start-up of new activities.

6.1.2. Indicators used to test hypothesis

Two types of methods were used to test this hypothesis:

(a) the opinion of the insurers (= their subjective feelings), and
(b) indicators from secondary sources, where they exist.

To obtain the opinion of the insurers on this subject, the following propositions were put to the interviewees:

---

[23]   'The Economics of 1992', *European Economy*, No. 35, March 1988. The Price Waterhouse sub-study on 'The Cost of Non-Europe in Financial Services', *Basic Findings*, Vol. 9, did not focus exclusively on insurance but was based on the prices for 16 financial products or services – seven in banking, five in insurance services and four in brokering or securities services.

[24]   Cf. 'Deregulation of financial services: the world after Cecchini', E. Gardner and P. Molyneux, Conference paper at IVIE Conference on Productivity, Efficiency and Profitability in Banking, University of Valencia, 25–26 May 1995.

[25]   'The Economics of 1992', op. cit.

A.   'Owing to insufficient size or performance, there has been a rapid increase in the number of insurance companies closing down';

B.   'New entrants have appeared on my national market';

C.   'There have been changes in foreign investment: fewer mergers/acquisitions, more new undertakings set up';

D.   'In order to improve their competitiveness, companies have endeavoured to cut their general operating expenses';

E.   'Companies' results have improved in terms of profitability'.

For the interviewees, the greatest changes occurring on the European market, in order of importance, are:

(a) the efforts made to be competitive by cutting general operating expenses (proposition D);
(b) the appearance of new entrants (proposition B).

On the other hand, the other aspects of market change:

(a) closures of undertakings (proposition A);
(b) change of investments towards the creation of more undertakings (proposition C);
(c) the improvement of the profitability of undertakings (proposition E);

are far less perceptible, as shown in Table 6.1.

Table 6.1.   Opinion of the interviewees on the changes in competition on their market

Proposition	Average score
A. Owing to insufficient size or performance, there has been a rapid increase in the number of insurance companies closing down	1.4
B. New entrants have appeared on my national market	2
C. There have been changes in foreign investment: fewer mergers/acquisitions, more new undertakings set up	1.3
D. In order to improve their competitiveness, companies have endeavoured to cut their general operating expenses	2.5
E. Companies' results have improved in terms of profitability	1.7

NB: The average scores result from a scale of 0 to 3, 0 meaning that the interviewee does not agree at all, 3 meaning total agreement.

There are few differences in perception between undertakings regarding the improvement of profitability through the endeavour to cut general operating expenses: a large majority is in agreement on this point. On the other hand, it is the large undertakings, the undertakings belonging to France, Luxembourg, the Netherlands and the UK which were the most sensitive to the new entrants.

The undertakings of southern Europe (Spain, Greece, Italy, Portugal), specialists in life assurance and small and medium-sized undertakings were hit harder by the increase in closures of undertakings. The effort made by undertakings to be competitive was seen particularly by the large undertakings, by those belonging to France, Luxembourg, the Netherlands and the UK and by the life assurance undertakings and general non-life insurance undertakings.

Figure 6.1. Changes in competition within the European Union: Variation in the opinions of undertakings according to their characteristics

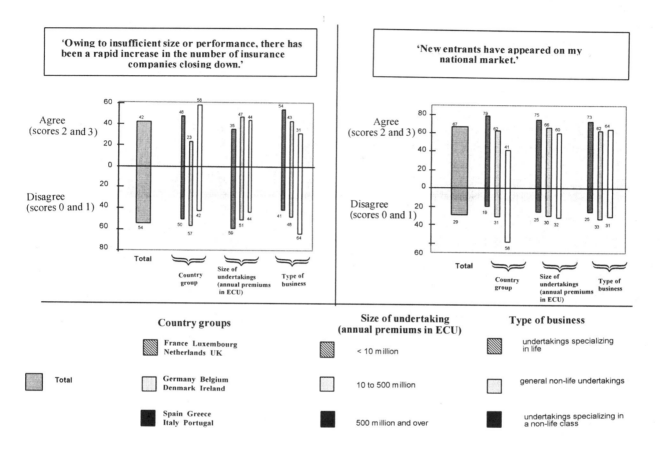

Figure 6.1. continued

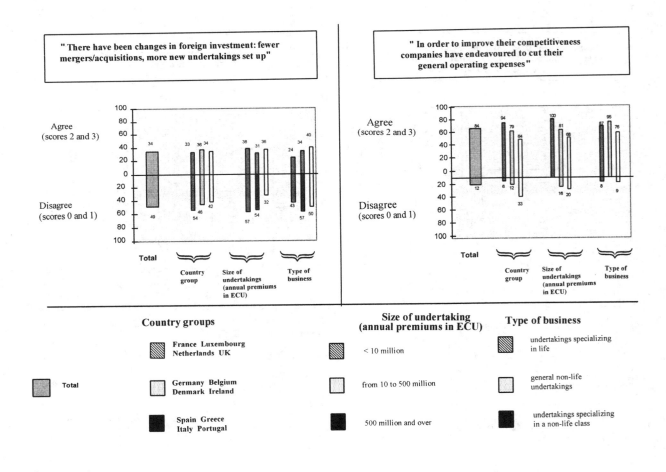

Figure 6.1. continued

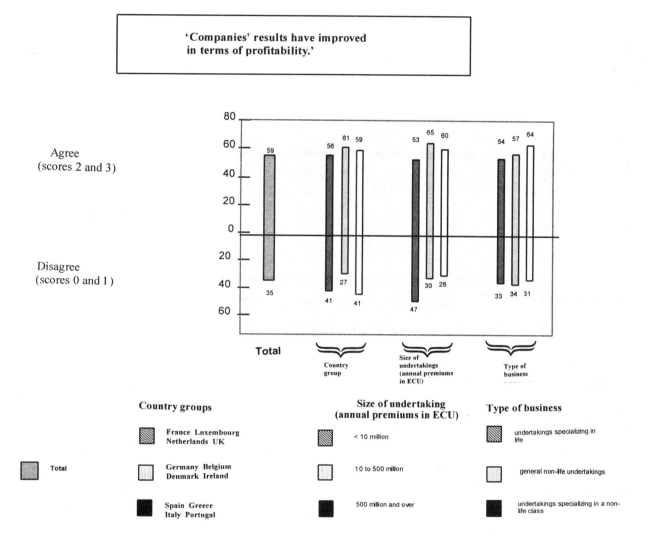

6.2. Case studies

The opinions gathered from the case study undertakings are very consistent with those of the sample group.

The closure of undertakings: the case study undertakings consider that, to date, few closures have actually taken place since, in the case of buy-out, the undertaking continues to operate, even if it is integrated into another group. The general opinion (UAP, Cecar, Mapfre) is nevertheless still that the movement is likely to gather pace in the future, in particular because of:

(a) the restructuring carried out in each country by certain groups (UAP);
(b) the high investments which will now have to be made to be competitive (information technology).

The new entrants: the opinions vary considerably according to the undertaking interviewed. UAP and Victoria consider that they have not really seen any evidence of this movement in their own countries, Mapfre and Fortis slightly more.

Changes in the pattern of investments: fewer mergers/acquisitions, more creations of new undertakings: on this point, the undertakings interviewed did not see any effect deriving from the single market.

For UAP, it is above all a question of:

(a) *markets:* in certain countries where management costs are high, it is better to establish than to buy;
(b) *opportunities:* it all depends on the potential purchases still existing in the target country, at a reasonable cost.

The efforts made with regard to general operating expenses: the case study undertakings are also unanimous on this point. For some undertakings, this effort has become necessary on account of the results of competitors and in particular of the new distribution channels (UAP), the group's development targets (Fortis), international competition between brokers (Cecar) or simply the shareholders' objectives (Victoria).

The improvement of profitability: the interviewees all disagree with this assertion, for the following reasons:

(a) the general increase in recent years in the loss burden;
(b) competition, which erodes the margins.

Concerning changes in the degree of concentration at national, Community or world level, the following propositions were submitted for assessment by the interviewees:

(a) '*In my country,* the degree of concentration of undertakings in the insurance business has increased';
(b) 'There has been concentration in the insurance business *at European level.*'
(c) 'There has been concentration *at world level.*'

For all the undertakings interviewed, it is clear that there has been a concentration movement in the insurance industry in the past five years, both at national and European levels, as shown in Table 6.2, by the average scores obtained by each proposition. On the other hand, this concentration is less obvious at world level.

Table 6.2.   Opinion of the interviewees on the trend in concentration in the insurance business in their country and in Europe

Proposition	Average score
A. 'In my country, the degree of concentration of undertakings in the insurance business has increased.'	2.3
B. 'There has been concentration in the insurance business at European level.'	2.2
C. 'There has been concentration at world level.'	1.6

NB: The average scores result from a scale of 0 to 3, 0 meaning that the interviewee does not agree at all, 3 meaning total agreement.

Variation in opinion according to the characteristics of the undertakings (size, nationality, business sector):

The concentration of the insurance sector at national level is perceived in particular by:

(a) the undertakings of northern Europe: Germany, Denmark, Netherlands, Luxembourg;
(b) the medium-sized undertakings;
(c) the general non-life undertakings.

At European level, the following were particularly sensitive to this concentration:

(a)   undertakings belonging to the following countries: Ireland, France, Netherlands, Spain;
(b)   small undertakings;
(c)   general non-life undertakings.

At world level, this concentration was felt more (see Figure 6.2):

(a) in Ireland, France and the Netherlands;
(b) in the smallest undertakings;
(c) in the general non-life undertakings.

In general, the interviewees consider that in the past five years there has only been a concentration movement *at national level*, the reasons for which are linked above all to the undertakings' poor performance (management, commercial weakness, unsuitability of the products on offer).

On the other hand, this movement seems to them still to be limited at European level and non-existent at world level.

Figure 6.2.   The trend in concentration of undertakings in the insurance sector: Variation in the opinions of undertakings according to their characteristics

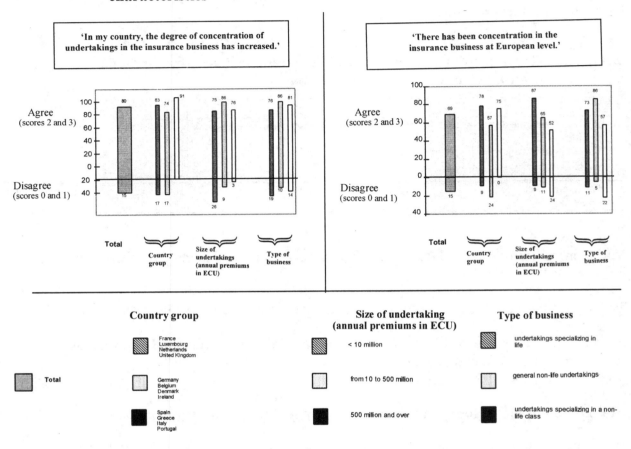

Figure 6.2. continued

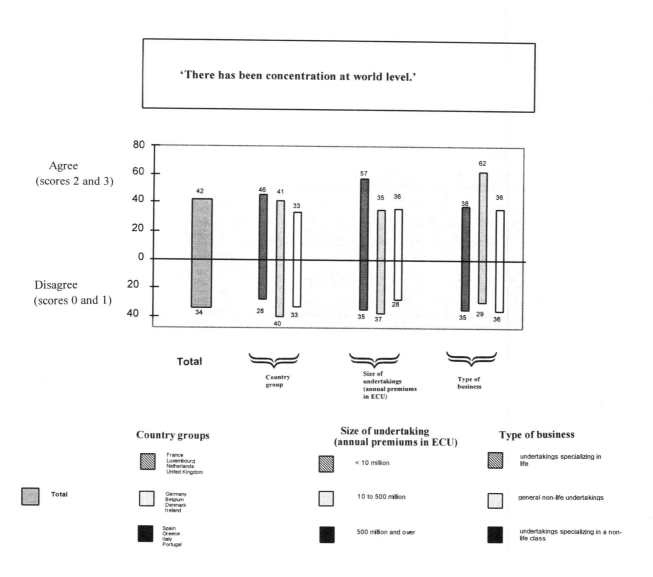

To study the subject of the protectionist measures taken by the States of the undertakings themselves, the undertakings were asked to agree or disagree with the following propositions:

(a) 'Some Member States have adopted protectionist attitudes, especially by granting government aid to their national companies';
(b) 'The insurers' federations and associations have developed protectionist behaviour'.

6.3. Opinions of the undertakings

6.3.1. Aggregate results

In general, the undertakings interviewed noticed little or no protectionist behaviour on the part of either the federations or governments, as shown in the results of Table 6.3.

Table 6.3.   Opinion of the interviewees on the development of protectionist behaviour by insurers' associations or governments

Proposition	Average score
A. 'Some Member States have adopted protectionist attitudes, especially by granting government aid to their national companies.'	1.4
B. 'The insurers' federations and associations have developed protectionist behaviour.'	1.2

NB: The average scores result from a scale of 0 to 3, 0 meaning that the interviewee does not agree at all, 3 meaning total agreement.

6.3.2. Variation in opinion according to the characteristics of the undertakings (size, nationality, business sector)

Protectionism of governments

The undertakings which most noticed protectionism on the part of governments come from the UK and Denmark.

It is the medium-sized undertakings which are the most sensitive to it, and, in our sample, the specialists in life assurance.

Protectionism of the associations

This type of protectionism did not seem to be very apparent to the interviewees.

Only the large undertakings of a few countries (France, Spain) were a little more sensitive to this than the others.

Figure 6.3.   The existence of protectionist attitudes: variation in the opinions of the undertakings according to their characteristics

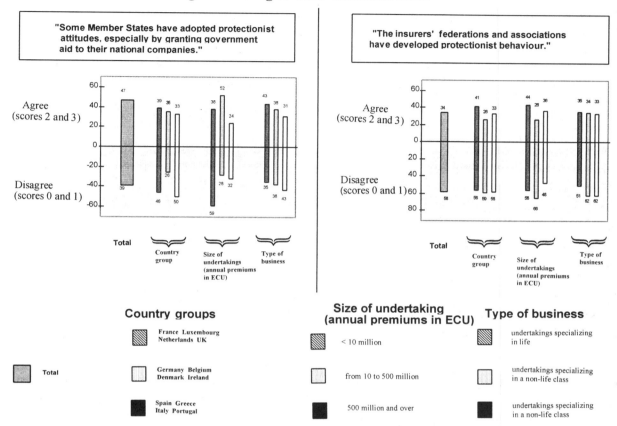

The typical undertakings interviewed share the sample group's opinion: there has been little or no protectionist behaviour over the past five years, especially on the part of the associations.

It is the governments which would be considered more protectionist, especially through aid granted to nationalized undertakings (Fortis).

6.4.   Secondary sources

Eurostat[1] expects an increase in the number of enterprises in the coming years for those EU States where the effects of deregulation are the greatest. However, a breakdown by Member State of the development within the period of reference of this report does not always confirm this trend.

6.4.1.   Changes in EU market share: breakdown by country

Belgium

Following the introduction of new regulatory controls, especially more stringent solvency requirements, the number of insurance undertakings decreased from 322 in 1980 to 283 in 1993. While the number of life assurance undertakings increased in the period under review, non-life and composite insurance undertakings declined considerably.

---

[26]   *Insurance in Europe*, 1996.

The Belgian insurance market (life and non-life) as a whole is dominated by composite insurance undertakings. The five largest undertakings accounted for 32.4% of the total market. Several composite insurance undertakings are among the largest in terms of market share (AG 1824 is the country's biggest insurer).

The specialist reinsurance market is dominated by three large firms which together command over 60% of the market. All three belong to an insurance group.

Germany

Between 1980 and 1990, the number of insurance undertakings rose only slightly. However, between 1990 and 1992, there was a distinct increase, particularly in life and health insurance. The majority of new undertakings were set up within existing insurance groups. Broadening one's range of services is a common way of forestalling the drift of customers to other companies. Specialist undertakings were also set up to handle special products or serve new groups of customers. German unification, however, played no part in the number of new undertakings set up.

The degree of concentration in individual insurance categories, measured by gross premiums earned, varies considerably but is generally low in life assurance (30.8%) and even more so in the non-life category (22.5%).

Sigma similarly characterizes the supply structure of the German insurance industry as interesting for two reasons: the level of concentration is low, not only compared with the UK and France but also with the Japanese market, which is also subject to substantive supervision. The regulation of German insurance has caused a relatively high degree of fragmentation in the industry. The other striking aspect is the stability of the supply structure: the changes which have taken place since 1980 are of a rather marginal nature. Only the top six to ten were able to make significant market gains.

Greece

The growth of the Greek insurance industry has been marked by its long domination by a number of large State-controlled insurers. The market is still generally underdeveloped, because many people are still without any form of insurance cover.

In 1994 some 68% of the life assurance market was controlled by five undertakings. In non-life insurance, the degree of market concentration was much lower, with only 38% of premiums written by the five biggest firms.

Spain

In 1993, trends in the Spanish insurance sector were dominated by a general climate of economic recession. The number of undertakings operating in the market fell as a result of mergers, takeovers and other forms of restructuring. The growth of some specialized companies led to a slight decrease in market concentration.

The number of insurance undertakings followed a sharply declining curve from 1985 onwards. This was mainly due to effects of the regulatory legislation introduced from 1984 onwards, to the restructuring prompted by the regulatory authorities and the pressure of market discipline.

In the life assurance sector, there were 63 life assurance undertakings and 443 private mutuals in 1993. The above-mentioned restructuring process has resulted in a greater concentration and specialization of activities in the insurance sector in Spain.

The five leading undertakings in the field of life assurance amassed 46.6% of all gross life insurance premiums between them in 1993. The value of business was more widely dispersed among undertakings specializing in non-life insurance, with the top five accounting for only 19.7%. When it comes to reinsurance alone, there is a strong concentration of activity in a single undertaking, 'Mapfre Re', which has 50.6% of the total premiums.

France

In the life assurance sector, the top five undertakings were limited companies controlling about 47% of the market. Among the 20 largest firms, there were only two mutuals and one subsidiary of a mutual, in comparison with 12 subsidiaries of banks or bank-like undertakings (such as CNP group) selling their products mainly through their network of outlets.

In the non-life sector, the top five places are evenly distributed between limited companies and mutuals, which between them command a market share of about 40%.

The top five specialist reinsurers wrote almost 70% of business ceded by undertakings active in the French market.

Ireland

The number of life undertakings has increased in the last decade from 21 in 1980 to 33 in 1993, and this trend is likely to continue. The number of non-life undertakings active in the market has nearly doubled since 1980 (from 38 to 74). This is due, in particular, to the activities of the International Financial Services Centre.

The life market is dominated by Irish Life Assurance which, in 1993, accounted for 32.1% of total gross life premiums written.

In the non-life sector in 1994, 50.5% of gross premiums were written by the five biggest undertakings.

Italy

Market concentration in Italy seems lower than in many other Member States. Measured against its relatively low market volume, the Italian insurance industry is fairly fragmented, even though there is an unmistakable trend towards concentration among suppliers. Small and medium-sized suppliers have dropped out of the market, because they were not able to survive in the difficult environment of government price regulation. The top ten insurance undertakings doing life business account for 60% of total premiums in this class, five of them being composite undertakings. In non-life insurance, the top ten firms, seven of which are composite insurers, generated 51.9% of total premiums. Looking at the total business, the top ten firms, eight of which are composite insurers, accounted for 48.5% of premiums.

Luxembourg

There was a noticeable upward trend in the number of life assurance firms, from 15 in 1986 to 45 in June 1995. Over the same period, a drop in the number of branches set up in the Grand Duchy of Luxembourg (from 35 in 1986 to 23 in 1993) mirrored a rise in start-ups of Luxembourg-registered firms (from 13 in 1986 to 50 in 1993). Some foreign firms converted their branches into Luxembourg-registered subsidiaries, while others gave up their branch status in order to carry on business in the Grand Duchy under the freedom to provide services from their head offices.

Netherlands

The number of life assurers has been fairly stable since 1985. However, especially in the 1980s a number of new life assurers entered the Dutch market.

Non-life mutuals rather than limited companies seem to dominate. However, careful interpretation of this picture is essential. Often the company group as a whole is set up on a mutual basis whilst the separate life and non-life companies of the group are limited companies (see, for example the Achmea, and the Interpolis Group).

Austria

Since 1984, the number of insurance undertakings has remained more or less constant. However, it should be noted that many mutuals have taken advantage of the possibility of transferring their insurance business to a limited company. This has led to the emergence of mutuals that are no more than holding organizations for the limited companies in question. In 1993 alone, there were five transfers of this kind.

As regards market concentration, composite undertakings had particularly substantial market shares. The five largest accounted for 42.6% of total life and non-life business. By contrast, the market share of the five biggest firms specializing in life assurance was only 20% of the total life assurance market.

Portugal

The 44 undertakings with head offices in Portugal comprised 12 life assurers, 22 non-life insurers, nine composite insurers and one specialist reinsurer. Composite insurance undertakings alone, the oldest and largest undertakings, accounted for 53% of the entire Portuguese insurance market.

The four largest undertakings are composite insurers and together account for a 44% share of the market. The largest non-life undertakings occupy the fifth and sixth places, while the largest life assurance undertakings is only seventh.

In life assurance, the top 15 hold 89.2% and in non-life 83.3% of the market with life concentration for the top five and ten increasing, whereas for non-life the situation is stagnating or sharing a slight decrease in market concentration.

Finland

Among the many non-life undertakings was a large number of mutual societies with only local significance. Increasing competition has forced many of the smaller units to merge and such undertakings have declined in number from 230 in 1980 to 118 in 1993. In 1994, 15 non-life undertakings generated about 99.6% of gross non-life premiums written.

Sweden

There was originally a large number of insurers, but merger and acquisition activity in the 1960s reduced the number of undertakings. Restrictions on establishing new undertakings were lifted in the 1980s, but the number of newly authorized firms has remained small.

In life and non-life business, the ten largest undertakings account for about 90% of the market.

UK

Composite groups are the major players in the UK non-life insurance market, but with over 600 undertakings authorized to undertake non-life business (although many fewer are actively underwriting), the market is not heavily concentrated by comparison to other European countries. Specialist non-life insurance undertakings tend to be smaller in size than the specialist life undertakings. They usually operate in one or two particular fields (such as marine, aviation, employers' liability, etc.). There are only a handful of mutuals among them and a number are subsidiaries of non-insurance groups or of overseas parent insurance undertakings.

The insurance market at Lloyd's of London – unique to the UK – is included in the above figures as one domestic non-life undertaking although, strictly speaking, it is not a corporate body. The number of undertakings does not include friendly societies: there are thousands of these, mainly active in the non-life business, but their gross premiums written are very small.

There are about 200 undertakings of a significant size in the UK, but effectively the market is dominated by about 15 undertakings and Lloyd's. The London market is less concentrated than the domestic market. Only two UK undertakings figure in the world's top 30, Prudential Corporation and Royal Insurance, with the largest, Prudential, ranking 19th according to Sigma/Swiss Re figures. However, examination of the top 20 European insurers shows that half of these are UK undertakings. The UK insurance industry has strength in its depth.

The expected shake-out of the EU market has not yet taken place. The five leading companies represent 50% to 75% of the market in seven EU countries (B, DK, GR, IRL, NL, P, E). There have been movements towards less concentration in the UK, Italy, Spain and Germany, whereas the inverse trend can be seen in the Netherlands, Denmark and Portugal which have seen their markets become more dominated by relatively few players. Figures[27] on the 'new' Member States (Sweden, Austria and Finland) show an increase in concentration for Austria and (less clearly) Finland, and a decrease for Sweden.

---

[27]   *European Insurance in Figures*, CEA, Paris, 1995.

Table 6.4.   Market share of the 5, 10 and 15 leading life assurance companies from 1989 to 1994 (percentages except for the 'premiums' column)

	1989				1991				1992			
	Premiums	5	10	15	Premiums	5	10	15	Premiums	5	10	15
B	2,273	56	69.9	79.7	2,684	53.3	67.5	77.2	2,997	54.6	68.7	78.4
D	23,816	33.3	47.9	58.8	30,727	32.1	51.9	62.8	34,335	31.5	46.5	57.3
DK	1,668	62.4	83.4	94.4	2,197	74.0	93.0	100	2,528	77.0	93.0	100
E	3,412	58.3	69.3	78.1	5,045	41.5	56.8	69.9	5,769	45.6	61.2	69.8
GR	217	76.1	89.1	96.3	426	72.0	86.0	93.2	506	68.7	82.9	90.6
F	27,740	47.4	68.1	78.3	33,802	49.1	68.8	79.3	40,258	46.4	68.2	80.3
I	4,844	64.5	78.4	85.8	6,883	57.5	71.1	79.9	7,229	53.9	68.4	77.1
IRL[1]	1,558	70	88.7	n.a.	1,910	66.8	87.6	98.7	1,750	62.6	82.5	91.8
NL	7,362	52.9	70.4	78.9	10,505	52.8	72.0	79.5	11,396	57.5	74.9	81.5
P	268	44.3	62.7	66.7	521	47.8	74.2	88.8	716	49.4	73.6	89.7
UK	55,008	36.1	50.3	62.6	56,623	31.2	48.2	59.0	55,456	29.2	45.7	57.3

	1993				1994			
	Premiums	5	10	15	Premiums	5	10	15
B	3,357	55.7	71.3	79.7	4,140	55.4	70.6	79.9
D	38,914	31.4	46.6	57.9	43,510	30.9	45.7	56.9
DK	3,116	74	90	96	3,141	70	85	90
E	5,512	37.2	55.1	65.3	8,945	46.6	61.9	71.1
GR	581	68.0	83.6	91.7	610	n.a.	n.a.	n.a.
F	50,462	47.9	68.8	80.6	60,546	47.6	67.8	80.2
I	7,928	49.4	63.9	72.6	9,327	46.1	60.2	69.2
IRL[1]	2,075	57.5	81.6	96.1	2,205	55.7	83.5	97.1
NL	11,777	55.7	73.6	84.6	n.a.			
P	841	54.4	75.6	90.6	1,106	53.0	76.7	89.2
UK	61,581	30.4	46.6	57.2	58,774	28.0	43.5	53.6

[1] 1988 figures.
Premiums in million ECU.
Sources: CEA for the years 1991-1994.
For 1989:
Sigma for the Netherlands, Spain, France, Italy, Federal Republic of Germany and the UK;
The Danish Insurance Industry 1989 for Denmark;
Private Insurance Magazine for Greece;
Argus of 24.11.89 for Ireland in 1988;
OCA Report 89-90 for Belgium;
1989 Report of the Associaçao Portuguesa de Seguradores for Portugal.

The non-life insurance market in the EU is far less concentrated than the life sector. However, the trend is generally towards higher concentration (except Greece). The five leading companies control more than 75% of the market in Finland and Sweden,[28] and between 50% to 75% in Austria, Denmark, Ireland and Portugal.

---

[28]   *European Insurance in Figures*, CEA, Paris, 1995.

Table 6.5.   Market share of the 5, 10 and 15 leading non-life insurance companies from 1989 to 1994 (percentages except for the 'premiums' column)

	1989				1991				1992			
	Premiums	5	10	15	Premiums	5	10	15	Premiums	5	10	15
B	3,803	32.0	43.7	53.4	5,274	n.a.	n.a.	n.a.	5,785	34.9	46.1	56.1
D	30,452	24.4	36.7	46.6	50,487	21.2	33.2	42.6	52,523	23.5	36.2	46.4
DK	3,014	47.2	67.9	77.5	2,650	57.0	77.0	85.0	2,843	61.0	78.0	85.0
E	7,667	19.5	31.4	40.9	11,125	17.4	28.4	37.7	11,581	18.3	29.3	38.6
GR	366	51.4	66.2	75.1	505	41.3	53.4	60.9	544	39.3	50.9	59.1
F	24,359	41.5	61.9	75.5	30,828	41.6	61.3	74.9	34,952	40.7	59.5	73.2
I	14,760	36.2	51.2	59.6	18,937	33.6	50.0	57.9	18,982	33.8	50.9	60.1
IRL[1]	731	49.1	74.1	n.a.	1,348	48.5	75.9	89.7	1,467	47.4	75.5	89.4
NL	8,251	31.8	48.1	58.2	8,815	25.0	39.1	n.a.	10,010	40.4	61.3	71.6
P	1,008	55.8	76.4	83.3	1,442	53.7	60.3	86.0	1,752	54.7	76.6	86.1
UK	39,461	51.9	69.4	76.9	34,194	35.0	53.0	63.7	36,214	36.2	54.1	63.1

	1993				1994			
	Premiums	5	10	15	Premiums	5	10	15
B	6,088	36.1	47.1	57.1	6,499	39.0	52.5	62.7
DK	2,969	58.0	76.0	84.0	3,141	60.0	78.0	86.0
D	58,467	23.1	36.0	46.2	64,749	23.5	36.7	47.3
GR	626	38.8	51.3	59.5	695	38.7	51.6	60.5
E	11,268	19.5	30.9	40.2	11,879	19.7	31.9	40.0
F	38,125	40.9	59.5	72.9	40,256	40.8	59.5	72.9
IRL[1]	1,461	50.2	79.8	94.9	1,580	50.5	79.6	94.6
I	18,382	34.1	51.8	61.2	18,436	33 8	51.9	61.1
NL	11,066	44.0	64.9	74.9	15,002	n.a.	n.a.	n.a.
P	1,833	55.1	75.5	84.9	2,102	53.7	73.3	83.3
UK	41,078	36.5	53.9	62.0	40,535	28.7	43.9	52

[1] 1988 figures.
Premiums in million ECU.
Sources: CEA for the years 1991 to 1994.
For 1989:
Sigma for the Netherlands, Spain, France, Italy, Federal Republic of Germany and
the UK;
The Danish Insurance Industry 1989 for Denmark;
Private Insurance Magazine for Greece;
Argus of 24.11.89 for Ireland in 1988;
OCA Report 89-90 for Belgium;
1989 Report of the Associaçao Portuguesa de Seguradores for Portugal.

The indicators analysed above are established in each Member State for national undertakings as a legal entity. However, some of these undertakings form part of larger groups (for example, Royale Belge, an undertaking appearing among the five largest undertakings in Belgium, is part of an even larger European group, UAP). The trend in market share of these European groups, which have been formed over the past ten years, is also a very significant indicator of the concentration movement in the insurance business in Europe.

Taking the trend in Community turnover of the following nine groups Allianz, UAP, ING, AXA, Prudential, AGF, Generali, Fortis, Commercial Union (see Table 6.6), it is found that their market share in relation to the EU market has risen from 19.83% to 22.60%. Similar to the trend towards concentration at national level, there has therefore also been market concentration at European level.

Table 6.6.   Trend in market share in the EU of the nine leading European insurance groups (life and non-life)

	1989	1994
Turnover of the nine groups within the EU[1]	54,414	95,064
Total EU insurance market[1]	274,444	420,666
Market share of the nine groups	19.83 %	22.60 %

[1] Units in million ECU.
Source: Annual reports of the group.

The number of insurance enterprises in the EU has fallen during the reference period from an all-time high of 5,517 in 1985 to 3,586 in 1995. However, as seen from the table below, the total number employed in insurance enterprises has risen from 912,000 (1990) to 961,000 (1993) during the reference period so this change cannot be interpreted as a reaction to an increasingly competitive environment within the insurance sector of the EU. Rather, this tendency seems to reflect the above-mentioned trend towards increased concentration among the leading insurers in the EU, which for a number of years have been concentrating on consolidating their dominant national positions, by taking over small companies and certain niche players.

6.4.2. The Eurostat survey

The opinion poll conducted by Eurostat gives very interesting results on this subject. In fact, the percentage of insurers interviewed who consider that the number of their competitors has increased is as follows:

(a) concerning the number of competitors *on the national market*: 48.3% consider it has increased (42.9% consider there to have been no change);

(b) concerning the number of competitors *on the European market*: 42.1% consider it has increased (53.8% consider there to have been no change);

(c) concerning the number of competitors *on the market outside Europe*: 9% consider it has increased (86.4% consider there to have been no change).

6.5. Conclusion

Concentration movements at national level were actually seen over the past five years.

Cecchini and many industry commentators[29] predicted that market structures would begin to change in particular as a result of the deregulation of insurance prices and conditions. It is true

---

[29]   See, for example, op. cit – Sigma: *Deregulation and liberalization of market access: the European insurance industry on the threshold of a new era in competition*, 1996.

Table 6.7. Changes in number of enterprises

Country	Total number of enterprises recorded in the countries (1980–95) [1]						
	1980	**1985**	**1990**	**1992**	**1993**[2]	**1994**	**1995**
A	n.a.	66	69	67	66	62	62
B	322	298	282	276	266	175	169
D	493	497	509	530	526	454	462
DK	n.a.	n.a.	n.a.	230	253	250	241
E	665	1,660	1,043	933	888	847	468[3]
GR	160	151	156	177	182	148	n.a.
F	468	521	593	627	609	494	482
FIN	276	226	192	172	160	160	159
I	n.a.	206	244	n.a.	265	224	223
IRL	59	65	81	96	107	75	n.a.
L	38	42	60	68	73	60	66
NL	n.a.	829	793	769	766	385	376
P	21	21	35	41	43	47	50
S	121	93	115	124	131	138	136
UK[4]	n.a.	842	839	823	828	764	692
EUR-15	**2,623**	**5,517**	**5,011**	**4,933**	**5,394**	**4,283**	**3,586**
IS	28	28	26	23	23	24	18
N	n.a.	212	160	143	137	116	116
EEA	**2,651**	**5,757**	**5,197**	**5,099**	**5,554**	**4,423**	**3,720**
CH	97	103	118	121	123	126	n.a.

[1] Excluding specialist reinsurance enterprises.
[2] Including branches of all foreign enterprises up to 1993 and of third countries only from 1994 onwards.
[3] Excluding the social benefit institutions.
[4] Including specialist reinsurance enterprises.
Source: Eurostat.

that, especially in markets like Germany and Italy where price regulation until 1994 had been in force, the current tendency for companies to cooperate via cartel-like agreements is being replaced by more rivalry and competition. But this is a first reaction to deregulation within particular national markets where price competition hitherto had been stifled and it cannot disguise the fact that on balance the expected surge in competitive conditions causing greater fragmentation, i.e. reduced market shares for the major insurance companies, simply has not taken place within the insurance market of the EU.

Rather, what has been experienced during the reference period is consolidation by leading players of their position on their national markets. This consolidation has gone hand-in-hand with an increase in cross-border takeovers and mergers – the number of mergers notified (i.e. only the major ones) to the European Commission going from six in 1991 to 12 in 1996.

Table 6.8.   Changes in number of employees

Country	Insurance enterprises employees		
	1990	1992	1993
B	32,254	31,581	29,444
DK	13,697 [1]	13,700	14,637
D	218,573	255,149	254,484
GR	9,500	10,000	20,000
E	42,895	44,265	44,570
F	123,400	123,800	122,000
IRL	9,258	10,049	10,085
I	42,925	49,755	49,236
L	1,100	1,180	1,208
NL [2]	50,000	51,900	53,000
A	32,783	30,932	32,104
P	12,229	13,610	12,766
FIN	10,542	9,977	9,595
S	49,600	52,000	40,100
UK	263,300	260,000	267,800
EUR-15	**912,056**	**957,898**	**961,029**
IS	423	417	422
N [3]	8,437	10,442	12,599
EEA	**920,916**	**968,757**	**974,050**
CH	48,020	49,069	48,319

[1] Excluding specialist reinsurance employees.
[2] Including employees of pension funds.
[3] The increase in employment for the period 1992/93 may be more apparent than real due to methodological problems.
Source: Eurostat.

7. Productivity of undertakings

7.1. Aims of the legislation

The microeconomic benefits of the removal of barriers to competition were seen by Cecchini to be analogous to the impact of removing non-tariff barriers on individual economic units. The benefits of the resultant supply-side shock were modelled as an increase in consumer surplus as prices reduce and product choice and quality improve (with greater innovation). In the short term, producer profits would be squeezed, but Cecchini felt that the longer term benefits would more than outweigh these short-term adjustment costs. In the longer term, businesses were predicted to make various adjustments. Cecchini envisaged these adjustments, including the exploitation of economies of scale and scope of production (i.e. restructuring economies), reductions in X-inefficiency and a generally improved capacity to innovate.

7.1.1. Hypotheses to be tested

To analyse the trend in the productivity of undertakings during the reference period, it was decided to observe this productivity through two significant ratios of this sector:

(a) the trend in average premiums per employee;
(b) the trend in the 'net profit/capital' ratio.

Hypothesis: there was an improvement in productivity if:

(a) the premiums per employee have risen faster than the rate of inflation;
(b) the 'net profit/capital' ratio has improved.

7.1.2. Indicators

(a) trend in the level of employment;
(b) premiums/employee;
(c) net profit/capital.

7.2. Facts and figures from the survey of 100 undertakings

7.2.1. Trend in average premiums per employee

For the 100 undertakings of the sample group, the 'average premiums per employee' ratio improved considerably over the period from 1989 to 1995. In fact, the median value of the ratios announced (table below) rose as follows:

(a) ECU 311,000 in 1989;
(b) ECU 417,000 in 1995 (ECU 325,000 after deflation);

i.e. a 34% rise in current ECU and 4.8% after deflation.

Table 7.1.   Trend in productivity (percentage of the number of undertakings interviewed)

Gross premiums per employee in ECU	1989	1995
Below 50,000	9.7	–
Between 50,001 and 100,000	7.5	7.5
Between 100,001 and 200,000	15	3.8
Between 200,001 and 300,000	14	7.5
Between 300,001 and 400,000	21.6	28.3
Between 400,001 and 500,000	7.5	13.2
Between 500,001 and 600,000	4.3	7.5
Between 600,001 and 1,000,000	6.4	15.1
Between 1,000,001 and 2,000,000	4.3	2.0
2,000,001 and over	9.7	15.1
Total replies (= 100 %)	93	53

This increase obviously varies considerably depending on the undertakings and the country. It is particularly large:

(a) in the following countries: France, Luxembourg, UK, Netherlands, Italy;
(b) in the small and medium-sized undertakings;
(c) in the undertakings specializing in life assurance;

as shown in Table 7.2.

Table 7.2.   Trend in average premiums per employee from 1989 to 1995 (median data observed in '000 ECU)

	1989	1995		Variation	
		Current ECU	Constant ECU	Current ECU (%)	Constant ECU (%)
Total	311	417	325.8	+ 34	+ 4.8
By country					
A: France, Luxembourg, Netherlands, UK	313	456	356.3	+ 45.7	+ 13.74
B: Germany, Belgium, Denmark, Ireland	309	381	297.6	+ 23.3	– 3.7
C: Spain, Greece, Italy, Portugal	137	NS	NS	NS	NS
By size of undertaking (annual premiums in ECU)					
Large: 500 million and over	409	554	432.8	+ 35.45	+ 5.8
Medium-sized: 10 to 500 million	255	385	300.8	+ 50.9	+ 17.9
Small: < 10 million	168	350	273.4	+ 108.3	+ 62.8
By type of business activity					
Specialist life assurance	323	570	445.3	+ 76.5	+ 37.9
General non-life insurance	311	442	346.0	+ 42.1	+ 11.2
Specialist non-life insurance	294	377	294.5	+ 28.3	+ 0.2

NS: not significant.

7.2.2. Trend in the 'net profit/capital' ratio

For the group of 100 undertakings as a whole, the net profit/capital ratio is falling: the median ratio observed fell from 12.06% in 1989 to 9.5% in 1995.

Table 7.3.   Trend in productivity: net profit/capital ratio (% of interviewees)

Result categories	1989	1995
Result equal to or below (loss) 0%	12.5	13
0 to 4.9%	12.5	19
5 to 9.9%	15	21
10 to 14.9%	16	8
15 to 24.9%	15	13
25 to 49%	7	13
50% and over	22	13
Total replies (= 100%)	87	53
Median	12.06	9.5

An analysis of the trend, undertaking by undertaking, of these ratios shows, however, that:

(a) for nearly half the undertakings, the results deteriorated during the reference period (these undertakings almost all had a high yield in 1989);
(b) for about one-third, they remained identical (these undertakings are also among those with high or low yield);
(c) for only 20%, they improved (but these were undertakings with a low yield in 1989).

Table 7.4.   Variation in the net profit/capital ratio by undertaking between 1989 and 1994[1]

Results category in 1989	Total number of undertakings in category	Trend in results in 1994			
		Deterioration	Identical	Improvement	Don't know
Result equal to or below 0%	11	-	4	5	2
0 to 4.9%	11	-	5	6	-
5% to 9.9%	13	6	5	2	-
10% to 14.9%	14	10	3	1	-
15% to 24.9%	13	7	3	3	-
25% to 49%	6	4	2	-	-
50% and over	19	13	6	-	-
Total undertakings replying	87 = 100%	40 = 46%	28 = 32%	17 = 20%	2 = 2%

[1] Comparison not possible in 1995, since not all the undertakings replied.

Results by type of undertaking

The undertakings with the greatest deterioration in their net profit/capital ratio during the reference period were the following:

(a) the very large or very small undertakings;
(b) the undertakings specializing in life or non-life;
(c) the undertakings from the following countries: UK, Belgium, Denmark, France.

Table 7.5.   Variation in the net profit/capital ratio between 1989 and 1995 (observed value: median)

	1989	1995
Total	12.06	9.5
By country		
A: France, Luxembourg, Netherlands, UK	10.3	12.1
B: Germany, Belgium, Denmark, Ireland	11.6	7.9
C: Spain, Greece, Italy, Portugal	12.6	10.8
By size of undertaking (annual premiums in ECU)		
Large: 500 million and over	10.0	8.7
Medium-sized: 10 to 500 million	15.5	9.5
Small: < 10 million	13.0	5.3
By type of business activity		
Specialist life assurance	8.09	4.7
General non-life insurance	10.1	8.7
Specialist non-life insurance	12.7	NS

NS: not significant.

7.2.3. Undertakings' explanations of trends in average premium per employee and the net profit/capital ratio

Concerning the trend in average premiums per employee, the undertakings where this ratio is rising gave the following explanations:

(a) the development of the market;
(b) the efforts made by the undertaking to cut wage costs;
(c) the enlargement of their market, especially through opening up to Europe, and the keener competition.

Concerning the trend in the net profit/capital ratio, the interviewees explain the change in this ratio, whether up or down, by symmetric reasons:

(a) first, the impact of the technical results;
(b) then, the trend in the general operating expenses ratio.

In both cases, it is the performance (or non-performance) of these two indicators which led to the final result.

7.3. Results from the case studies

A. UAP

Trend in the average premiums per employee

This ratio has risen considerably, as shown by the figures below:

	1989	1994	Variation (%)
Average premiums per employee (million FF)	2.15	2.97	+38.1
Average premiums per employee (current ECU)	306,267	445,946	+45.6
Average premiums per employee (constant ECU)	306,267.0	359,638.8	+17.42

This rise is linked to both:

(a) the group's commercial efforts (especially in life);
(b) the productivity efforts made in the organization of the undertaking and especially the efforts made either to restructure certain units or, more generally, regarding general operating expenses. On this latter point, plans were implemented everywhere and substantial progress was made in the group in Germany, Belgium and France.

Trend in the net profit/capital ratio

The ratio, on the other hand, deteriorated substantially during the reference period:

	1989	1994
Net profit/capital ratio of the UAP group (%)	20.3	4.04

UAP explains this decline as follows:

(a) substantial reduction in financial income over the same period (this fell from 31% of turnover in 1989 to 23.3% in 1994);
(b) reduction in capital gains realized (10.8% of turnover in 1989, 3.7% in 1994);
(c) losses incurred by the Worms banking subsidiary.

B. Victoria

Trend in average premiums per employee

In Germany only, this ratio rose during the reference period as follows:

	1989	1994	Variation (%)
Average premiums per employee (in DM)	817,944	1,098,089	+ 34.2
Average premiums per employee (in current ECU)	395,142	560,249	+ 41.7
Average premiums per employee (in constant ECU)	395,142	451,814	+ 14.3

Considering the Group as a whole, the change was as follows:

	1989	1994	Variation (%)
Average premiums per employee (in DM)	357,163	698,327	+ 90.2
Average premiums per employee (in current ECU)	177,373	356,289	+ 100.8
Average premiums per employee (in constant ECU)	177,373	287,330	+ 61.9

This growth is the fruit of:

(a) an improvement in productivity (staff training, improvement in management systems);
(b) the determined strategy of the Group not to disperse over too large a number of activities (products or countries) but to seek profitability of operations before growth.

Trend in the net profit/capital ratio

For the Group as a whole, this ratio (expressed in terms of pre-tax profit, including extraordinary profits or losses over average capital of the company) fell over the period from 1989 to 1994, as shown in the table below:

	1989	1994
Return on own funds (%)	32.3	11.0

The reasons for this fall in the rate of return are the following:

(a) the capital increases made from 1992 to 1994;
(b) the deterioration in the technical results, in general, in Germany, over the same period: increase in crime, resurgence of natural disasters (storms/hail).

C. Mapfre

Trend in the average premiums per employee ratio

	1990	1994	Variation (%)
Spain (only)			
Average premium per employee (million PTA)	29.07	42	+44.5
Average premium per employee (current ECU)	222,912	296,966	+33
Average premium per employee (constant ECU)	222,912	239,489	+7.4
Group total (Spain + international)			
Average premium per employee (million PTA)	18.07	32	+77
Average premium per employee (current ECU)	138,562	226,260	+63
Average premium per employee (constant ECU)	138,562	182,468	+31.7

The increase in average premiums per employee at Mapfre in Spain is firstly attributable to the company's strong commercial development. The volume of insurance premiums in fact rose over the same period (1990–94) by 105%.

This commercial success was made possible:

(a) first by the development of the Spanish insurance market (expenditure per inhabitant on non-life: +31% over the same period);
(b) by the commercial efforts made by the Group to retain and develop its market shares.

Trend in the net profit/capital ratio

The trend in the Mapfre Group's rate of return (consolidated accounts of 'Mapfre Mutualidad') was as follows:

	1989	1994
Net return on capital (%)	32.9	22.3

The (falling) result derives from several factors:

(a) the fall in the financial profit/premiums ratio (which declined from 17% in 1990 to 10.6% in 1994);
(b) the claims ratio rose by 52%;
(c) the general operating expenses rose from 28% to 30%.

D. Fortis

Trend in average premiums per employee

The ratio rose by 17% between 1989 and 1994, but fell by 5.7% in deflated value.

	1989	1994	Variation (%)
Average premiums per employee (in current ECU)	207,853	243,166	+17
Average premiums per employee (in constant ECU)	207,853	196,101	−5.7

Trend in net profit/capital ratio

The ratio remains constant, at the relatively high level of 12%.

	1989	1994
Net profit to own funds (%)	12.6	12.8

The buoyancy of the net profit/capital ratio is attributable to:

(a) the effective control of the technical results (the claims ratio rose from 67% in 1989 to 69.5% in 1994),

(b) the pressure exerted on general operating expenses (40.7% in 1989, 38.2% in 1994). On this latter point, the productivity efforts focused on:
   • progress in computerization;
   • the reclassification of functions, in certain cases the merger of companies within the same country (Netherlands).

E. Cecar

Average premiums per employee rose considerably:

	1989	1994	Variation (%)
Average premiums per employee in '000 FF	620	870	+40.3
Premiums in current ECU	88,319	130,630	+47.9
Premiums in constant ECU	88,319	105,347	+19.3

This increase is linked to:

(a) the rise in turnover, which tripled over the same period;
(b) concentrated rationalization through a complete renewal of computer equipment.

The company did not wish to give figures for its net profit/capital ratio.

7.4. Secondary sources

Eurostat[30] has looked at productivity changes from 1992 to 1995 for non-life insurance undertakings in the EU on the basis of two parameters: gross claims incurred as a percentage of gross direct premiums written and gross operating expenses as a percentage of gross direct premiums written.

7.4.1. Gross claims

Table 7.6.   Non-life insurance products: gross claims incurred in 1992 (as % of non-life gross direct premiums written)

	Motor vehicle	Accident and health	Fire and other damage to property	General liability	Other non-life products[1]	Total non-life insurance products[2]		Exchange
	%	%	%	%	%	m ECU	%	1992
A	n.a.	n.a.	n.a.	n.a.	n.a.	n.a.	n.a.	14.2169
B	70.7	54.6	53.3	49.3	56.0	2,997	61.6	41.5932
D[3]	94.9	34.4	69.0	66.0	68.4	30,848	74.9	247.026
DK	89.8	95.2	64.4	113.4	102.6	2,423	83.1	7.80925
E	79.6	70.1	61.8	89.4	55.1	8,603	71.0	132.526
GR	n.a.	n.a.	n.a.	n.a.	n.a.	n.a.	n.a.	247.026
F	85.8	84.9	81.4	95.7	77.8	24,818	84.2	6.84839
FIN	n.a.	n.a.	n.a.	n.a.	n.a.	n.a.	n.a.	5.80703
I	68.7	74.1	70.6	72.7	99.4	17,412	84.6	1,595.1
IRL	90.9[4]	41.0[5]	61.4	85.2	75.5	1,283	80.7	0.76072
L	83.3	41.1	54.7	54.3	95.9	384	81.7	41.5932
NL[6]	81.0	98.3	62.4	n.a.	64.3	6,985	83.1	2.27482
P	80.5	65.7	45.7	105.0	71.3	1,199	73.0	174.714
S	84.0	88.3	n.a.	n.a.	81.5	3,428	82.7	7.53295
UK	n.a.	n.a.	n.a.	n.a	n.a.	34,027	61.6	0.73765
EUR-15								
IS	57.5	70.6	50.3	35.4	67.9	99	57.7	74.6584
N	n.a.	n.a.	n.a.	n.a	n.a.	n.a.	n.a.	8.04177
EEA								
CH	76.4	69.3	60.2	65.7	n.a.	10,868	94.9	1.81776

[1] Such as marine, aviation and transport insurance and credit and suretyship insurance.
[2] Covering the direct business of non-life and composite insurance undertakings.
[3] In percentage of direct premiums earned.
[4] Referring to motor vehicles on land.
[5] Excluding permanent health insurance.
[6] Net amounts.
Source: Eurostat.

---

[30]   *Insurance in Europe*, 1996.

Table 7.7. **Non-life insurance products: gross claims incurred in 1994 (as % of non-life gross direct premiums written)**

	Motor vehicle	Accident and health	Fire and other damage to property	General liability	Other non-life products[1]	Total non-life insurance products[2]		Exchange
	%	%	%	%	%	m ECU	%	1994
A[3]	73.7	74.5	56.9	79.8	57.1	4,087	69.2	13.5395
B	80.8	64.5	52.8	80.9	53.6	3,617	69.7	39.6565
D	84.4	63.6	61.3	70.4	72.0	47,030	71.4	1.9237
DK	89.8	84.7	60.4	58.7	72.4	2,297	74.4	7.54328
E	78.7	71.4	61.8	89.6	51.7	8,097	69.8	158.919
GR	n.a.	n.a.	n.a.	n.a.	n.a.	n.a.	n.a.	288.026
F	94.7	78.5	67.0	85.6	85.1	33,532	83.3	6.58263
FIN	91.2	91.9	61.3	110.5	142.5	1,712	94.0	6.19077
I	88.6	67.1	62.7	92.3	55.3	14,670	79.4	1915.06
IRL	88.6[4]	46.7[5]	45.8	91.2	33.3	1,143	77.2	0.793618
L	82.1	38.7	39.3	38.0	55.1	323	58.7	39.6565
NL	82.5	83.2	56.9	n.a.	72.0	8,939	76.4	2.15827
P	67.8	75.8	44.6	56.3	60.7	1,275	66.5	196.896
S	87.1	155.6	52.7	n.a.	82.8	3,357	83.3	9.16308
UK[6]	55.7	46.1	31.4	49.5	n.a.	n.a.	n.a.	0.775902
EUR-15								
IS	66.1	56.2	49.7	49.2	49.9	98	56.7	83.3015
N	67.4	46.0	64.6	66.1	52.8	1,754	59.4	8.3742
EEA								
CH	65.4	64.8	60.9	65.7	55.7	8,593	63.0	1.62124

[1] Such as marine, aviation and transport insurance and credit and suretyship insurance.
[2] Covering the direct business of non-life and composite insurance undertakings.
[3] Gross direct premiums earned.
[4] Referring to motor vehicles on land.
[5] Excluding permanent health insurance.
[6] The premiums are for all business written in the UK, regardless of where the risk is situated, while the claims are in respect of UK risks only.
Source: Eurostat.

The claims ratios from 1992 to 1995 showed – for some countries and for some products – some volatility. Mostly due to changing loss experiences for motor vehicles insurance, the claims ratios for Germany declined by 12%. In contrast, the ratio increased for Italy by 21%.

The claims ratio for accident and health insurance in France and the Netherlands decreased by 10% and 6% respectively, but the most striking change is recorded for Sweden, with a claims ratio in this category which went from 88% in 1992 to 162% in 1995. Some of these changes are likely to be due to a revised composition of these products.

Looking at the claims ratio of the total direct non-life business throughout the EU, a general improvement can be noticed with some ratios falling under the 70% to 85% range. Sweden, with 85% of the gross direct premiums used on claims incurred, ranks highest.

Table 7.8.   **Non-life insurance products: gross claims incurred in 1995 (as % of non-life gross direct premiums written)**

	Motor vehicle	Accident and health	Fire and other damage to property	General liability	Other non-life products[1]	Total non-life insurance products[2]		Exchange
	%	%	%	%	%	m ECU	%	1995
A	72.5	70.3	54.1	81.8	64.2	4,234	67.6	13.18239
B	75.5	63.6	43.8	78.4	48.7	3,550	64.4	38.55189
D	82.0	60.4	59.0	72.0	74.7	49,484	69.1	1.87375
DK	84.1	81.6	63.9	57.2	66.7	2,517	73.4	7.328043
E	76.4	71.1	59.9	88.5	53.6	8,310	69.0	163
GR	n.a.	n.a.	n.a.	n.a.	n.a.	n.a.	n.a.	302.9886
F	75.4	74.5	63.8	128.9	67.7	23,910	74.5	6.525055
FIN	87.5	97.4	69.8	66.2	65.9	1,591	80.9	5.708546
I	89.4	67.0	60.0	96.6	60.6	14,439	80.2	2130.143
IRL	n.a.	n.a.	n.a.	n.a.	n.a.	n.a.	n.a.	0.8155245
L	84.9	38.4	37.3	49.6	79.1	401	70.6	38.55189
NL	79.5	82.0	53.8	n.a.	63.4	9,181	73.6	2.098914
P[3]	n.a.	n.a.	n.a.	n.a.	n.a.	1,446	69.0	196.1047
S	87.3	162.3	56.1	n.a.	67.8	3,398	85.1	9.331923
UK	58.9	36.7	39.6	48.3	4.6	14,122	28.6	0.8287888
EUR-15						**136,583**		
IS	71.1	64.6	76.4	55.2	50.9	104	67.6	84.68527
N	n.a.	n.a.	n.a.	n.a.	n.a.	n.a.	n.a.	8.285745
EEA								
CH	n.a.	n.a.	n.a.	n.a.	n.a.	n.a.	n.a.	1.54574

[1] Such as marine, aviation and transport insurance and credit and suretyship insurance.
[2] Covering the direct business of non-life and composite insurance undertakings.
[3] Provisional information.
Source: Eurostat.

All these observations, whether towards an improvement or an aggravation of the claims ratios, should be interpreted with care, because in some cases they could well represent a change in methodology (e.g. new regroupings of products, changed contents of the gross claims incurred, comparison of premiums and claims with a different coverage) rather than a definite change in loss experience.

7.4.2. Gross operating expenses

Table 7.9. **Non-life insurance products: gross operating expenses in 1992 (as % of non-life gross direct premiums written)**

	Motor vehicle	Accident and health	Fire and other damage to property	General liability	Other non-life products[1]	Total non-life insurance products[2]		Exchange
	%	%	%	%	%	m ECU	%	1992
A	n.a.	n.a.	n.a.	n.a.	n.a.	n.a.	n.a.	14.2169
B	39.9	37.6	48.0	50.0	40.9	2,072	42.6	41.5932
D	13.6	39.4	29.6	33.3	32.8	10,214	24.8	2.02031
DK[3]	n.a.	n.a.	n.a.	n.a.	n.a.	n.a.	n.a.	7.80925
E	29.7	24.1	36.5	37.6	43.5	3,949	32.6	132.526
GR	n.a.	n.a.	n.a.	n.a.	n.a.	n.a.	n.a.	247.026
F	30.6	22.7	35.4	32.7	32.5	8,973	30.5	6.84839
FIN	n.a.	n.a.	n.a.	n.a.	n.a.	486	24.7	5.80703
I	49.9	27.7	24.9	27.4	2.6	3,935	19.1	1,595.51
IRL	12.2[4]	15.1[5]	16.5	11.3	15.9	210	13.2	0.76072
L	17.8	19.5	19.8	29.0	8.0	67	14.2	41.5932
NL	n.a.	n.a.	n.a.	n.a.	n.a.	n.a.	n.a.	2.27482
P	32.1	38.0	39.6	35.2	35.1	581	35.3	174.714
S	30.3	26.5	n.a.	n.a.	26.0	1,135	27.4	7.53295
UK	n.a.	n.a.	n.a.	n.a.	n.a.	n.a.	n.a.	0.73765
EUR-15								
IS	n.a.	n.a.	n.a.	n.a.	n.a.	n.a.	n.a.	74.6584
N	n.a.	n.a.	n.a.	n.a.	n.a.	n.a.	n.a.	8.04177
EEA								
CH	n.a.	n.a.	n.a.	n.a.	n.a.	4,475	39.1	1.81776

[1] Such as marine, aviation and transport insurance and credit and suretyship insurance.
[2] Covering the direct business of non-life and composite insurance undertakings.
[3] In percentage of gross premiums earned.
[4] Referring to motor vehicles on land.
[5] Excluding permanent health insurance.
Source: Eurostat.

Table 7.10. **Non-life insurance products: gross operating expenses in 1993 (as % of non-life gross direct premiums written)**

	Motor vehicle	Accident and health	Fire and other damage to property	General liability	Other non-life products[1]	Total non-life insurance products[2]		Exchange	Gross direct premiums written
	%	%	%	%	%	m ECU	%	1993	m ECU
A	n.a.	n.a.	n.a.	n.a.	n.a.	n.a.	n.a.	13.6238	5.618
B	38.6	36.5	49.0	49.8	35.2	2,081	41.5	40.4713	6.463
D[3]	13.5	38.6	28.2	32.7	31.6	11,178	23.7	1.93639	60.432
DK	n.a.	n.a.	n.a.	n.a.	n.a.	n.a.	n.a.	7.59359	2.982
E	28.8	23.8	35.0	35.0	42.8	3,725	31.9	149.124	11.682
GR	n.a.	n.a.	n.a.	n.a.	n.a.	n.a.	n.a.	268.568	567
F	29.5	23.0	34.0	32.4	32.0	9,560	29.7	6.63368	33.874
FIN	n.a.	n.a.	n.a.	n.a.	n.a.	414	24.2	6.69628	1.711
I	14.8	26.4	24.6	26.8	16.5	3,461	18.9	1,841.23	18.331
IRL	13.2[4]	12.4[5]	14.3	10.2	10.6	208	12.6	0.79995	1.644
L	15.5	18.5	17.8	15.6	9.7	79	13.1	40.4713	603
NL[6]	31.4	14.1	42.4	n.a.	38.0	2,488	26.2	2.17521	9.484
P	31.3	38.7	39.6	34.2	37.1	623	34.7	188.37	1.777
S	28.8	27.6	n.a.	n.a.	16.7	909	20.0	9.12151	4.533
UK[7]	n.a.	n.a.	n.a.	n.a.	n.a.	9,001	16.5	0.77999	54.464
EUR-15									
IS	n.a.	n.a.	n.a.	n.a.	n.a.	n.a.	n.a.	79.2528	159
N[8]	n.a.	n.a.	n.a.	n.a.	n.a.	728	26.9	8.30954	2.710
EEA									
CH	n.a.	n.a.	n.a.	n.a.	n.a.	4,689	37.0	1.73019	12.678

[1] Such as marine, aviation and transport insurance and credit and suretyship insurance.
[2] Covering the direct business of non-life and composite insurance undertakings.
[3] In percentage of direct premiums earned.
[4] Referring to motor vehicles on land.
[5] Excluding permanent health insurance.
[6] Net amounts.
[7] Including Lloyds. Including management expenses and commissions minus reinsurance commission received.
[8] In percentage of direct premiums earned.
Source: Eurostat.

Table 7.11. Non-life insurance products: gross operating expenses in 1994 (as % of non-life gross direct premiums written)

	Motor vehicle	Accident and health	Fire and other damage to property	General liability	Other non-life products[1]	Total non-life insurance products[2]		Exchange
	%	%	%	%	%	m ECU	%	1994
A	26.3	19.1	35.4	36.0	34.6	1,632	27.7	13.5395
B	36.8	20.4	48.3	48.0	48.1	2,061	39.7	39.6565
D[3]	13.3	18.8	27.3	31.7	29.3	13,569	20.6	1.9237
DK	34.2	33.0	28.1	27.2	30.6	957	31.0	7.54328
E	28.4	23.3	34.7	32.5	42.4	3,647	31.4	158.919
GR	n.a.	n.a.	n.a.	n.a.	n.a.	n.a.	n.a.	288.026
F	28.4	23.4	34.1	33.0	25.0	11,216	27.9	6.58263
FIN	n.a.	n.a.	n.a.	n.a.	n.a.	457	25.1	6.19077
I	14.6	25.7	24.4	26.3	17.4	3,430	18.6	1,915.06
IRL	16.7[4]	40.0[5]	25.7	17.1	20.5	287	19.4	0.793618
L	17.7	20.8	20.6	16.3	8.1	77	13.9	39.6565
NL[6]	14.5	9.2	14.2	n.a.	18.6	1,499	12.8	2.15827
P	29.4	34.9	37.8	35.2	39.5	624	32.6	196.896
S	29.6	37.5	27.0	–	22.3	1,163	28.9	9.16308
UK[7]	18.8	19.6	27.7	18.4	n.a.	n.a.	n.a.	0.775902
EUR-15								
IS	16.1	14.8	12.7	12.6	7.7	22	13.0	83.3015
N	n.a.	n.a.	n.a.	n.a.	n.a.	663	22.5	8.3742
EEA								
CH	n.a.	n.a.	n.a.	n.a.	n.a.	5 149	37.8	1.62124

[1] Such as marine, aviation and transport insurance and credit and suretyship insurance.
[2] Covering the direct business of non-life and composite insurance undertakings.
[3] Referring to motor vehicles on land.
[4] Excluding permanent health insurance.
[5] Excluding general expenses.
[6] Gross direct premiums earned.
[7] The premiums are for all business written in the UK, regardless of where the risk is situated, while the expenses are in respect of UK risks only.
Source: Eurostat.

Table 7.12.   Non-life insurance products: gross operating expenses in 1995 (as % of non-life gross direct premiums written)

	Motor vehicle	Accident and health	Fire and other damage to property	General liability	Other non-life products[1]	Total non-life insurance products[2]		Exchange
	%	%	%	%	%	m ECU	%	1995
B	37.8	34.5	46.7	48.2	31.3	2,203	40.0	38.55189
DK	20.0	20.0	20.0	20.0	20.0	686	20.0	7.328043
D	13.7	19.0	29.2	32.8	21.9	15,243	21.3	1.87375
GR	n.a.	n.a.	n.a.	n.a.	n.a.	n.a.	n.a.	302.9886
E	28.2	23.2	34.0	30.7	41.4	3,732	31.0	163
F	38.0	24.0	33.7	34.6	20.4	10,657	33.2	6.525055
IRL	n.a.	n.a.	n.a.	n.a.	n.a.	n.a.	n.a.	0.8155245
I	14.9	25.6	24.5	25.9	19.0	14,439	80.2	2,130.143
L	21.5	26.3	28.0	17.2	9.5	98	17.2	38.55189
NL	26.9	13.8	34.6	n.a.	30.1	2,887	23.1	2.098914
A	27.1	18.7	33.0	35.5	37.6	1,719	27.4	13.18239
P	n.a.	n.a.	n.a.	n.a.	n.a.	558	26.6	196.1047
FIN	21.7	13.8	25.0	16.9	12.5	373	19.0	5.708546
S	30.1	22.1	27.5	–	20.3	1,054	26.4	9.331923
UK	18.8	19.0	26.5	14.5	4.0	6,814	13.8	0.8287888
EUR-15						60,463		
IS	18.3	16.9	13.5	14.7	11.8	24	15.6	84.68527
N	n.a.	n.a.	n.a.	n.a.	n.a.	n.a.	n.a.	8.285745
EEA								
CH	n.a.	n.a.	n.a.	n.a.	n.a.	n.a.	n.a.	1.54574

[1] Such as marine, aviation and transport insurance and credit and suretyship insurance.
[2] Covering the direct business of non-life and composite insurance undertakings.
[3] Provisional information.
Source: Eurostat.

Operating expenses in non-life insurance depend on the class of business, but on average for all classes they are clearly higher than those for life assurance. The highest average cost ratio is shown by Italy, followed by Belgium and Spain. The Netherlands is found at the lower end with 12.8%. However, here again, one should bear in mind that operating expenses will only follow harmonized definitions starting from the 1995 reference year.

7.4.3. Combined ratios

When looking at the combined ratio presented in the graph below covering the gross claims incurred and the gross operating expenses, three Member States (France, Finland and Sweden) exceed 110%. It should be noted that the investment return on assets is available to offset the above ratios, so that a loss is not necessarily made even when these ratios exceed 100%.

Figure 7.1.   Gross premiums written by branches of third country enterprises in the host country in 1994 (as % of the total gross premiums written)

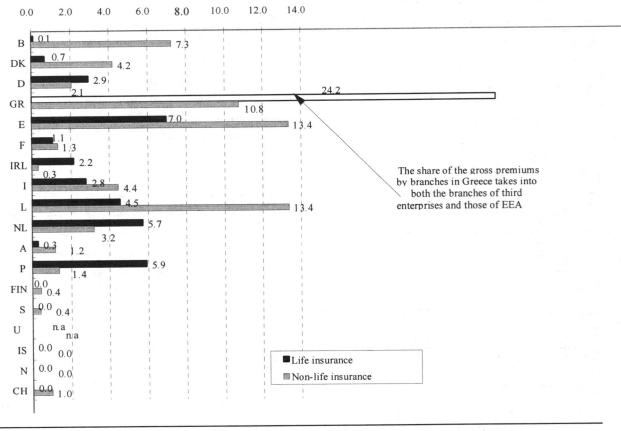

Figure 7.2. Combined ratio in 1994 (gross claims incurred and gross operating expenses as % of non-life gross direct premiums written)

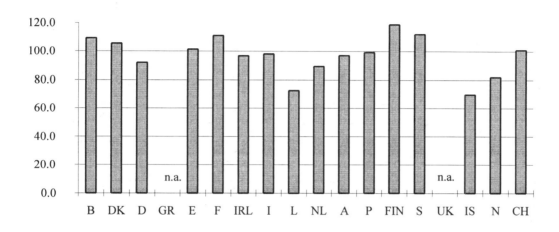

Source: Eurostat.

As far as life assurance is concerned, Table 7.13 compares the premiums to the claims and costs and to the change in life assurance provision for the total life assurance business of life and composite insurance undertakings. The change in life assurance provision derives from investment income as well as from premiums.

Depending on the various accounting practices and on the different mathematical techniques used in life assurance, the ratios of the gross claims incurred and of the change in life assurance provision show large differences between Member States. Any comparison between EEA Member States is very difficult.

7.4.4. OECD

During the reference period, the gross premiums of European companies according to the OECD increased by just over 50% in value.

Strengthened by this situation, the ratio of gross premiums written to the number of employees rose by nearly 30% over the period 1989–94 in constant ECU, and by 6.9% in deflated value.

Table 7.13.   Profit and loss account in life assurance in 1993[1]

	Gross premiums written (m ECU)	Gross claims incurred (%)	Change in gross life assurance provision (%)	Gross operating expenses (%)
B	3,445	70.77	51.06	25.42
DK	3,107	78.79[2]	128.59	9.26
D[3]	39,243	53.42	60.32	19.65
GR	630	–	–	–
E	6,881	65.76	54.26	13.59
F	50,034	52.26	72.16	9.30
IRL	2,231	82.80	–	22.18
I	9,117	30.64	58.83	15.14
L	504	22.50	94.29	10.91
NL[4]	10,644	40.00	81.13	16.42
A[3]	2,949	43.26	49.19	18.12
P[5]	766	29.76	80.95	13.01
FIN	461	113.30	27.25	18.19
S	5,596	57.60	49.64	8.64
UK	63,892	78.81	–	16.75
EUR-15	**199,502**	–	–	–
IS	6	37.26	–	36.21
N[3]	1,904	71.24	115.1	17.05
EEA	**201,412**	–	–	–
CH	14,867	68.78	52.35	12.93

[1] Including life business of composite insurance undertakings.
[2] Claims paid.
[3] Gross premiums earned.
[4] Net premiums written.
[5] Gross direct premiums written.
Source: Eurostat.

The variations by country: the situation shows a few contrasts and the countries can be classified in three groups:

(a)   the countries with little progress or a negative trend (Spain, Ireland);
(b)   the countries with less than 30% productivity increase: the following countries come in this group: Denmark, Luxembourg, UK;
(c)   more than 30%: Germany, Belgium, France.

The largest increases in productivity were therefore achieved in countries where the business is more mature and the search for greater productivity has been in progress for several years.

Figure 7.3 encapsulates the trend in productivity indicators.

Table 7.14. **Trend in productivity in the insurance sector in Europe: gross premiums written per employee (million ECU)**

Member State	Gross premiums per employee			
	1989	1994 (current ECU)	1994 (constant ECU)	Variation as % 89–94 in constant ECU
Belgium	227.5	396.2	319.8	+40%
Denmark	361.2	542.1	437.2	+21%
Germany	319.6	560.1	451.6	+41%
Greece	76.2	143.8	116	+52%
Spain	387.3	486.1	392	+1%
France	468.9	814.5	656.9	+40%
Ireland	350.3	399.1	321.9	−8%
Italy	498.4	692.8	558.7	+12%
Luxembourg	272.5	408	329	+20%
Netherlands	290.3	n.a.	n.a.	n.a.
Portugal	91.1	216	174.2	+91%
UK	301.6	442.5	356.8	+18%
Total EUR-12	338.6	541.6	436.8	+29%

Source: OECD.

Figure 7.3. **The insurance industry in the EU: comparative trends 1989–94**

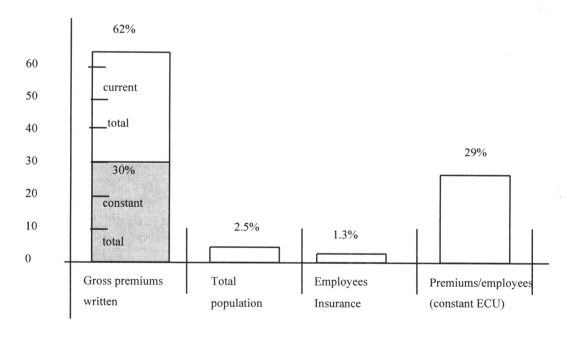

Source: OECD.

7.4.5. Comparison with the outside world: the results in the USA

Referring to the average premium per employee ratio, the productivity of the European insurance business over the past five years has improved more than that in the USA.

In fact, during the same period (1989–94) and taking comparable bases (OECD source), the average premium per employee ratio rose from US$ 358,623 to US$ 435,884 for the market as a whole, life and non-life together, which corresponds to an increase in productivity of 21.5% in current dollars and of 3% in constant dollars.

As regards productivity measured in terms of net profit on capital, there is a tendency in the USA, as in Europe, for the yield on capital invested to fall, as shown for the life sector by the 'return on equity' ratio (US GAAP, according to the source AMBest), which fell from 15% in 1989 to 9.7% in 1994. In the non-life sector, the results are tending to improve at present: 9.1% in 1989, 10.5% in 1993, after a weaker period in 1990–91.

7.5. Conclusion

In all the undertakings encountered, the average premiums per employee ratio rose considerably during the reference period. In constant ECU:

(a) this ratio rose by 4.8% in constant ECU in the undertakings of the sample group;
(b) it varied from 7.4% to 19.3% in the case study undertakings, although one undertaking experienced a decline.

Among the reasons given by the insurers of the sample group to explain the substantial change in this ratio, mention should be made:

(a) first (48% of the replies), of the efforts made by the undertakings to control their general operating expenses and to limit (or reduce) the number of their employees;
(b) then (36% of the replies), of the development of the market and the premium receipts of the company;
(c) followed (12%) by the expansion of the market, attributable in particular to the creation of the EU;
(d) and, finally (8%), of the development of competition in insurance, especially in the life sector.

The detailed interviews with the case study undertakings confirmed this information and provided further details:

(a) Concerning the average premiums per employee ratio: the undertakings all refer to the general development of the market (especially in the life sector), but also to their constant concern to boost the productivity of the workforce: maintenance or reduction of the staff, training measures, modernization of management systems. Only commercial investment is still unaffected.
(b) On the other hand, the net profit/capital ratio has deteriorated in at least half the undertakings.
(c) This is the case for 46% of the undertakings of the sample group.
(d) This is the case for three of the four case study undertakings.

The reasons given are always the same, whether this ratio has improved or deteriorated: first, the technical results; and second, the trend in general operating expenses.

The possible explanations for the less favourable trend in the net profit/capital ratio are bound up with a whole series of reasons, the main ones of which are the following:

(a) the operating results of the insurance sector in general: in recent years, costs and the frequency of claims have risen almost across the board;

(b) the fall in financial income and capital gains, linked to the fall in interest rates and the crisis on the property markets;

(c) the general climate of actual or anticipated keener competition, which causes undertakings to be prudent about raising their prices;

(d) finally, the measures taken by undertakings to improve their competitiveness (fall in general operating expenses) are, on the one hand, slow to implement and, on the other, cannot offset the difficulties mentioned above in terms of value.

The results from the primary sources lead to no firm conclusions: productivity measured as premium per employee shows an increase, whereas the second ratio of net profit on capital shows a general decrease. The primary results are remarkably consistent for both the sample group and the case studies. However, the ratio premium per employee is somewhat unreliable because Member States define employees in different ways. Since the number of employees in general has not gone down, their productivity seemingly has indeed increased. Net profit on capital as a ratio is obviously dependent on the general economic environment so a fall in the general level of interest rates during the reference period might explain a part of the fall in the ratio.

Secondary sources are equally short on information in that gross operating expenses show this ratio going down in Belgium, Denmark, Germany, Finland and Sweden, but up in Italy, Spain, Luxembourg, the Netherlands and France.

Results of gross claims incurred as a ratio of premiums should be interpreted with caution over such a short period, but it is significant that all Member States except Belgium and Sweden actually show decreasing ratios, indicating increased productivity over this reference period.

In conclusion, three out of four parameters show a degree of increased productivity throughout the reference period. However, before this trend can be validated it needs to be confirmed by more data from the period after 1 July 1994.

8. The international competitiveness of insurance undertakings

8.1. Aims of the legislation

Among the anticipated effects of creating the single market, the Cecchini Report mentioned increased competitiveness through economies of scale. The effects of this improvement in competitiveness should include enabling European undertakings to be more competitive on the non-EU markets.

8.1.1. Hypotheses to be tested

If the single market has really had such an impact on the international competitiveness of European insurance undertakings, it should be possible to observe a twofold effect:

(a) over the reference period, there were moves towards expansion towards non-EU countries by European insurers;
(b) over the reference period, there was a limitation of the activity of foreign insurers within the single market, particularly on account of the improved competitiveness of the European insurers on their own market.

8.1.2. Indicators used to test these hypotheses

The indicators proposed to test the hypothesis of this international expansion are the following:

(a) increase in the proportion of turnover of the European insurers from outside the EU;
(b) increase in the number of European insurers operating outside the EU (through subsidiaries or branches);
(c) increase in the number of non-EU countries where European insurers operate.

The indicators proposed to test a possible limitation on the operations of foreign insurers in the single market are the following:

(a) trend in market share held by foreign insurers;
(b) (subjective) assessment by the insurers of the trend over the reference period in the pressure of foreign competition.

8.2. Facts and figures from the survey of 100 undertakings

In 1989, 16 undertakings from the sample group (out of 100) engaged in insurance business outside the EU. In 1995, this figure had risen to 18 undertakings.

8.2.1. Aggregate results

During the reference period, the number of undertakings with subsidiaries outside the EU stayed the same, in both the life and the non-life sectors.

On the other hand, the number of subsidiaries in non-life increased, as shown in Table 8.1.

Table 8.1.   The international development of the undertakings of the sample group through non-European subsidiaries between 1989 and 1994

	Life business		Non-life business	
	1989	1994[1]	1989	1994[1]
Number of undertakings of the sample group with one or more subsidiaries in non-European countries	7	7	5	5
Total number of non-European subsidiaries of these undertakings	35	35	83	98
Mean number of subsidiaries per undertaking	5	5	16.6	19.6
Number of undertakings concerned = operating internationally outside the EU	16	19	16	19

[1] These figures could not be updated in 1995 since replies were not received from all the undertakings interviewed.

The total turnover of the life subsidiaries rose by 88%. The total turnover of the non-life subsidiaries rose by 32%.

8.2.2. Results by type of undertaking

During the reference period, the undertakings showing the greatest international dynamism outside Europe were:

(a)   the large undertakings;
(b)   the general non-life undertakings;
(c)   undertakings of the following countries: the UK, France, Germany.

The number of European undertakings having set up international branches outside Europe varied very little over the reference period.

On the other hand, these undertakings increased the number of their branches significantly, especially in the life sector.

Table 8.2.   The international development of the undertakings of the sample group through non-European branches between 1989 and 1994

	Life business		Non-life business	
	1989	1994[1]	1989	1994[1]
Number of undertakings of the sample group with one or more branches in non-European countries	3	3	5	7
Total number of non-European branches of these undertakings	9	15	26	35
Mean number of branches per undertaking	3	5	5.2	5
Number of undertakings concerned = operating internationally outside the EU	16	19	16	19

[1] These figures could not be updated in 1995 since replies were not received from all the undertakings interviewed.

Table 8.3.   **The business of the 100 undertakings of the sample group outside Europe: mean number of countries where the main insurance products were sold in 1995**

Products	1989		1995	
	Number of undertakings	Mean number of countries	Number of undertakings	Mean number of countries
Health/accident	6	4.0	7	2.9
Motor vehicle	7	3.7	8	2.9
Fire and other damage to property	6	4.5	7	3.0
Marine, aviation, transport	4	5.0	4	1.8
Liability	5	4.6	6	2.8
Credit insurance	2	1.5	2	1.0
Legal expenses and/or aid	2	5.5	2	5.5
Business interruption	2	8.5	4	2.8
Life (assurance in the case of survival, in the case of death, endowment)	8	2.3	7	2.7
Annuity	5	1.8	3	3.3
Contingency, death, disablement	2	4.0	2	4.0
Long-term sickness insurance	2	4.0	2	4.0
General mean	**4.3**	**4.1**	**4.5**	**3.1**

Certain products were slightly more widely distributed in 1989 than others. These were:

(a) insurance against business interruption;
(b) marine, aviation and transport insurance;
(c) fire and other damage to property.

Other products were little distributed:

(a) credit insurance;
(b) annuity insurance.

In general, product by product, there was no increase in the geographical area covered outside the EU between 1989 and 1995, but rather a cut-back, except for the contingency, sickness and legal expenses insurance.

8.3. Case studies

A. UAP

International development through subsidiaries and branches outside Europe

The number of subsidiaries and branches in the life sector remained stable in the reference period.

	Life business		Non-life business	
	1989	1994	1989	1994
Subsidiaries	12	12	19	17
Branches	10	10	25	17

In non-life, on the other hand, the figures tended to fall, particularly through the closure of small branches.

The turnover outside the EU of these subsidiaries and branches

During the reference period, turnover rose in both life and non-life. The trend in turnover (subsidiaries and branches) was as follows.

	Life business		Non-life business	
	1989	1994	1989	1994
Million FF	0.5	1.4	1.7	3.7
Million ECU	0.07	0.21	2.4	5.55

Number of countries where the products are sold

In total (excluding the EU), UAP was present in 38 countries in 1989 and 32 in 1994:

Country	1989	1994
Africa	14	12
French Overseas Departments and Territories	6	6
Middle East	6	3
South America	4	4
Australia / Pacific	2	2
Asia	6	5

Motor vehicle and fire insurance are sold everywhere, liability insurance and life assurance a little less frequently, and credit and legal expenses insurance rarely.

B. Victoria

As mentioned above, the Group's policy is to invest in only a few countries, but to develop them in depth.

Establishments outside the EU

Outside the EU, the Group has developed essentially in Austria, the Czech Republic and Switzerland, solely through subsidiaries.

In 1989, the Group had two subsidiaries outside the EU (both in Austria).

In 1994, the Group had five subsidiaries outside the EU, of which two in Austria, two in the Czech Republic and one in Switzerland.

The Group's turnover in Austria more than doubled over the same period, rising from ECU 76 million in 1989 to ECU 146 million in 1994.

Presence in other countries in the world

Through its two partnerships, the Group has access:

(a)   for life assurance and through the partnership with IGP (International Group Program), to 50 different countries;

(b)   for non-life insurance and through the partnership with INI (International Network of Insurance), to 60 different countries.

C. Mapfre

The Mapfre Group has the particularity of having a relatively low level of presence in the EU (Portugal and Italy only), compared to its establishment in the rest of the world. But on account of the Group's recent efforts in Portugal, development has been particularly rapid in the EU over the past five years.

Distribution and trend in the turnover of the Mapfre Group from 1989 to 1994 was as below (direct insurance in million ECU).

	1989	1994	Variation (%)
Spain	972	1,839	+ 89
EU	12	70	+ 483
Rest of the world	211	964	+ 228
Total	**1,195**	**2,603**	**+ 117**

Establishment in the world (outside the EU)

Mapfre developed its establishments outside the EU considerably between 1989 and 1994 especially through subsidiaries (life three to seven, non-life seven to 11).

	Life business		Non-life business	
	1989	1994	1989	1994
Number of subsidiaries	3	7	7	11
Turnover (million ECU)	8.88	102.26	83.44	612.62

The number of branches of the Mapfre Group outside the EU rose from 125 to 551.

Countries covered

All the products are sold outside the EU in seven or eight countries, with the exception of credit insurance, which is sold in only four countries.

Products	Number of countries where these products were sold in 1994
Health/accident	7
Motor vehicle	8
Fire and other damage to property	7
Marine, aviation, transport	7
Liability	7
Credit insurance	4
Legal expenses and/or aid	7
Business interruption	7
Life (assurance on survival, in the event of death, endowment)	8
Annuity	8
Contingency, death, disablement	8
Long-term sickness insurance	8

D. Fortis

Establishment: branches and subsidiaries outside the EU

The number of subsidiaries remained stable:

Country	1989	1994
USA	7	7
Australia	4	4
Hong Kong	1	0
Singapore	1	1

The turnover of these subsidiaries rose by 93% over five years.

The group has no branches outside the EU.

The number of countries outside the EU covered

The number of countries outside the EU where the Group sold the various insurance products remained virtually unchanged between 1989 and 1994. It roughly corresponds to the countries referred to above, as shown in the table below.

The international development of Fortis and the number of countries where the Fortis sold products are listed below.

Products	1989	1994
Health/accident	-	-
Motor vehicle	4	3
Fire and other damage to property	3	2
Marine, aviation, transport	3	2
Liability	2	2
Credit insurance	3	3
Legal expenses and/or aid	2	2
Business interruption	2	2
Life (assurance on survival, in the event of death, endowment)	-	-
Annuity	-	-
Contingency, death, disablement	-	-
Long-term sickness insurance	-	-

E. Cecar

Cecar's establishments outside the EU are recent.

In 1989, the Group only had one subsidiary outside the EU, in Brazil.

In 1994, the Group developed by setting up four other subsidiaries.

(a)   Austria (with extensions in the Czech Republic and Hungary);
(b)   Turkey;
(c)   Argentina;
(d)   Hong Kong.

Cover of the rest of the world is achieved through agreements with correspondents.

Analysis of the case studies presented above shows highly contrasted situations. Two undertakings developed their international activities significantly (Mapfre and Victoria), but in accordance with a policy of 'proximity' specific to them: Eastern Europe for Victoria, Latin America for Mapfre. Over the same period, the other two groups essentially channelled their resources into Community development (UAP and Fortis).

8.4. Secondary sources

8.4.1. Trend in turnover of ten large European groups

To refine the information, we finally analysed the figures for the EU and non-EU turnover of the ten leading European groups, which enables us, through another approach, to assess the comparative trend in business conducted by these groups within and outside the EU.

This analysis (see Table 8.6) yields the following results:

(a)   The consolidated world turnover of these 10 undertakings increased substantially over the 5 years, by 84% in absolute terms and by 49% in real terms (constant ECU).
(b)   However, this increase was chiefly achieved in the other EU countries (in relation to the home country) since the increase in total EU turnover in real terms was nearly double that of the home country (41.1% compared to 23.1%).
(c)   Lastly, turnover outside the EU grew even faster (73.4% in real terms).

8.4.2. Insurance flows between the EU and the rest of the world

It is very difficult to measure the insurance flows between the EU and the rest of the world, since the official statistics for each country usually group all these movements together under the heading 'foreign', without drawing a distinction between other Member States and non-European countries.

It was nevertheless possible to gather these data for four countries (see Tables 8.4 and 8.5). Analysis of the movements between 1989 and 1994 would tend to indicate the following facts:

(a) the penetration of foreign insurers into the markets of the four countries did not increase between 1989 and 1994, but remained stable (Table 8.4);

(b) exports outside the EU of three out of four of these countries represent an increased proportion of their business (Table 8.5).

Table 8.4. Penetration of the European market by foreign insurers: gross premiums written by non-EU insurers on the markets of four European countries (million ECU)

Country	1989			1994		
	Total market[1]	of which		Total market	of which	
		Written by national or EU insurers (%)	Written by non-EU insurers (%)		Written by national or EU insurers (%)	Written by non-EU insurers (%)
France[2]	45,910	96.28	3.72	85,919	97.00	3.00
Spain	15,006	95.06	4.94	20,634	94.93	5.07
Italy[3]	21,503	97.50	2.50	23,944	98.09	1.91
Germany	57,276	94.19	5.81	113,067	95.31	4.69

[1] Premiums issued on their market by national insurers, plus premiums issued by insurers of other countries (EU + non-EU).
[2] 1989 replaced by 1990.
[3] 1994 replaced by 1993.
Sources: Germany, Spain, Italy: Supervisory authorities; France: FFSA.

Table 8.5. Trend in exports by European insurers: gross premiums written by the insurers of four European countries on (a) the domestic market, (b) the markets of other EU countries, (c) the non-EU markets (million ECU)

Country	1989				1994			
	Total gross premiums written by national insurers	of which premiums written on:			Total gross premiums written by national insurers	of which premiums written on:		
		Domestic market (%)	EU market (%)	Non-EU market (%)		Domestic market (%)	EU market (%)	Non-EU market (%)
France	52,137	76.64	20.86	2.50	02,782	70.59	20.26	9.15
Spain	14,053	98.93	1.02	0.04	19,305	99.48	0.47	0.06
Italy[1]	21,323	96.75	2.91	0.35	23,686	98.47	0.78	0.75
UK[1]	104,176	72.27	6.76	20.97	106,744	74.47	7.53	18.00

[1] 1994 replaced by 1993.
Note: Figures expressed as net premiums.
Sources: Spain, Italy: Supervisory authorities; France: FFSA; UK: Association of British Insurers.

Table 8.6. Turnover of the ten leading European insurance undertakings in 1994 (million ECU)

Undertaking	Domestic turnover			Turnover in Europe (12)			Turnover outside Europe			Consolidated world turnover		
	1989	1994	variation (%)	1989	1994	variation (%)	1989	1994	variation (%)	1989	1994	variation (%)
AGF	3,787	5,678	49.95	4,649	7,810	67.97	795	2,619	229.32	5,445	10,429	91.54
		4,579	*20.91*		*6,298*	*35.48*		*2,112*	*165.67*		*8,410*	*54.46*
AXA	4,282	6,023	40.64	5,585	8,881	59.01	779	7,032	802.33	6,365	15,913	150.03
		4,857	*13.43*		*7,162*	*28.24*		*5,671*	*627.98*		*12,833*	*101.62*
UAP	6,339	8,093	27.67	8,649	19,610	126.73	431	766	77.47	9,080	20,375	124.39
		6,527	*2.96*		*15,815*	*82.85*		*618*	*43.33*		*16,431*	*80.96*
ING (1990 instead of 1989)	5,194	6,790	30.72	6,308	7,770	23.18	3,970	5,645	42.20	10,278	13,415	30.53
		5,740	*10.51*		*6,568*	*4.12*		*4,772*	*20.20*		*11,340*	*10.33*
Generali	3,007	4,991	65.99	6,253	12,761	104.07	1,674	4,129	146.62	7,927	16,890	113.06
		4,025	*33.85*		*10,291*	*64.58*		*3,330*	*98.92*		*13,621*	*71.83*
Commercial Union (1993 instead of 1994)	1,914	2,898	51.39	3,520	4,848	37.71	1,741	2,522	44.89	5,261	7,370	40.09
		2,337	*22.11*		*3,910*	*11.07*		*2,034*	*16.82*		*5,944*	*12.97*
Allianz	9,234	18,947	105.19	13,066	25,307	93.68	2,312	8,412	263.83	15,378	33,718	119.26
		15,280	*65.47*		*20,409*	*56.20*		*6,784*	*193.42*		*27,192*	*76.82*
Prudential	3,865	4,960	28.33	4,202	4,960	18.04	3,564	4,080	14.48	7,766	9,040	16.40
		4,000	*3.49*		*4,000*	*-4.81*		*3,290*	*-7.68*		*7,290*	*-6.13*
Fortis	1,512	1,093	-27.70	2,181	3,118	42.94	1,864	1,443	-22.59	4,045	4,561	12.75
		881	*-41.70*		*2,515*	*15.29*		*1,164*	*-37.57*		*3,678*	*-9.07*
Gan	3,322	5,330	60.46	3,793	6,991	84.31	117	441	277.30	3,910	7,432	90.07
		4,298	*29.39*		*5,638*	*48.64*		*356*	*203.97*		*5,994*	*53.29*
Grand total	42,456	64,803	52.64	58,207	102,055	75.33	17,248	37,090	115.04	75,455	139,143	84.41
		52,260	*23.09*		*82,302*	*41.40*		*29,911*	*73.42*		*112,212*	*48.71*

Note: Figures in italic: constant ECU. The figure in italic is the deflated value (in million ECU) of the preceding line.
Sources: Company annual reports.

8.5. Conclusion

Overall, the international development (outside the EU) of European undertakings progressed little during the period 1989 to 1994.

The effort towards establishment (through subsidiaries or branches) is almost always undertaken by undertakings already established outside the EU before 1989.

The geographical area for the international dissemination of products (measured in terms of the number of countries where they are sold) is tending to decline.

However, a small number of undertakings, among the most dynamic, did conduct a real international strategy during this same period. They developed their establishment (subsidiaries or branches) and saw a considerable increase in their international turnover. All the case study undertakings saw a substantial increase in their international turnover during the reference period, each, however, targeting their strategy differently.

Finally, the analysis of the ten leading European groups shows more rapid growth in their international turnover (+ 73.4%) than in Europe (+ 41.4%) or on their domestic markets (+ 23%).

Overall, the secondary sources for the trend in the EU's insurance flows (unfortunately incomplete) would tend to show that the EU is defending its single market effectively against insurers from the other major regions of the world and that export capacity varies depending on the EU countries.

The reasons given by the undertakings for their international development are essentially strategic: the interest of possible target markets (growth rate, market size, openness and administrative facility to conduct business there, etc.), the appropriateness of possible acquisitions, etc. Conversely, the reasons given by undertakings which did not undertake any international development essentially concern lack of resources: human or financial.

In fact, to date there have been few economies of scale achieved by European undertakings as a result of the introduction of the single market of a nature to improve their international competitiveness.

Internationalization demands substantial resources. To be able to invest internationally, it is found that, in this respect, the case study undertakings had:

(a) either a highly selective establishment policy (see Victoria, Mapfre, Fortis);
(b) or a resources rationalization policy (restructuring of establishments, search for business through partnership agreements, which is less costly in terms of investment).

9. Price changes

9.1. Aims of the legislation

One of the expected effects of forming the single market was greater convergence in the prices applied by insurers in the various Member States and a general reduction in these prices, on account of the greater internal competition.

The main provisions of the Framework Directives, i.e. the abolition of prior control of policy conditions and premium rates and the introduction of the single licence, were expected to lead to greater competition within the Member States and greater cross-border competition from foreign suppliers. It follows that increased competition and its pressure on prices was expected to have its greatest effect on strongly regulated markets with a large number of small uncompetitive enterprises of low capitalization. Price reductions on 'good' risks were, at least in part, expected to be compensated by price increases for aggravated risks, but overall the Cecchini Report anticipated increased price competition to lead to smaller margins and an increase in the volatility of technical results.

The Cecchini Report (1988) on the 'Cost of non-Europe in financial services' also brought out both the difficulty in comparing the various insurance prices throughout the Member States and the considerable divergences in prices existing throughout Europe for similar services. For each of the five insurance products analysed (see list below), Cecchini showed substantial divergences in costs between the least expensive and the most expensive countries. These divergences are encapsulated in the multipliers below.

Table 9.1.   Divergences in prices for one and the same insurance product in Europe

	Multiplier (between the cheapest and the most expensive products)	Cheapest country	Most expensive country
Life assurance	2.51 (5-year contracts)	UK	Belgium, Italy
	2.41 (10-year contracts)	UK	Belgium, Italy
Homeowner's comprehensive policy	2.25	Belgium	UK, Italy
Motor vehicle insurance	2.98	UK	Italy, Luxembourg
Fire and theft insurance for business premises	4.06	Luxembourg	Italy, France
Business liability insurance	2.59	Netherlands	France, Italy

Source: Cecchini Report: 'Cost of non-Europe in financial services'.

9.1.1. Hypotheses to be tested

To be able to establish whether the single market started to have the impact described above, it would be necessary to find greater convergence in the prices of insurance throughout the EU.

9.1.2. Indicators

Declaration by insurers of their strategy:

(a) convergence of prices in the sample group;
(b) convergence of products;

(c) the secondary indicators in the field of convergence of prices.

The object of this chapter is therefore to deal with the impact of the single market on the trend in insurance prices in the EU and, more specifically, by analysing each of the following topics.

9.2.   Facts and figures from the survey of 100 undertakings

9.2.1.   Development of strategies to place identical products in several EU Member States

Of the 39 undertakings in the sample group engaging in insurance business in the EU in 1995, 13 undertakings were already selling one (or more) identical products in several countries in 1989, with this number rising to 18 undertakings in 1995, i.e. 46%.

In general, it is the undertakings specializing in life assurance which are the champions of the 'European product'.

These are quite often small or medium-sized undertakings, first situated in Luxembourg (100% of the sample concerned), the UK (60%), France (50%) or Germany (50%).

The undertakings having recently (i.e. during the reference period between 1989 and 1995) decided to create 'European products' were asked to explain the reasons for this strategy.

A detailed analysis of these cases is given in Table 9.2. It indicates a few possible explanations, which are as follows.

For four out of five of these undertakings, it was the opening of the frontiers, and more especially the facilities offered under the freedom to provide services, which led them to embark on 'international' business and to do so on the basis of European products. Looking at these cases in greater detail, it is found that:

(a) these undertakings have no sales organization outside their country;
(b) they are still at the start of their operations in Europe and their turnover there is very low;
(c) these five undertakings stated that they wish to work under the freedom to provide services.

Table 9.2.   Five cases of undertakings which, in the past five years, decided to sell the same product in several EU Member States

Case number	Insurer's home country	Undertaking's business activity	Size of undertaking	Organization in the EU	Why they have decided to sell an identical product in the EU
1	UK	Specialist in life	Large	No subsidiaries or branches No partnership	Decision to start operating internationally in 1990 (4% of total turnover in 1994 came from the EU)
2	Germany	Composite life and non-life	Medium-sized	Existence of an organization in the EU: three subsidiaries and two branches Existence of partnership in fronting	The opening of the frontiers (26% of total turnover in 1994 came from the EU and 28% from the rest of the world)
3	Netherlands	Specialist in indemnity	Medium-sized	No structure in the EU	Start-up of business in 1992 (1% of total turnover comes from the EU)
4	Italy	Indemnity	Medium-sized	No structure in the EU or partnership	The opening offered by the freedom to provide services in 1992 (1% of total turnover in 1992 came from the EU, 10% from the rest of the world)
5	Luxembourg	Specialist in life	Small	No structure in the EU but partnership agreements	The opportunity offered by the freedom to provide services (99% of turnover comes from Germany, 1% from the rest of the world)

9.2.2.   Standardization of prices and policy conditions

Despite a slight trend towards the development of European products, the harmonization of their prices and conditions is not one of the insurers' particular concerns.

In fact the question *Do you concern yourself with standardizing the prices and policy conditions of similar products sold to several European countries?*, provoked the following replies:

(a)   as regards prices, only four undertakings out of 36 were concerned in 1989, with the number rising to five in 1995 (adding together the replies 'often' and 'sometimes'),

(b)   as regards policy conditions, the results are equally low, since in 1989 and in 1995 only five undertakings concerned themselves with these.

Table 9.3.   **The standardization of prices and policy conditions where similar products are sold in Europe (number of undertakings concerning themselves with the harmonization of prices or policy condition where similar products are sold in Europe)**

	Harmonization of prices		Harmonization of policy conditions	
	1989	1995	1989	1995
Yes, often/always	3	4	3	4
Yes, sometimes	1	1	2	1
Yes, occasionally	1	1	1	1
No, never	3	8	3	8
Don't know	5	4	5	4
Undertakings selling one and the same product in Europe	13	18	13	18
Total number of undertakings in sample	100	100	100	100

Harmonization/non-harmonization of prices: the reasons for the strategies

The undertakings which opted for 'often' or 'sometimes' having a price harmonization policy (four undertakings in 1989, five in 1995) did so for the following reasons:

(a) they consider that there is no difference between risks from one country to another;
(b) their international customers required the same contract for everyone;
(c) the will to 'wipe out' the differences associated with the exchange rate;
(d) to avoid the complexity of management associated with different scales.

The undertakings 'never' or 'occasionally' seeking to harmonize their prices explain this as follows, in order of importance:

(a) the need to adapt to local market conditions (competition, service, different regulations);
(b) the freedom left to subsidiaries to draw up their own price strategy;
(c) the level of business which is (still) too low to justify such practices;
(d) the difference in the products sold;
(e) other reasons of different kinds are given, such as the difference in mortality tables between different countries (for life products).

Harmonization/non-harmonization of policy conditions: the reasons for the strategies

The undertakings generally follow the same strategies and the same logic with respect to harmonizing prices or policy conditions. Hence, the following reasons are to be found:

(a) in favour of standardizing policy conditions:
   • the similarity of risks (indemnity or goods);
   • the undertaking's wish for simplification;
(b) against the standardization of policy conditions:
   • the need to adapt to specific local characteristics (competition, regulations);
   • the independence of the local subsidiaries;
   • the scale of operations being too small.

9.3. Case studies

A. UAP

Product standardization

UAP offers an interesting example of a product created to be sold in various countries of the EU. This is the life product of Paneurolife, a company set up in Luxembourg for the sole purpose of offering the European market a life product 'which would be a combination of the best European products'.

Launched in 1991, this product underwent rapid development to achieve a turnover in 1994 of LFR 9.9 billion. It is currently sold mainly in Belgium, France and Germany.

UAP developed an identical product for these various countries for the following reasons:

(a) it found that on its target market (up-market life), there was a European clientele with the same needs and the same requirements;
(b) the desire to construct an efficient product taking advantage of the experience of various European markets;
(c) the desire to develop in the target customer segment with reasonable profitability, which resulted in choosing not only a simplification of the supply, but also a place (Luxembourg), which, from the practical point of view, increased its feasibility (trilingual staff, favourable geographical location, etc.).

The standardization of prices and policy conditions: in this field, UAP respects the autonomy of its subsidiaries and branches.

B. Victoria

Victoria's foreign subsidiaries offer similar products in all the countries. On account of market differences, it is impossible to sell identical products at the same price in all the countries. Nevertheless, Victoria's subsidiaries exchange information on their experiences of the different products.

C. Mapfre

Even though Mapfre sells the same products in Spain and Portugal, this company does not apply either the same prices or the same policy conditions, considering that market conditions do not permit this.

D. Fortis

The Group's only European product is a life product developed in Luxembourg.

The Group endeavours to find joint ideas, shares experience and information. However, the products remain different because the markets are different. Consequently, even for a product as 'commonplace' as personal motor vehicle insurance and countries as close as Belgium and the Netherlands, where methods of payment and taxes differ from one country to the other, Fortis has not yet been able to harmonize products, prices or policy conditions.

9.4. Secondary sources

During the reference period, various studies were conducted to try to measure the differences in premium rates for insurance products from one country to another; these include:

(a) Produktspiegel 1994 – Internationale Produktkonzeptionen der Assekuranz aus 16 Ländern im Vergleich (classes of motor vehicle insurance, fully comprehensive, third-party and legal expenses insurance);
(b) EuroLeben 1995 – Lebensversicherungsprodukte im internationalen Vergleich (both published by SCG St Gallen Consulting Group); and
(c) House Insurance in Europe – Consumers suffer through failure of the single market (Beuc/Test Achats, April 1996).

The first two studies compare product design, the third the prices and quality of the product. By way of example, the last-mentioned study highlights the differences in quality and price of house insurance (fire, storm, water damage, etc.) policies of 60 companies in 12 Member States.

According to the study, the quality and price of house insurance policies vary substantially from one country to another across Europe. The quality of policies was judged using 30 criteria, including scope of cover, exclusions, how the insured value was established, the reimbursement to be paid and the reconstruction obligation, etc. France, Spain and the UK ranked highly on quality, whereas Greece and Italy were shown to be mediocre. Differences relating to three of the most important criteria are set out below.

The premium which European consumers have to pay to cover the risk of destruction (total or partial) of their house can be up to as much as five times more expensive in one country than in another. Of course, it should be borne in mind that the extent of cover differs from country to country, from company to company. Several factors may influence the amount of premiums: not only the extent of the cover and the value insured, but equally, for example, the type of building materials used, the geographical location, the age of the building, the existence of an anti-burglary system, a fire or leakage detection system, etc. The 12 countries are classified according to premium levels, for three types of risk areas (low, medium, high). These are the average premiums asked from house owners to cover the building and its contents (including burglary).

The study concludes that it is clear that Europe's consumers are not on a level playing-field in relation to insurance. However, they are not free to shop around and buy insurance under more favourable conditions in other Member States. European legislation specifies that the law applicable to insurance contracts is the law of the country of residence of the consumer. This means, for example, that a French insurance company wishing to offer its policies to an Italian consumer would have to adapt its general conditions in order to comply with Italian laws. In practical terms, this means that an Italian consumer would not be able to benefit from the same advantages as a French consumer who purchased an insurance policy from the same French firm.

BEUC and Test Achats call on the EU to introduce legislation to improve consumers' rights and level of protection in relation to insurance contracts, not only for house insurance, but also for other types of insurance. BEUC and Test Achats want to see common minimum requirements established at European level for insurance contracts. This does not mean total harmonization or the suppression of all differences between countries. Instead, EU legislation should have as one of its main objectives the limitation of the ability of the insurance companies to refuse to honour a contract (for example, based on an incorrect statement of the risk or an exclusion clause in the contract) and thus allow consumers to benefit from fair payment in the event of a claim.

BEUC and Test Achats also call on the EU to introduce legislation which would set common rules on information to be provided to the consumer about the insurance policy he or she is buying, establish efficient, rapid and independent redress mechanisms for handling consumers' complaints, and define clearly compulsory insurance.

These studies, although carried out on very different bases, tend towards the same conclusion: although there is strong evidence, especially in the life sector, that deregulation means greater competition and innovation, not only does the divergence in premium prices not seem to have narrowed, the most expensive (and the least expensive) countries often stay the same.

The current difficulty in comparing the prices of various insurance products has to be admitted. In fact, even if it is sought to compare the prices of two 'comparable' products in two countries (i.e. covering similar risks), the cost of this risk for the insurer will be different and so, too, will the price paid by the policyholder. The main sources of divergence in cost between countries are in fact associated with the following variables:

(a) the policyholder's personal characteristics (age, profession, length of time of holding the driving licence in the case of motor vehicle insurance, etc.);
(b) the physical characteristics of the market: state of the roads or proportion of motorways for the motor vehicle risk, frequency of natural disasters in certain regions for the insurance of property, the weather, etc.;
(c) the legal characteristics: system of compensation granted by the local courts in the case of physical injury, regulations in the field of liability;
(d) the economic characteristics, including the level of local competition, taxation, etc.

Another reason why establishing premium rate trends over a reference period is extremely uncertain is that despite increasing internationalization of insurance and capital markets, the insurance cycle in the key countries still fails to run in parallel.[31]

---

[31]   Sigma Studies 5/95 and 3/96.

9.5. Conclusion

Few undertakings are yet concerned today with harmonizing their prices and policy conditions for similar products from one Member State to another (this fact is incidentally confirmed by the studies conducted by BEUC, which show substantial divergences in premium prices for the standard products analysed, which may reach divergences of 1 to 3 for life products and 1 to 10 for motor vehicle products).

The results of the sample group show that no progress is being made in these efforts towards harmonization, even among the undertakings with a European products policy. The reasons behind this hesitation are discussed in Chapter 3 concerning access to other EU markets, and can be summarized as follows: regulatory obstacles based on Member States' different interpretations of the concepts of the 'general good'; the demarcation between freedom to provide services and freedom of establishment; the absence of a harmonized or partially harmonized EU contract law; the absence of harmonized legislation on insurance intermediation, and divergent systems and rates of taxation.

Nevertheless, since 1989, there has been a slight increase in undertakings introducing 'European' products (i.e. identical insurance products for several European countries).

Today, half the undertakings of the sample group operating in Europe have developed one or more European products.

This trend is developing particularly in the life sector (for example, the Luxembourg products), or the contingency insurance programmes, but is also starting to emerge in the indemnity products.

The reasons directly linked to the SMP include:

(a) *the opening up of the European market*, and more specifically the freedom to provide services. It is in fact to be able to benefit from a market which is now open and more specifically relying on the freedom to provide services that four of the five undertakings which recently had the idea of a European product introduced such products. One of the particularly convincing examples is the creation and development of Paneurolife's products (UAP group), which pushed the reasoning to the limit by creating a special operating structure for these products;

(b) The concern for standardization, mentioned by one undertaking already long established on the European market, which corresponds to a will on the part of the undertaking to *simplify and cut costs*; this cost reduction is made both possible and essential (competitiveness) by the SMP.

Another reason is also starting to favour the 'European product' in undertakings: the demand from international customers (contingency insurance contracts or employer's liability coverage).

The SMP has had little direct impact among the factors which led to undertakings harmonizing their prices and conditions.

Indeed, for the undertakings, it was first a matter of:

(a) the finding that certain risks are identical from one country to another (especially in the damage to property sector);
(b) (international) customer demand;
(c) the concern to simplify the management.

On the other hand, a large number of factors still limit this harmonization in undertakings:

(a) some are associated with the absence of a single market, especially where it is a matter of the difference in regulations from country to country;
(b) others are associated with causes of another kind: the difference in markets (competition, practices and customs, nature and cost of the risks, mortality tables, etc.) or the autonomy left to subsidiaries to conduct their own policy.

There is real development in undertakings of 'European' products. This tendency is most marked at present in the life and contingency activities and it is possible to link this development directly with the introduction of the single market (use of the freedom to provide services, recognition by undertakings of the existence of a 'European consumer', etc.).

However, even in these undertakings, the standardization of prices and policy conditions is making only a very little progress. The undertakings justify this situation by both reasons not linked to the single market (technical difference, economic difference of the various markets) and reasons linked to the limits to the single market: legal differences (law of contract) still exist.

Overall, what is missing most would not appear to be so much the wish for harmonization of prices, but a real possibility for customers to compare the products with one another. In this context, the lack of true European distribution, and therefore means of 'carrying' these products in part does not contribute to this non-harmonization and hence calls for a convergence in prices. The transparency resulting from EMU and the introduction of the Euro, on the other hand, should contribute considerably to overcoming the difficulties for consumers of comparing different products offered by different markets and create cross-border pressure on both economic operators to harmonize policies and prices and on regulators to adopt harmonized legislation allowing operators to do so.

10. Contribution to the protection of the environment

10.1. Aims of the legislation

The Community wanted responsible development for its Member States, especially with regard to protection of the environment. Insurers are particularly concerned by this aspect of the Community's philosophy, since through their activities relating to business liability insurance, they contribute to awareness of the costs and to preventive measures.

Consequently, in the countries where national legislation is most stringent in terms of undertakings' liability for pollution, specialized insurance products have developed in this field (for example, northern Europe).

10.1.1. Hypotheses to be tested

The Community's action has really had an effect on the insurance market if the demand for insurance products covering business liability associated with pollution can be seen to have developed. Have policyholders become more aware of their responsibility and risks in the field of environmental protection as a result of the single market programme?

As a result, have they made more efforts to obtain cover for such risks through new contracts?

10.1.2. Indicators

Declarations by insurers of the development of such products in their general business activity; the marketing of these products (and more particularly the demand expressed by policyholders).

During recent years, it was possible to observe both the rise in the influence of the ecological parties (especially in northern Europe) and the growing public awareness of disasters affecting the quality of the environment. Everyone is increasingly aware that the impact of disasters is not limited by frontiers (for example, pollution of the Rhine) and that international harmonization of the regulations in the field of liability and compensation is necessary.

Various discussions and projects have been launched to this end, including:

(a) at the OECD: work of the group of economic experts on insurance against pollution and the compensation funds for accidental pollution;
(b) at the European Commission: proposal for a European Directive on liability for damage caused by waste, drawing up of the Green Paper, etc.

The object of this chapter is to examine the extent to which insurers, through market demand, have come to develop such products.

10.2. Facts and figures from the survey of 100 undertakings

Twenty per cent of the undertakings of the sample group have in fact developed such products.

10.2.1. Characteristics of the undertakings

It is mainly:

(a) large undertakings;
(b) general non-life insurance undertakings;
(c) undertakings from Germany, Denmark and the Netherlands

which have developed this type of product.

Table 10.1.   Details, by country, of the 20 undertakings of the sample group having developed insurance products linked to the environment

Germany	9 undertakings out of 16 interviewees	= 56%
Denmark	4 undertakings out of 8 interviewees	= 50%
France	4 undertakings out of 23 interviewees	= 17%
Netherlands	2 undertakings out of 7 interviewees	= 27%
Spain	1 undertaking out of 5 interviewees	= 20%
Total	20 undertakings out of 100 interviewees	= 20%

10.2.2. Reasons for developing the products

The 20 undertakings of the sample group which developed such products stated that they did so for the following reasons (in descending order):

(a) first, *market demand*: the recognition of the existence of a need, the specific demand of a particular customer;
(b) *the trend in national legislation,* which extends the liability of undertakings;
(c) *the position of leader or specialist in industrial risks*, which requires the development of increasingly specific products;
(d) participation in a pool or in programmes with other insurers;
(e) the hope of possible future (commercial) development in this field.

Of the 80 undertakings of the sample group which have not developed products covering environmental risks, 21 undertakings gave the reasons for this:

* 62% consider that this type of insurance is too difficult to devise technically or financially;
* 52% consider that there is no market or no demand for such policies;
* 19% consider that this product offers few prospects of profitability;
* 14% finally, consider that the insurer's obligations may become excessive.

Figure 10.1. Characteristics of undertakings having developed products covering environmental risks

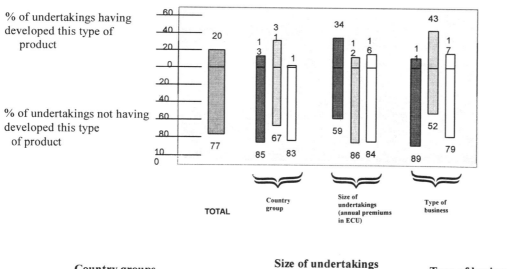

% of undertakings having developed this type of product

% of undertakings not having developed this type of product

TOTAL   Country group   Size of undertakings (annual premiums in ECU)   Type of business

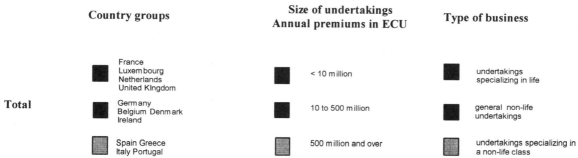

Total

Country groups

France
Luxembourg
Netherlands
United Kingdom

Germany
Belgium Denmark
Ireland

Spain Greece
Italy Portugal

**Size of undertakings
Annual premiums in ECU**

< 10 million

10 to 500 million

500 million and over

Type of business

undertakings
specializing in life

general non-life
undertakings

undertakings specializing in
a non-life class

10.3. Case studies

A. UAP

UAP finds that protection against environmental risks has become a growing preoccupation on the market. UAP has therefore set up its own think tank ('Ecorisk'), born of cooperation between UAP and Woodwork Clyde. This is a discussion team, currently providing engineering services, available to the various units of the group, but not covering the risks directly.

In France, UAP insures only the risks located in France, with the support of the Assurpol pool.

B. Victoria

Victoria already covered environmental risks well before 1989 and especially risks associated with water pollution, in the form of liability policies.

In 1990, a law was promulgated in Germany making a large number of industrial and commercial sectors liable for damage to property or personal injury as a result of pollution.

New insurance products were then devised by Victoria, which take the form of separate insurance policies.

C. Mapfre

Mapfre is not currently developing any products covering environmental risks.

D. Fortis

In its liability contracts for professionals, the group offers insurance covering the risks associated with protection of the environment, but does not seek to develop them, particularly on account of the difficulties in limiting precisely the length of time for which policyholders are liable.

10.4. Secondary sources

10.4.1. The development of the supply

For some years, and especially as a result of certain countries passing laws dealing specifically with the liability of polluters (for example, 1990 Law in Germany), demand has developed on the part of undertakings and authorities for insurance covering pollution risks.

In various European countries, insurers have gradually organized themselves to meet this demand, either individually (for example, in Germany) or by setting up co-reinsurance pools, as in France, Italy, Denmark, Spain and the Netherlands.

Table 10.2.   Overview of the co-reinsurance pools specialized in covering environmental risks created in the EU

Pool/Country	Year set up	Number of members	Premiums 1993 (million ECU)	Premiums 1994 (million ECU)	Capacity (million ECU)
Assurpol (France)	1989	50 insurance companies, 15 reinsurance companies	4.6	8.2	33 (1995)
Inquinamento (Italy)	1982	75 members	7	6.7	25
MAS	1984	58 members	0.66	0.67	8.5
Dansk Pool (Denmark)	1993			0.08	13
Médio ambiantales (Spain)	1995			0.05	6

Source: Miscellaneous.

10.4.2. Development of skills, introduction of tools

The development of these initiatives, whether individual in insurance companies or by co-reinsurance groups, has enabled technical competence to be developed allowing the risks to be defined more accurately and the customer undertakings to be advised regarding preventive measures to be implemented.

For instance, Assurpol has introduced:

(a) a method of prior audit of the risk;
(b) a subscription guide, enabling its members to classify and price the risks;
(c) participation by the pool, in the most difficult cases, in studying the risk alongside the insurer.

Since 1993, AXA has a specialized 'environment' sector which has developed a methodology for analysing compulsory risks when the policy is written. AXA has signed a cooperation agreement with the BRGM (Bureau des Recherches Géologiques et Minières) enabling it to dispose of data concerning the water flow and the nature of the subsoil.

AGF has invested in prevention, with the recruitment of a team of six specialized engineers to counsel undertakings in prevention.

UAP has set up a small think tank 'Ecorisk', born of the cooperation between UAP and the American consultants Woodwork Clyde: this is a discussion team, currently providing engineering services, available to the units of the group, but not covering the risks directly.

Allianz has a technical centre in Munich employing more than 100 engineers. The technical expertise available to Allianz in this way enables it both to analyse the causes of an industrial disaster and to recommend preventive measures.

10.5. Conclusion

Twenty per cent of the insurers interviewed for this study have already developed products covering environmental risks.

It is therefore noted that there is in fact a trend towards the development of this type of product, even though insurers are very prudent when dealing with a risk which they still consider today to be ill-defined and sometimes difficult to measure.

Among the undertakings interviewed, the largest proportion developing this type of policy or including specific clauses relating to pollution in their contracts come from northern Europe. This proportion is as high as 50% of the undertakings interviewed from Germany and Denmark.

On the other hand, the undertakings of the south (in the sample group and case studies) are still distinctly less concerned.

It is very clearly the demand of the policyholders which, as a priority, led insurers to propose cover against risks linked to pollution.

This demand is supported and stimulated by:

(a) the trend in national legislation; or
(b) the fact that the insurer, as a leader in industrial risks, wishes to meet the needs of its customers.

However, other reasons also play a role (albeit less important) in the undertakings' strategy to develop these products. These are:

(a) the hope of gain or of future development through this activity;
(b) participation in an insurance pool.

11.   The impact of the single market on insurers' costs

11.1. Aims of the legislation

According to Cecchini, the impact of greater competition (resulting from the dismantling of barriers) on the insurance sector would start with a squeeze on margins (associated in particular with the pressure on prices). However, in the medium term, the insurers, benefiting from a larger market, could achieve substantial reductions in their costs, in particular through the following effects: restructuring of the insurance sector, economies of scale, experience curve and increased innovation.

11.1.1. Hypotheses to be tested

It will in fact be possible to say that the single market has had the effects described above if the insurers were able to see a reduction in their costs during the reference period.

It will also be possible to establish a link between these reductions and the single market if undertakings started to make 'economies of scale' during the reference period, i.e. to group certain functions together at European level.

11.1.2. Indicators

(a) Trends in costs grouped under the term 'general operating expenses' during the reference period.
(b) Trend towards integration of certain functions of the undertaking at multinational level.

The 'costs' concerned here are all the operating costs of insurance undertakings, except:

(a) the cost of claims (refunds made to customers);
(b) financial costs.

This, therefore, refers to what are generally known as 'general operating expenses' by insurers, which cover all their operating costs, i.e.:

(a) distribution costs;
(b) marketing, advertising and promotion costs;
(c) administrative costs: production and administration of contracts, handling of claims;
(d) other operating costs: operational departments, general management, accounting, etc.

The general operating expenses ratio is usually expressed as a percentage of turnover.

11.2. Facts and figures from the survey of 100 undertakings

To be able to make hypotheses about the impact of the single market on insurers' earnings and costs, the undertakings interviewed were asked in which three functions (from the list below) they had achieved the greatest productivity gains in the past five years and to explain how they were achieved.

List of functions analysed:

(a) marketing, development of new products;
(b) advertising and promotion services;
(c) accounting and financial services;
(d) general management;
(e) information technology;
(f) personnel management and human resources management;
(g) sales departments and sales staff;
(h) claims management.

The replies indicate one function in which nearly half the undertakings have made significant gains: information technology. Nearly a quarter of undertakings then mentioned:

(a) marketing and development;
(b) sales departments;
(c) claims management.

Conversely, very few undertakings made productivity gains in:

(a) human resources management;
(b) accounting;
(c) advertising and promotion.

These results are illustrated in Figure 11.1.

Figure 11.1.   Business functions where productivity gains were made

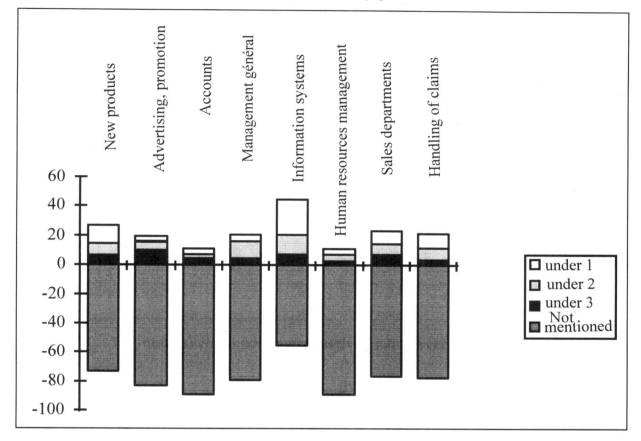

11.2.1. The gains in information technology

The majority stated they had renewed their equipment (new system, new software, general reorganization of the architecture) or used more modern technologies.

Others alluded to fuller, more extensive use: better sharing of information between departments, equipment of all departments, issuing of portables to sales staff, etc.

Some undertakings mentioned the standardization of previously ill-assorted systems.

11.2.2. Marketing/development of new products

The gain factors were:

(a) introduction of new products and innovative measures;
(b) targeting niches;
(c) efficiency from know-how shared between several countries;
(d) simplification of products;
(e) adaptation to a changing market, to increased competition;
(f) more competent staff, efforts to train sales staff;
(g) general reorganization of the company.

11.2.3. Sales departments and the sales staff

The gain factors were:

(a) improvement of the sales staff's tools especially through the introduction of information technology;
(b) improvement of the professionalism of sales staff especially through training and support;
(c) the introduction of new distribution networks, to obtain better coverage of national territory;
(d) improvement of customer service;
(e) reduction in staff;
(f) sales productivity efforts.

11.2.4. The 'claims' department

The gain factors were:

(a) the use of information technology (which allows better knowledge of the costs, faster processing, etc.), the introduction of new methods;
(b) more prevention;
(c) decentralization of decisions;
(d) cuts in staff or operating costs;
(e) international handling of claims in a network.

11.2.5. Administration and general management

The gain factors were:

(a) a change in direction or personnel (of better quality);
(b) reorganization of the functions leading, in particular, to a reduction in the number of managers.

11.2.6. Advertising and promotion

Few gain factors were mentioned, apart from:

(a) improvement of the teams' techniques and skills;
(b) respect of budgets;
(c) a better concept and better targeting of activities.

11.2.7. Accounts

The gain factors were:

(a) new information technology tools;
(b) better use of information technology resources, especially sharing with other undertakings.

11.2.8. Human resources management

The gain factors were:

(a) boosting service, the recruitment of specialized managerial staff;
(b) training measures;
(c) a cut in staff or better use of staff.

During the reference period, the general operating expenses of the undertakings interviewed fell on average for the group as a whole by 4.5%, dropping from 22.7% to 18.2% between 1989 and 1995.

These data are not very meaningful in their raw form. In fact, each country records its general expenses differently. But the important factor is the trend in the general operating expenses of European insurers during the reference period, which is clearly falling. This trend is confirmed by the secondary sources (see Table 11.1).

This decrease is not the same for all types of undertakings. Those achieving the greatest gains are:

(a) small undertakings;
(b) undertakings specializing in life assurance;
(c) the following group of countries: France, Luxembourg, Netherlands, UK.

Table 11.1.   Trend in general operating expenses (as a % of premiums) according to undertakings' characteristics

	1989	1995	Variation 1995/89
General mean	22.7	18.2	− 4.5
By country group			
Group A[1]	25.8	21.6	− 4.2
Group B[2]	20.8	17.0	− 3.8
Group C[3]	18.8	13.2	− 5.6
By size of undertaking			
Large	17.3	11.8	− 5.5
Medium-sized	18.2	19.2	+ 1.0
Small	35.0	21.1	− 13.9
By type of business activity			
Specialist life	23.9	16.0	− 7.9
General non-life	22.5	12.0	− 10.5
Specialist non-life	21.6	21.3	− 0.3

[1] France, Luxembourg, Netherlands, UK.
[2] Germany, Belgium, Denmark, Ireland.
[3] Spain, Greece, Italy, Portugal.

11.3. Case studies

All the case study undertakings also experienced a substantial reduction in their general expenses over the reference period.

A. UAP

The trend for UAP was as follows:

General expenses	1989 (%)	1994 (%)
Life + non-life business of the group (general operating expenses net of commissions)	17.4	13.3
Non-life business only (general operating expenses + commissions)		
France	29.9	26.7
Belgium	37.8	36.8
Germany (Colonia)	37.9	34.3
Life business Percentage intermediation[1] (group)	4.44	2.73

[1] Administrative and marketing costs as % of mathematical provisions

These results are linked to:

(a) *the rise in premiums* (which increased during the same period by 53.9% in France and by 76.7% in the other EU Member States);

(b) *the constant efforts* of the group to keep general operating expenses stable. Business restructuring plans were introduced in various European countries to achieve this.

The group did not really reorganize functions at group level. Excluding top management ('group strategy committee'), the European management was, on the contrary, decentralized through the creation of 'regional profit centres'.

The group human resources management endeavours to internationalize the management by organizing international mobility of executives and an exchange of skills. This function does not replace those already existing in the European regional profit centres.

An example of regrouping activities is the case of Paneurorisk, a European economic interest grouping set up on behalf of the group's European subsidiaries working in large risks. By pooling expertise and joint reinsurance negotiations, the European economic interest grouping enables economies of scale to be achieved in reinsurance prices and the costs of risk assessment without merging activities.

Restructuring, on the other hand, is carried out at national level in certain countries by regrouping acquisitions which do not attain the critical size or which offer possibilities of synergies.

A. UAP (continued)

For the group, it is difficult to cite services or functions where major productivity gains were achieved over the past five years. In fact, the gains are made specifically in each national unit, since there are no centralized functions.

The gains are essentially made at national level by restructuring and merging the small units, which leads to reductions in personnel and general operating expenses.

B. Victoria

The trend, for Victoria was:

General expenses	1992 (%)	1994 (%)
Health		
acquisition costs	16.7	10.8
general operating expenses	4.9	4.1
Life		
acquisition costs	4.13	3.72
general operating expenses	4.9	4.0
Non-life		
acquisition costs + general operating expenses	30.6	26.4

The very favourable trend in the general operating expenses ratio is linked to a twofold trend:

(a) the sustained growth in premiums recorded by Victoria during the past three years, largely associated with the development of the new *Länder*. For instance, in 1994, 50% of the new contracts recorded in non-life insurance (motor vehicle, housing, liability) were concluded in these new *Länder*;

(b) the constant efforts made from 1992 to 1994 to stabilize (and even reduce) wage and equipment costs, after the investments made in 1990–92 to develop in these *Länder*.

Victoria has not, for the time being, regrouped functions between various European countries.

For Victoria, it is not so much the effects of the single market which have generated the increased productivity as the following reasons:

(a) considerable reductions in costs of staff, equipment, acquisition costs;

(b) the renewal of the data processing system;

(c) the introduction of a new management system for the accounts, life assurance and motor vehicle insurance.

C. Mapfre

The trend in general operating expenses at Mapfre was as follows:

Mapfre Mutualidad	1989	1994
General operating expenses (including life and non-life commissions) compared to net premiums collected (%)	28.8	24.5

This positive trend is attributable to:

(a) the very sharp increase in net premium receipts, which rose by 15% during the same period;

(b) the application of strict management rules already in force before 1989, which enabled the rate of growth of expenses to be contained.

The case of Italy having to be considered separately, the only European country where Mapfre is present is Portugal, which is covered by a branch and considered as an additional 'region'. As a result, the commercial and claims management resources are decentralized there, but all the other functions are grouped together with those of Spain (general management, human resources, information technology, etc.).

Mapfre has long been involved in productivity efforts which focus primarily on:

(a) portfolio monitoring (selection of the risks) and claims management: introduction of a price scale for repairs, a network of experts, etc.;

(b) other gains were made in sales departments with the computerization of the sales staff, the introduction of telephone reception and information units for customers ('hot lines');

(c) finally, the information technology and management systems are being standardized for all the countries covered by Mapfre.

D. Fortis

The trend, for Fortis, was as follows:

	1989	1994
General operating expenses as a % of net premium receipts	40.7	38.2

Over the same period, Fortis saw its turnover rise by 63.7% while costs only rose by 53.7%.

The Fortis Group has regrouped virtually no functions at European level, apart from a small accounts unit for the production of the consolidated accounts (but the fact that it has chosen to develop through subsidiaries rather than branches means that it has to continue to produce accounts in each country, according to the standards of the country, for presentation to the national authorities) and human resources management.

Conversely, the Group's philosophy is to decentralize responsibilities and decisions as far as possible and to achieve economies of scale first at national level, rather than at international level.

This philosophy is summed up in the formula 'Fortis does not consider itself as an *international* group, but rather as a group composed of *several national companies*'.

Consequently, whereas the information technology systems are still different between Belgium and the Netherlands, in the Netherlands the management is currently endeavouring to regroup the banking and insurance activities by restructuring them into seven 'business units' oriented to each market, with a single information technology system and creating joint functions for accounts, human resources and general services.

In total, for the time being 'the group does not believe in the effects of size at horizontal (European) level, but at vertical (national) level'.

The productivity efforts focused on:

(a) *the overhaul of the information technology*, to standardize it between the various units of each country. However, there is no regrouping of information technology *between* countries;

(b) *the commercial efforts of 'cross-selling'*: better use of the existing networks to sell all the group's products.

E. Cecar

Each unit of the Cecar Group is independent (monitoring of customers, claims management, accounts, etc.).

The only joint function for the time being is communications, in order to give a strong unity of image in each country.

11.4. Facts and figures from the survey of 100 undertakings: aggregate results

Another question is that of the extent to which any progress in integration has enabled economies of scale to be made (and therefore costs to be reduced) among European insurers.

To discover this, the following question was put to the companies: 'Has there been any effort, over the past five years, to integrate or coordinate any of the following functions between two or more EU Member States?'

List of functions:

(a) marketing, development of new products;
(b) advertising and promotion services;
(c) accounting and financial services;

(d) general management;
(e) information technology;
(f) personnel management and human resources management;
(g) sales departments and sales team;
(h) claims management.

Of the 36 undertakings of the sample group operating in Europe, 12 undertakings (i.e. 33%) did in fact start to integrate or coordinate some of their functions at European level.

These were:

6 undertakings in Germany;
2 undertakings in Luxembourg;
1 undertaking in the UK;
1 undertaking in France;
1 undertaking in the Netherlands;
1 undertaking in Spain.
(Total: 12 undertakings).

The functions where the undertakings interviewed were able to achieve the most coordination over the past five years are the following (12 undertakings, 39 replies):

(a) information technology: 10 replies
(b) marketing/development: 8 replies
(c) general management: 5 replies
(d) advertising/promotion: 4 replies
(e) human resources management: 4 replies
(f) sales departments: 3 replies
(g) claims department: 3 replies
(h) accounts: 2 replies
Total number of replies: 39 replies
Total number of undertakings: 12 undertakings.

The reasons for these efforts at regrouping were as follows.

11.4.1. Information technology

(a) to share knowledge and experience;
(b) to be able to exchange information (compatibility of systems);
(c) to exchange between subsidiaries and branches;
(d) to cut costs through standardization.

11.4.2. Marketing/development

(a) to exchange information on products and markets, benchmarking, to benefit from the ideas of other countries;
(b) to standardize;
(c) to cut costs through standardization.

11.4.3. General management

(a) to standardize strategy;
(b) to make the structure more adaptable and more flexible.

11.4.4. Advertising/promotion

(a) to have an identical image;
(b) to make oneself known everywhere;
(c) to exchange ideas.

11.4.5. Human resources management

(a) to share experience;
(b) to develop training.

11.4.6. Sales departments

(a) to have new distribution networks, to develop;
(b) to develop training.

11.4.7. Claims management

(a) to exchange experience, initial training;
(b) use of an international network.

11.4.8. Accounts

(a) improvement of reporting.

11.5. Secondary sources

11.5.1. Supervisory authority

The trend in costs may be observed on the basis of the data produced by the supervisory authorities in their annual reports. However, since the definitions and accounting methods are not the same from one country to another, this observation does not allow results to be compared between countries. It does, however, give good indications of the trend within each country.

11.5.2. Trend in general operating expenses

The situation regarding general operating expenses is very different in the life and the non-life sectors.

Whereas the general operating expenses ratios have fallen considerably in the life sector in almost all countries, and sometimes to a very considerable extent:

(a) gains of five points in Italy over five years;
(b) gains of ten points in Portugal over the same period, etc.

in the non-life classes, the tendency has also been to fall, but far more gradually.

Table 11.2.   **Trend in general operating expenses from 1989 to 1993 in seven European countries**

Member State	1989	1990	1991	1992	1993	1994
Life						
Spain	12.8	13.4	11.6	12.3	13.4	
France	12.0	12.9	12.6	8.6	7.2	
Ireland	18.2	22.1	22.0	25.1	21.7	
Italy	25.1	23.5	22.2	21.6	19.8	
Luxembourg	29.4 [1]	n.a.	23.7	12.1	10.6	7.9
Portugal	21.6	20.1	17.9	17.2	14.3	11.6
UK	21.0	22.0	20.0	19.0	19.0	
Non-life						
Spain	34.1	32.0	31.8	32.0	32.7	
France	29.9	30.3	30.7	29.5	28.8	
Ireland	20.8	18.2	19.1	19.3	19.3	
Luxembourg	32.9 [1]	n.a.	27.5	29.1	26.4	28.3
Netherlands	13.7 [1]	14.4	15.1	14.5	13.8	
Portugal	38.8	37.6	37.9	36.2	35.6	32.4
UK	30.0	31.0	31.0	30.0	30.0	

[1] 1986 figures.
Sources: Questionnaires sent to the supervisory authorities.

11.6. Conclusion

During the period of reference there is a clear trend towards insurance operators achieving considerable reductions in overall cost. This trend tallies with the fact that Chapter 7 on the productivity of the undertakings established that, during the period from 1989 to 1995, there was a slight tendency among European insurers to improve their productivity. This tendency appears in the undertakings of the sample group and in the case studies.

In the majority of cases, it is clearly reasons internal to the undertakings interviewed, or reasons associated with their direct environment, which are the cause of the productivity gains recorded.

More specifically, the insurers indicate that the economies were made through measures for modernization and reorganization of information technology: about one undertaking in two had made productivity gains in this field. Even where other functions are mentioned, it is often thanks to information technology that productivity gains were made there (for example: the improvement in the sales staff's tools and information in the case of the 'sales departments', the use of information technology for 'claims management', the new information technology tools for 'accounts').

For one-third of undertakings, four other sources of productivity gains were also mentioned:

(a) *marketing/development* in various forms: innovation, adaptation of products, simplification of ranges, training of staff in the product;
(b) *sales departments*: measures involving methods and tools, professionalism, but also network construction;

(c) *claims management*: improvement of the service (speed) and the management methods (supervision, prevention, decentralization of decisions);

(d) reorganization of the management to make it more flexible and more modern.

However, these efforts also have an effect on the competitiveness of the undertakings and the question arises of the extent to which increased awareness of the threats of competition, associated in particular with the creation of the single market, has accelerated or facilitated the introduction of these productivity measures in undertakings.

In a more limited number of cases, the impact of the single market is indicated more clearly:

(a) efforts at simplification and standardization among units of the same group in the field of information technology, products, etc.;

(b) pooling of resources or sharing of know-how at international level in the areas of product design, claims management, sales networks;

(c) and, in general, all the efforts specifically designed to increase competitiveness: improvement of the claims department, innovative measures to adapt products to the market, etc.

It is therefore difficult to establish a direct link between these measures and the SMP, but indirectly it is clear that the prospect of the creation of the single market promoted an awareness among insurers of the threats of competition (real or to come) and of the importance of improving their level of competitiveness by taking action regarding their operating costs, on the one hand, and the quality of the way they conduct their business (claims management) and the improvement of their customer service, on the other.

Economies of scale were measured through the efforts made by undertakings to integrate one or more business functions at European level over the past five years. The study shows that real progress was made towards this: about one-third of the undertakings operating at European level started to integrate some of their functions at European level.

This effort focuses first on information technology and product marketing. For the other functions, some instances exist, but they are less common. The undertakings state that they have integrated one or more of their functions at European level because they hope to achieve savings in so doing, especially in the following fields:

(a) information technology: better quality and speed of reporting, thanks to standardization of information technology tools and sharing of databases;

(b) product marketing: time saved in research and preparation of formulas, sharing of ideas on efficient products.

Hence, *the sharing of information* on markets and the effort made to unify advertising messages correspond to recognition on the part of the undertakings that there is a true single market, with a consumer capable of moving round and choosing, directly linked to the introduction of the freedom to provide services and the single passport.

On the other hand, *standardization of the information technology resources* between subsidiaries, the setting up of databases and surveys for claims management, is more a question of good resources management in a group run as such, and possibly of preparation for further integration in the future.

Finally, the case studies show that, in the case of large groups, the greatest progress in the field of integration and economies of scale is first made at national level, then at the level of 'European regions'. This would tend to indicate that economies of scale at European level are limited where the national units are already large.

12. The impact of the single market on the strategy of insurance undertakings

The object of this chapter is to analyse:

(a) the impact of the single market on the factors determining the strategic choices of the undertakings,
(b) the nature of the responses adopted by undertakings to cope with the new market conditions thus created.

It is a matter of determining here the extent to which the creation of the single market influenced undertakings' strategy and, more specifically, in the major choices concerning:

(a) the design and choice of products and/or services;
(b) market preparation and distribution methods;
(c) search for financing;
(d) provision of services;
(e) marketing and efforts to improve the performance of products and/or services.

What part was played by the following concerns:

(a) the operating costs and investments needed to be competitive;
(b) the fear of new entrants;
(c) the pressure of certain major customers;
(d) the existence of substitute products or services;
(e) the strength of the current competitors?

To be able to analyse the respective significance of these various factors, undertakings were asked to indicate the significance of each of these factors on a scale of 0 to 3, first in 1989 and then in 1994, when drawing up their strategy.

Table 12.1.   Proportion[1] of insurance undertakings whose strategy was influenced significantly by one of the following factors (% – 1989)

	General mean	Country group[2]			Size of undertaking[3]			Type of business activity		
		A*	B**	C***	Large	Medium-sized	Small	Life	General non-life	Specialist non-life
The volume of investment necessary to be competitive	55	58	48	67	66	53	44	54	77	46
The fear of new entrants	32	37	23	41	41	32	20	33	29	33
The pressure of major customers	28	16	43	33	25	39	12	25	34	29
The emergence of substitute products or services	34	41	24	41	41	33	28	41	24	34
The strength of competitors	64	68	64	50	69	67	52	51	76	79
Total = 100 %	100	46	42	12	32	43	25	37	21	42

[1] Total scores '2' and '3'.
[2] Country group: * France, Luxembourg, Netherlands, UK; ** Germany, Belgium, Denmark, Ireland; *** Spain, Greece, Italy, Portugal.
[3] Size of undertakings (annual premiums in ECU): large: 500 million and over; medium-sized: 10 to 500 million; small: < 10 million.

12.1.   Facts and trends from the survey of 100 undertakings

12.1.1. The order of priorities of the undertakings in 1989 and 1994

Among the factors mentioned above, in 1989 it was above all the fear of competition in all its possible forms which dominated:

(a) first that of the current competitors (64%), but also that of the appearance on the market of newcomers (32%) or substitute products or services (34%);
(b) second (and consequently), the amount of investment or the efforts to be made to become competitive oneself (55%);
(c) finally, the amount of pressure or the influence brought to bear by major customers or suppliers (28%).

During the following five years (1989–94), a greater awareness developed of the threats linked with competition and its constraints.

Table 12.2. Proportion[1] of insurance undertakings whose strategy was influenced significantly by one of the following factors (% – 1994)

	General mean	Country group [2]			Size of undertaking [3]			Type of business activity		
		A*	B**	C***	Large	Medium-sized	Small	Life	General non-life	Specialist non-life
The volume of investment necessary to be competitive	73	78	67	75	84	74	56	79	81	64
The fear of new entrants	52	54	41	66	53	60	28	54	57	43
The pressure of major customers	43	37	50	42	57	46	32	32	52	47
The emergence of substitute products or services	55	65	43	58	61	58	40	57	57	53
The strength of competitors	73	76	69	75	81	73	64	73	86	67
Total = 100%	100	46	42	12	32	43	25	37	21	42

[1] Total scores '2' and '3'.

[2] Country group: * France, Luxembourg, Netherlands, UK; ** Germany, Belgium, Denmark, Ireland; *** Spain, Greece, Italy, Portugal.

[3] Size of undertakings (annual premiums in ECU): large: 500 million and over; medium-sized: 10 to 500 million; small: < 10 million.

It is striking that, comparing the replies given for 1989 with those for 1994 to the same question, undertakings had become distinctly more aware in five years of the threats coming from their economic environment and of the efforts which had become necessary to become competitive.

The order of the factors stays the same, although there is far greater awareness of all the factors: the pressure from major customers, the possibility of a change in market conditions (new entrants, emergence of new products or services).

Figure 12.1. Development between 1989 and 1994 of the importance of certain factors in the strategy of insurers

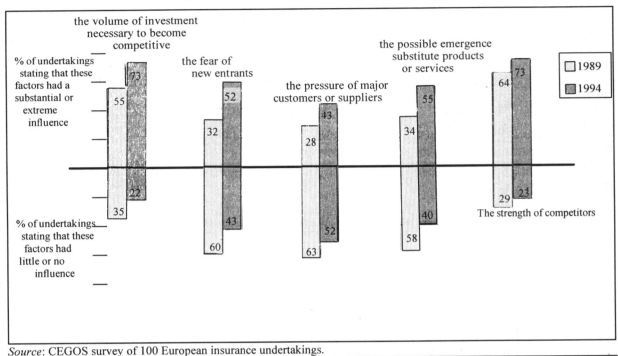

Source: CEGOS survey of 100 European insurance undertakings.

This perception varies considerably, however, depending on the size of the undertakings, their home country in the EU, or the class of insurance (type of risks) they cover.

12.1.2. The influence of the size of undertakings

The large undertakings (annual premium receipts in excess of ECU 500 million) were already those which, as early as 1989, were both the most attentive to the possible threats from competition and the most aware of the investments to be made to become competitive. This trend would be reinforced in 1994 and supplemented by a keener awareness of the pressure from their customers and suppliers.

At the other extreme, the small undertakings (annual premium receipts under ECU 10 million) were influenced very little by such concerns. During the past five years, they seem to start to become aware, since nearly half of them state that they are aware of the strength of their competitors and the financial efforts needed to achieve the required level of competitiveness.

12.1.3. Influence of the 'class of insurance' provided by the undertakings

Of all the types of undertakings, it is the general non-life insurance undertakings which were the most aware in 1989 of the threat of competition and aware of the efforts to be made to become competitive. The same was true in 1994, with more general concern among the undertakings of this type.

Conversely, in 1989, as well as five years later, it is the specialized undertakings, i.e. those located in *niches,* which are on the whole the least concerned about the threats mentioned above.

12.1.4. Variation in opinions by country of origin

In the EU Member States where insurance is the least developed (essentially southern Europe), the fear of competition dominated in 1989, not so much in the present form as in that of its possible future developments (new entrants, substitute products), as well as the importance of the efforts for competitiveness to be made to cope with it. This tendency was greater in 1994.

In the countries where insurance is the most highly developed, the strategy of half the undertakings was already inspired by the need to become competitive and the threats of their present competition as early as 1989. In 1994, this trend had not changed in nature, but amplified, and the concern is now shared by three-quarters of the undertakings.

12.2. Case studies

A. UAP

The following aspects had a significant impact on UAP's strategy.

The administrative costs and necessary investments: general operating expenses have influenced the Group's strategy, especially since 1992. The Group is endeavouring to reduce the ratio by introducing in each country both a cost reduction plan and, where appropriate, restructuring (through merger) of the units acquired in the same country.

The fear of new entrants and the strength of competitors: from the 1980s, the Group decided to prepare for the creation of the single market, which it considered unavoidable. Its strategy will be both defensive (bring competition to the territory of the others in order to protect oneself more effectively from their activities in the national territory) and offensive (gain market shares in Europe).

The influence of major customers: UAP has a large proportion of its business in large risks. It was taking these customers into account which led UAP to set up a specific unit, the European economic interest grouping Paneurorisk, which allows coordination of the various subsidiaries in handling these risks.

Existence of substitute products: this had little influence on UAP's strategy.

B. Victoria

Founded in 1853, the Group was greatly affected by the history of Europe and Germany during the 20th century. This large insurance group, present in 20 different countries, was in fact forced to lose most of its business abroad following the two world wars. Later, the division of Germany after the Second World War led to it losing its sales sectors in Eastern and Central Germany, which was its traditional stronghold. It is not so much the influences attributable to the single market as the concentration on a certain number of objectives which marked the Group's strategy during the reference period:

(a) *cost cutting and increase in productivity*, which led to the Group having a prudent policy abroad, especially in relation to the EU;
(b) *reconstruction of trade with the new Länder*, which led to the Group investing primarily in its newly expanded national market;
(c) *defence and further development of the national market*, through the introduction of banking cooperation with the Vereinsbank Group;
(d) *development of trade abroad through partnerships*.

C. Mapfre

For Mapfre, whose European activities focus essentially on Spain (as well as Portugal and, to a limited extent, Italy), the main inspiration behind its strategy is the identification of development opportunities which, for the company, have proved to be of particular interest in the past ten years in Latin America.

D. Fortis

In 1989, the main concerns of Amev (which became the Fortis Group in 1990 after its merger with AG) were:

(a) *competition*: the fear of seeing new entrants arriving on their market, the strength of the present competitors, the fear of substitute products;
(b) *the scale of the investments necessary to become competitive.*

Although in 1989 Amev, with a turnover of ECU 4.6 billion (of which 44% in the Netherlands), was number three on the Dutch market, this company considered that it was too small for a market which had become European. It was the search for a critical size enabling it to measure up to the other European giants which would dictate its strategy during the years 1989–94, which was characterized by a series of business combinations, the most spectacular of which are the merger with the VSB savings bank in 1990, then with the AG Group to create Fortis in 1990.

D. Fortis (continued)

On the other hand, the *pressure of major customers* was then felt to be of little importance (but Amev operated mainly on the personal market).

In 1994, the ranking of these concerns was still the same, although with greater emphasis on the fear of seeing the arrival of new entrants.

E. Cecar

Cecar's strategy was essentially dominated by the *pressure exerted by its major customers,* who are becoming increasingly international and globalizing their buying strategy (widespread use of risk managers).

This pressure leads to growth in order to be able to support customers, *both geographically and in terms of skills,* and finally to be able to handle *all* their risks.

12.3. Conclusion

The main aim of this chapter is to show how the opinions of the undertakings have evolved over the five years of the reference period and, consequently, how certain preoccupations of the undertakings have become predominant or, on the contrary, have lost their importance.

The trend in this awareness is illustrated by the following summary table.

Table 12.3.   Proportion[1] of insurance undertakings whose strategy was influenced significantly by one of the following factors (%)

	1989	1994	Variation 1994/89
The volume of investments necessary to be competitive	55	73	+ 18
The fear of new entrants	32	52	+ 20
The pressure of major customers	28	43	+ 15
The emergence of substitute products or services	34	55	+ 21
The strength of competitors	64	73	+ 9

[1] Total scores '2' and '3'.

The first point to note is the substantial increase in concern about the intensification of competition represented by two main subjects:

(a) 'the fear of new entrants' (+ 20);
(b) 'the emergence of new substitute products or services' (+ 21);
     and 'investments to be made to remain competitive' (+ 18).

To a lesser extent, the *pressure of major customers* is also becoming more important (+ 21), but this concern only has an impact on the strategy of the undertakings specializing in large risks, which explains why, in our sample, this only concerns 43% of the sample in 1994.

The *strength of competitors* is and always has been strongly felt, rising from 64% to 73% of the undertakings during the reference period.

Among the factors which influenced the strategy of insurance undertakings during the period 1989 to 1994, the very strong role of the fear of competition and investments to be made to remain competitive should therefore be stressed. In general, these are the two guiding principles in the undertakings' strategy and, although they have changed little between 1989 and 1994, their significance – and therefore the awareness of undertakings – have simply become stronger in 1994.

The single market has had the following impact on this awareness:

(a) *first through the anticipatory effect*: the fear of competition and of possible new entrants which emerges from 1989 is clearly linked, in the interviewees' replies, to the prospect of the market opening up in 1992; in anticipation of this announced event, each of the undertakings interviewed would develop a defensive strategy specific to it: for instance, UAP constructed most of its European presence before 1989, the Amev/AG merger took place in 1990, etc.;

(b) *then through the confirmation of these fears in 1994*: indeed, the fear of competition and the efforts to be made to be competitive played a larger role, in our study, in the strategic implications for undertakings in 1994 (compared to their importance in 1989).

Clearly, it is not possible to attribute this increased awareness entirely to the creation of the single market, since purely national forms of competition developed in parallel during the same period, such as those of the banks or the new distributors. Depending on the 'class' of insurance, competition will take a different form: international for insurers selling to undertakings, more national for insurers targeting the personal market and facing the emergence of new distribution systems, such as the banks, direct selling and network distributors.

13. The types of strategic responses

Insurers may adopt a variety of strategies to respond to the change in market conditions. These include:

(a) the internationalization of their business activities (within or outside the EU);
(b) the adjustment of their production capacity (financial or resource organization);
(c) choices concerning the location of their activities;
(d) cost-cutting measures;
(e) the redefinition (or adaptation) of their supply of products or services;
(f) the reorganization of the management of the undertaking;
(g) innovative measures;
(h) setting up cross-border partnerships.

To analyse the extent to which the single market has influenced the implementation of these strategies (and in particular which), the insurers interviewed were asked to indicate, on a scale of 0 to 3, the extent to which their undertaking's strategy had been characterized by each of these actions:

(a) first in 1989;
(b) then in 1994.

The purpose of this survey is therefore to establish the extent to which insurers are aware that their undertaking had to reverse or change its strategy over the past six years on account of the creation of the single market.

13.1. Facts and trends from the survey of 100 undertakings

13.1.1. Aggregate results

Adding the scores '2' and '3' allocated to each of these strategic choices, we find the following.

In 1989, undertakings' strategy was mainly focused on the search for productivity and on deepening the insurance profession, i.e. (in order of priority):

(a) the reduction of operating costs (66%);
(b) innovative measures (61%);
(c) redefinition of the supply of products/services (48%).

The other concerns, and especially those relating to the internationalization of business, only affected a minority of undertakings and only the largest at that time.

In 1995, an intensification of efforts is to be seen in the same areas (productivity, innovation and redefinition of supply), but also a rise in internationalization strategies.

As shown in Table 13.1, the hierarchy of the strategic choices has stayed largely the same over six years. However, whereas almost all undertakings are implementing cost-cutting and innovative measures, the concern for internationalization has progressed, with the priority still on Europe for the majority of undertakings.

Table 13.1.   **The strategic options of insurance undertakings in the EU: trends between 1989 and 1995 (% of undertakings stating that their strategy was affected to a significant extent by the following decisions)**

Strategic options	In 1989	In 1995
Internationalization strategy		
Internationalization of business activities within the EU	25	38
Internationalization of business activities outside the EU	15	25
Setting up of cross-border partnerships	20	33
Search for productivity		
Cost-cutting measures	66	83
Reorganization of management	33	53
Location of business activities	24	40
Innovation and redefinition of supply of products/services		
Innovative measures	61	80
Redefinition of the supply of products/services	48	75
Positioning		
Effort to ward off competition	35	48

The specific characteristics of the undertakings (size, class of insurance supplied, home country within the EU) nevertheless led to them implementing a wide variety of strategic responses.

13.1.2. Influence of the size of the undertakings

The large undertakings of the sample questioned are those showing themselves to be the most active in the internationalization of their business activities, especially outside the EU. This trend has gathered pace during the period from 1989 to 1995, with half then declaring that they were internationalizing their business outside the EU and entering into cross-border partnerships.

It is also striking to see that in 1995 almost all of them came to implement cost-cutting strategies, redefine their supply of products and services and introduce innovative measures.

The small undertakings follow the general trend, but whereas internationalization only concerned barely 10% of them in 1989, this proportion doubled in 1995 and mainly applies to the introduction of strategies within Europe.

13.1.3. Influence of the type of business of the undertakings

The undertakings specializing in life assurance are those which seem to have changed their strategies the most over the past six years: strong impetus to the internationalization of their activities (the proportion of undertakings concerned doubled over the period from 1989 to 1995), search for innovation and redefinition of the supply of products or services, which in 1995 affected three-quarters of the undertakings of this sector.

The general non-life insurance undertakings adopted strategies characterized more by the rationalization of their activities and their organization: in the space of six years, the proportion of these undertakings having redefined their supply and reorganized their management practically doubled.

The specialized non-life insurance undertakings, which in 1989 were already putting a lot of effort into cost-cutting strategies and redefining their supply, continued and amplified these strategies.

13.1.4. Difference according to country groups

It is in the countries where the insurance markets are the most highly developed (UK, France, Luxembourg, Netherlands) that the efforts towards internationalization of business activities over the period from 1989 to 1995 were the most marked:

(a) nearly half the undertakings of these countries stated that they had a European strategy and that they took decisions concerning the location of their business activities;
(b) over one-third are internationalizing outside Europe and over one-third have entered into cross-border partnerships.

It is also in these countries that the cost-cutting strategies are the most developed (89% of undertakings in 1995) or those to stand out from the competition: innovative measures (92%), efforts to ward off competition (63%).

Table 13.2.   **The strategic options of European insurance undertakings in 1989: variation according to the specific characteristics of the undertakings (% of undertakings stating that their strategy was strongly influenced by the following decisions)**

	General mean	Country group[1]			Size of undertaking[2]			Type of business activity		
		A*	B**	C***	Large	Medium-sized	Small	Life	General non-life	Specialist non-life
Internationalization of business activities in the EU	25	26	27	16	47	17	12	19	43	22
Internationalization of business activities outside the EU	15	20	10	16	29	7	12	16	24	10
Cost-cutting measures	66	72	60	67	69	72	52	54	62	78
Redefinition of the supply of products/ services	48	52	45	41	69	42	32	38	43	60
Reorganization of the management	33	39	24	42	35	37	24	27	38	36
Innovative measures	61	69	52	59	72	61	48	57	76	57
Efforts to ward off competition	35	50	26	8	35	40	28	38	34	33
Cross-border partnerships	20	22	21	8	50	7	4	16	43	12
Decision concerning the location of business activities	24	30	17	25	35	21	16	17	52	17
Total = 100 %	100	46	42	12	32	43	25	37	21	42

[1] Country group: * France, Luxembourg, Netherlands, UK; ** Germany, Belgium, Denmark, Ireland; *** Spain, Greece, Italy, Portugal.

[2] Size of undertakings (annual premiums in ECU): large: 500 million and over; medium-sized: 10 million to 500 million; small: < 10 million.

Table 13.3. **The strategic options of European insurance undertakings in 1995: variation according to the specific characteristics of the undertakings (% of undertakings stating that their strategy was strongly influenced by the following decisions)**

	Total	Country group[1]			Size of undertaking[2]			Type of business activity		
		A*	B**	C***	Large	Medium-sized	Small	Life	General non-life	Specialist non-life
Internationalization of business activities in the EU	38	46	36	17	50	39	20	35	58	31
Internationalization of business activities outside the EU	25	35	17	17	44	19	12	30	34	17
Cost-cutting measures	83	89	79	75	97	86	60	78	81	88
Redefinition of the supply of products/services	75	78	73	67	88	77	56	73		
Reorganization of the management	53	57	48	59	47	63	44	56	57	48
Innovative measures	80	92	67	84	94	83	56	84	81	76
Efforts to ward off competition	48	63	31	50	44	51	48	54	53	41
Cross-border partnerships	33	37	33	17	53	26	20	32	38	31
Decision concerning the location of business activities	40	52	26	42	50	42	24	36	52	38

[1] Country group: * France, Luxembourg, Netherlands, UK; ** Germany, Belgium, Denmark, Ireland; *** Spain, Greece, Italy, Portugal.

[2] Size of undertakings (annual premiums in ECU): large: 500 million and over; medium-sized: 10 million to 500 million; small: < 10 million.

13.2. Case studies

A. UAP

UAP's strategic options were the following.

Internationalization in the EU: this was the priority in 1989, the objective being to double the Group's market share there and to reach a critical size in each country.

Internationalization outside the EU took second place: the Group traditionally had a strong presence in Africa and wished merely to maintain it, as well as in South America. Today, this concern has become a priority, but it relates mainly to Asia.

The search for partnership: this preoccupation was constant both in Europe and regarding internationalization outside Europe: Japan, Brazil, China.

Cost-cutting measures and the reorganization of the management became prime concerns from 1992. It can be said that after an establishment stage, UAP passed on to a rationalization stage. Recent reorganization includes:

(a) Netherlands: merger of UAP Nederland and Nieuw Roterdam (formerly Vinci);
(b) Spain: merger of Iberica and two subsidiaries of Vinci;
(c) Germany: regrouping within Colonia Konzern AG (CKRAG) of the activities of Colonia and Nordstern.

In parallel, the Group organized its European management into 'European regions' which have become 'profit centres': France, CKRAG, Royale Belge, Sun Life and UAP International (for the rest).

Innovation and the redefinition of the supply of products/services: each country has an independent product strategy. In 1991, the Group created a European product, Paneurolife; the Group now considers it necessary to create other transnational products.

B. Victoria

The Group's strategic priorities in 1989 and 1995 were the following.

Rather than internationalization in the EU, priority has been given during the past five years to what the Group sees as its *natural market:*

(a) the former East German *Länder*;
(b) Austria;
(c) the Czech Republic.

In 1994, these strategic options were confirmed through the setting up of a subsidiary in the Czech Republic and the buy-out in Switzerland of the DAS company (which did not belong to the Group despite the similarity in name).

Internationalization outside Europe and the search for partnerships are undertaken via partnership agreements within IPG and INI (see Section 4.3).

Cost-cutting measures: the Group has always paid considerable attention to costs, especially in its foreign investment policy (seeking to establish itself thoroughly, but profitably, in a few countries, rather than spreading itself over a large number of countries). Since 1992, in addition, cost-cutting has become one of the Group's priority objectives.

On the other hand, the Group's strategy has been little influenced by the other possibilities proposed: the location of business activities, reorganization of the management, innovation, redefinition of the supply of products/services and effort to ward off competition.

C. Mapfre

Mapfre has endeavoured to defend its national market by adopting the following strategies:

(a) stepping up efforts to *cut costs* and increase its competitiveness;
(b) *innovation and development of new services/products:*
   • creation of a supply *of financial and banking products* (acquisition of a bank in 1989, converted into the 'Banque Mapfre' in 1990, then development of factoring and leasing units),
   • *development of new services* for the insurance clientele (telephone reception centre);
(c) *internationalization* was a major objective in 1989 and still is today. Mapfre developed (with the exception of Portugal) first in Latin America, with which the Group feels more cultural and linguistic affinities than with northern Europe (main countries of establishment: Brazil, Mexico, Puerto Rico, Argentina, Chile).

This strategic priority is still maintained today, the establishment objective being to ensure balance in the Spain/rest of the world ratio at 50%.

D. Fortis

In 1989, Amev's strategy was characterized by:

(a) the *efforts at internationalization* (in 1989, Amev's turnover was already distributed as follows: only 37% in the Netherlands, 41% in the USA, 17 % in the rest of Europe, 5% in the other regions of the world);

(b) the *cost-cutting measures* (see Chapter 11);

(c) the *innovative measures, adjustment of the range of products and services* on offer (especially from the merger with the VSB Bank), to distribute insurance and financial products through all the Group's distribution channels: banking outlets, agents and brokers.

In 1994 (and especially from the merger with AG), when the Group achieved a turnover of ECU 7.4 billion in insurance, *internationalization* is no longer considered to be a priority objective, but as an opportunity to be taken, provided it meets the following conditions: first involve one of the Group's basic business activities, and then contribute to the spread of the present activities.

The *search for partnerships* was one of the points which most marked Fortis's strategy, first internally (cooperation between banks and insurance companies), then through the creation of the Fortis Group, and finally, through the agreement signed with the Caixa in Spain.

The priorities of the present strategy of the Fortis Group include:

(a) special emphasis placed on *cost-cutting*. This is to be achieved through rationalization and the regrouping of certain administrative services, first at national level, by regrouping certain administrative services common to the banks and insurance companies;

(b) at commercial level, efforts are focused on the *optimization* (still at national level) of the existing sales systems, so that customers can buy both insurance products and financial products (*'Allfinanz'* concept) whichever company of the Group they contact. This strategy can be assimilated to both a development strategy and protection of the national market.

E. Cecar

Customer pressure led to the Group internationalizing, with the choice of countries being those where customers were developing (for example, supporting the customer Carrefour in Brazil). Internationalization by setting up subsidiaries or partnerships therefore strongly marked Cecar's strategy during the period from 1989 to 1995. The same applies to investment in skills, by recruiting increasingly specialized executives, a prerequisite to be able to cater for all the customer's requirements.

13.3. Conclusion

The undertakings' strategies have changed a great deal between 1989 and 1995, as shown in Table 13.4.

Table 13.4.   The type of strategic responses of the insurers: trends between 1989 and 1995

Decision	% of undertakings stating that their strategy was significantly influenced by the following decisions		
	1989	1995	Variation 1995/89
Internationalization of business activities in the EU	25	38	+ 13
Internationalization of business activities outside the EU	15	25	+ 10
Cost-cutting measures	66	83	+ 17
Redefinition of the supply of products/services	48	75	+ 27
Reorganization of the management	33	53	+ 20
Innovative measures	61	80	+ 19
Efforts to ward off competition	35	48	+ 13
Cross-border partnerships	20	33	+ 13
Decision concerning the location of business activities	24	40	+ 16

In decreasing order of importance, the following changes can be noted in the strategies of European insurers.

Innovation and the redefinition of the supply of products/services assumed major importance in undertakings' strategy. In 1995, 80% of the undertakings stated that their strategy included innovative measures and 75% a redefinition of the supply of products and services. This priority affects the large undertakings above all, but it must doubtless be linked to the search for competitiveness described in Chapter 12 as one of the undertakings' major concerns.

Reorganization of the management: the reorganization of certain functions: re-engineering, the re-think of organizations with fewer hierarchical echelons, the search for a more rapid reporting method, the integration of information systems in many functions of the undertaking, may be considered as contributing to the general effort to increase productivity described below.

Cost-cutting has become the major priority everywhere. The significance of this priority is shown by the fact that it now affects 83% of the undertakings of the sample group (66% in 1989), and the case studies show that each of these undertakings took specific account of this concern.

Internationalization within the EU is gaining ground. In 1989, a quarter of the undertakings of the sample group were concerned; in 1994, this percentage had risen to 38%. This effort affects both the small undertakings and the larger ones, but the most advanced in this respect are now reaching a phase of rationalization and economies, after the conquering phase.

Internationalization outside the EU is only so far affecting the large undertakings. It is true that progress is being made here too, but to a lesser extent. For the undertakings, it is often the subject of a choice between Europeanization or what may be considered as an even more natural market by the undertaking than Europe; the case studies provide us with two interesting examples: Mapfre and the choice of Latin America, Victoria and the choice of Central Europe.

The *setting up of cross-border partnerships* is developing to an increasing extent. These partnerships, if well-targeted, offer effective, rapid solutions. The Fortis Group provides the most successfully completed example: during the reference period, it signed major national partnership agreements with banks, allied with the Caixa and above all formed itself. It is in the small and medium-sized undertakings of the sample group that they are seen to have developed the fastest during the past five years. These various changes in the strategic movements may be attributed to varying degrees to the single market.

As regards *the progress of internationalization* of the undertakings within the EU, the creation of the single market had an influence especially through the awareness to which it gave rise: on the one hand, that a natural market exists around the national market in which, even if the market conditions are different, it is possible to find commercial synergies (Fortis), a critical size, or economies of scale (Mapfre in Portugal), and, on the other, that competition can now come from across frontiers.

The same is true of the *development of partnerships*, which are a means of conquering markets by seeking synergies and saving investments, which allow development on a market, while using national characteristics (distribution, know-how, regulations).

The progress of *internationalization outside the EU* seems less definitely linked to the single market. In fact, among the undertakings interviewed, those which are the most active outside the EU are those with few projects and establishments in Europe. Everything proceeds as though the European undertakings had to make a choice between their target markets and this choice, for reasons of geographical, historical or cultural proximity, is not always made in favour of Europe.

The efforts made to improve *productivity, to develop innovation* in the product field, to reorganize the range of products and services, essentially seem to be linked to the development of competition on the insurer's market. It is difficult, as stated above, to attribute all these efforts to the creation of the single market, on account of simultaneous development of all forms of competition. However, it is obvious that the single market has contributed, in part, to the awareness of insurers of this need to be more creative and in this way to acquire a competitive edge with their customers.

APPENDIX A

Methodology

A.1. Fields covered by the study

Insurance is a vast sector, covering a wide variety of trades, clienteles and types of undertakings. It is therefore appropriate to define the scope of this study.

A.1.1. Business areas

The definition of the business area covered by our study corresponds to NACE 82, which defines three major types of risks:

(a) life assurance;
(b) non-life insurance (health, accident, damage to property, etc.);
(c) endowment insurance (which comprises both the previous risks).

Under the NACE classification, reinsurance is not considered as a separate category, but included, as appropriate, under one of the above headings.

This study only covers the direct insurance industry (i.e. not reinsurance) in all the business sectors (life and non-life) and its customers: personal market and corporate market.

A.1.2. Types of undertakings

A wide variety of types of undertakings exists in the insurance sector, covering both companies with capital (joint stock companies) and mutual companies. In addition, in some countries, some of these companies belong to the public sector. The study covers all these undertakings, irrespective of their status.

A.2. Presentation of the case study undertakings

The characteristics of each of these undertakings are presented below.

A.2.1. Presentation of the five case study insurers

A. UAP (Union des Assurances de Paris, France)

UAP is a multinational group of insurance companies of European origin, controlled by the company UAP.

All the Group's direct insurance activities are grouped under five profit centres, which are: UAP France (40.7% of the Group's consolidated turnover in 1994); Colonia Konzern AG (20.7%), which encompasses the business activities in Germany and Eastern Europe; Sun Life, for life assurance in the UK (12.7%); La Royale Belge, which groups together the business activities in Benelux and Northern Europe (11.4%); UAP International, for the other countries in the world (8.2%).

The Group's cross-disciplinary activities and SCOR (reinsurance) for their part contribute 6.3% to the Group's consolidated turnover.

The Group operates in a large number of classes of insurance, covering both life and non-life activities, with a significant market share in large risks.

The leading insurance group in France, the Group is also the second largest insurance group in Europe, which is the result of a deliberate strategy, since Europe was considered from 1985 as the priority for development.

The growth of the Group in Europe was mainly effected through external growth. The main stages in this growth were:

(a) in 1987, acquisition of 40% of La Royale Belge;
(b) in 1992, acquisition of Sun Life;
(c) in 1993, acquisition of Colonia via the Vinci Group.

In 1994, the Group's total insurance amounted to ECU 20.37 billion (FF 135.7 billion).

B. Victoria (Germany)

Victoria is an insurance group comprising several companies: the life sector (Victoria Lebensversicherung AG); the non-life sector (Victoria Versicherung AG) through which Victoria has a majority holding in the legal expenses insurance company DAS (Deutscher Automobil-Schutz); health insurance (Victoria Krankenversicherung AG).

The Group's consolidated turnover amounted in 1994 to ECU 4.46 billion (DM 8.75 billion) distributed as follows among the Group's various insurance activities: life (40.8% of premiums), health insurance (6.5%), legal expenses insurance (11.1%), damage to property (8.9%), motor vehicle insurance, liability, accident (27.7%).

Its international development policy is strongly oriented towards Germany's traditional areas of influence: Austria, Czech Republic, Greece, Netherlands.

Victoria is both a medium-sized company and a company which can be described as a 'niche' player, especially for its legal expenses insurance business. In this sense, this case seemed to us to be of particular interest for this study.

C. Mapfre (Spain)

Mapfre is an independent insurance group, headed by a mutual company, Mapfre Mutualidad, the subsidiary of which, quoted on the stock exchange, Corporación Mapfre, is the holding company owning the shares of the majority of the Group's commercial companies. Mapfre Corporation's total turnover comes to ECU 1.257 billion (PTA 177.8 billion) and it operates in the following areas: personal motor insurance (it is the leading motor vehicle insurer in Spain with ECU 892 million in 1994), life assurance, and various other forms of insurance.

The Group's international development has focused mainly on Latin America, but Europe, with the exception of Portugal and a small establishment in Italy, does not yet account for a significant proportion of the Group's turnover.

D. Fortis (Belgium/Netherlands)

The Fortis Group was formed from the partnership, in 1990, between the companies AG (Compagnie Belge d'Assurances Générales), the leading Belgian insurer, and Amev/VSB, also one of the leading insurers in the Netherlands.

In 1994, the Group's total turnover came to ECU 16.3 billion and was distributed as follows among the Group's various establishments: Belgium (50% of turnover), the Netherlands (22%), the United States (18%), various other European countries (8%) and non-European countries (2%). In Belgium and the Netherlands, the Group is active in both the life and non-life sectors. In Belgium, the Group receives support from the ASLK-CGER Bank, and in the Netherlands from the VSB banking group. In the USA, the Group's activities focus mainly on health and contingency insurance and life assurance.

Finally, the Group signed a partnership agreement with the Spanish bank Caixa, to distribute life products in Spain.

This company was chosen for a case study essentially on account of its original development strategy (merger of two undertakings) in Europe and the strong use of bancassurance as a means of development.

E. Cecar (France)

Cecar is a brokerage company specializing in large risks. The breakdown of turnover by sector in 1994 was as follows: indemnity and special risks (28%), liability (25%), technical and construction risks (10%), marine, aviation and transport (16%), personal insurance (11%), motor vehicle and private individuals (10%).

With a volume of premiums of ECU 750 million (FF 5 billion), Cecar is the second largest French broker in terms of size and the tenth largest at European level.

The choice of a medium-sized continental broker (to be compared with the major international brokers of Anglo-American origin) was made to throw light on the difficulties, resources and strategies used by the intermediaries to achieve their objectives and develop in Europe.

A.3. Research methods and the information and themes analysed

To analyse the impact of the deregulation measures adopted, the following topics were analysed in turn and each formed the subject of a chapter in this report.

(a) changes in market access;
(b) the development of partnerships in the insurance industry (upstream or downstream of direct insurance);
(c) changes in the pattern of investments;
(d) changes in market concentration and competition;

(e) changes in insurers' productivity;

(f) changes in the international competitiveness of European insurers;

(g) changes in the price of insurance on the European market;

(h) the contribution of insurers to reasonable development;

(i) the impact of the single market on European insurers' costs;

(j) the impact of the single market on the strategies of insurance undertakings;

(k) the types of strategic responses.

Since the objective of the study is to ascertain, regarding all the points listed above, whether the behaviour of insurers or their results have changed as a result of the measures taken to complete the single market, it was necessary to solve a twofold problem:

(a) on the one hand, the problem of *measuring these trends*;

(b) on the other hand, *the problem of the explanation* to be given to these trends, and especially the role of the new conditions generated by the creation of the single market.

To solve the first part of this problem, it was decided:

(a) to measure the variations in the behaviour of the undertakings over a six-year period, starting in 1989, i.e. before the second and third generation Directives were translated into national legislation, then at the latest possible date, i.e. in 1995. This six-year period is referred to throughout the study as the 'reference period';

(b) to ask the undertakings interviewed to explain the variations in their behaviour or results. These explanations could include reasons associated with the existence (or absence) of Community measures, or other reasons relating to the operating characteristics of the sector or its economic environment;

(c) to make comparisons, where possible or relevant, with the situation of non-European countries, of comparable size to the European market, i.e. the USA or Japan.

A.4. The analytical model used and the presentation of the results

To present this research and interpret the results, each chapter sets out the information and discusses it according to the following plan and logic:

(a) reminder of the aims of the legislation;

(b) presentation of the hypotheses to be tested;

(c) proposed indicators to test the reality of these hypotheses;

(d) presentation of the results (indicators) deriving from the survey of 100 undertakings and explanations provided by the latter;

(e) illustration by describing the conduct and opinions of the case study undertakings;

(f) comparison of these results with secondary sources, where possible;

(g) conclusion and interpretation of all these results.

A.5. Research methods and the use of secondary sources

A.5.1. Presentation of the survey of 100 undertakings

A telephone survey of 100 European insurance undertakings was conducted in September/October 1995. The object of this survey was essentially to measure the change in behaviour and results of the undertakings over the selected reference period. In order to obtain the 1995 results (and therefore to have a five-year reference period), this survey was then updated by a second wave of measures in June 1996 involving the same undertakings. Sometimes, however, it is not possible to use the update of the results for 1995 since an insufficient number of undertakings were able to reply. In this case, our report states this clearly and we assume that the changes measured over five years (1989–94) can be considered to be sufficiently significant results.

This survey was then extended in June 1996, still using the same sample, by a series of supplementary questions designed to obtain explanations from the undertakings of the changes in their decisions, results or strategy.

The interviews were conducted by telephone (but preceded by a faxed questionnaire). The sample was constructed using the quota method, endeavouring to respect the following three criteria:

(a) size of undertakings (measured by the volume of annual premium income);
(b) country of origin;
(c) type of business activity of the undertaking.

The sample was selected from lists of undertakings and their turnover appearing either in the reports of the supervisory authorities or in the lists of trade federations in each EU Member State.

To be able to confirm the information obtained from the interviews of undertakings, the documentary sources publishing statistical data were analysed. The main official sources used (see details in the Bibliography) are:

(a) Eurostat: *Insurance in Europe* (1996);
(b) OECD: *Annuaire des statistiques d'assurances*, 1992 to 1995 editions;
(c) CEA: *L'assurance européenne en chiffres*, 1994 and 1995 editions;
(d) Supervisory authorities of the 12 Member States: latest annual reports published.

Concerning the supervisory authorities, a specific survey was addressed to them by written questionnaire in 1995 in order to gather the figures and observations on the flows of cross-border business in the insurance sector in Europe in recent years: imports and exports of insurance, preliminary data on the amount of business carried out under the freedom to provide services provision, notifications of companies stating that they would be operating under the freedom to provide services provision in another Member State.

Other sources which do not come under the concept of official publications were also consulted:

(a) Sigma (publications of the Compagnie Suisse de Réassurances);
(b) BEUC (European Bureau of Consumers' Unions);
(c) BIPAR (Bureau International des Producteurs d'Assurances et de Réassurances);
(d) *Financial Times*, and especially its studies on 'Insurance in the EC and Switzerland', 1992 and 1994, and 'The marketing and distribution of European insurance' (1995) (supervisory authorities).

The data thus collected are presented in the report under the heading 'secondary sources' to confirm, invalidate or explain the information from the survey of the sample group or the case studies.

The questionnaire submitted to the undertakings aimed:

(a) to measure the changes observed over the reference period;
(b) to explain them.

APPENDIX B

Taxation in the EU

Table B.1. **Comparison of Member States' tax arrangements governing life assurance in 1994 (percentages)**

Member State	Tax on contributions	Stamp duty	Parafiscal charges 1 2 3
Belgium	Exempt		
Denmark	Exempt		
Germany	Exempt		
Greece: contracts under 10 years	4.0	2.4	5.0
contracts over 10 years	Exempt	2.4	5.0
Spain	Exempt		
France	Exempt		
Ireland	Exempt	IRL 1 per IRL 1,000 amount insured	
Italy	2.5		
Luxembourg	Exempt		
Netherlands	Exempt		
Portugal	Exempt		1.0 – 0.1
UK	Exempt		

Source: 'Fiscalité indirecte des contrats d'assurance en Europe', CEA.

Table B.2. **Comparison of Member States' tax arrangements governing motor vehicle insurance in 1994 (percentages)**

Member State	Tax on contributions	Stamp duty	Firemen's tax	Parafiscal charges 1	2	3
Belgium						
Third party						
• cars and 2-wheel vehicles	9.25			10.00	7.50	0.25
• taxis, buses, passenger transport on behalf of third parties	9.25			5.00	7.50	0.25
Accidental damage						
• cars and 2-wheel vehicles	9.25			10.00	7.50	
• taxis, buses, passenger transport on behalf of third parties	9.25			5.00	7.50	
• legal expenses motor vehicle	9.25				7.50	
Denmark		DKR 0.25 per DKR 5,000 insured amount or 12.00% contribution[1] max DKR 8[2]				
Third party						
• lorries > 6 tonnes laden	15.00					
• buses	40					
• mopeds	DKR 230 (annual)					
• other vehicles	50					
France	18.00					
Third party	18.00			15.00	1.90	
• agricultural vehicles	Exempt			15.00	1.90	7.00
Accidental damage	18.00			FF 9	per contract	
• agricultural vehicles	Exempt			FF 9	per contract	7.00
• vehicles > 3.5 tonnes	Exempt			FF 9	per contract	
Germany	12.00					
Greece						
• all guarantees except fire	10.00	2.40		1.00	2.00	
• fire	20.00	2.40		1.00	2.00	
• third party	10.00	2.40		1.00	2.00	1.00
Ireland	2.00	IRL 1 per new contract				
Italy	12.50			1.00	6.50	1.50
Luxembourg	4.00					
Netherlands	7.00					
• vehicles registered in another EU country	Exempt					
Portugal		9	13.00	2.50	1.00	0.35 / 150 ESC
Spain						
• compulsory third party				0.50	3.00	
• voluntary third party				0.50		
• damage to vehicles				0.50		
UK	2.50					

[1] The insurer is free to choose the cheaper solution.
[2] Only applies to compulsory third-party motor insurance according to the Road Traffic Act.
Source: 'Fiscalité indirecte des contrats d'assurance en Europe', CEA.

APPENDIX C

European annual insurance statistics

Table C.1. **Trend in the exchange rate against the ECU of the currencies of Member States**

Currency	1984	1986	1988	1989	1990	1991
Belgian franc	45.44	43.80	43.43	43.38	42.43	42.22
Danish krone	8.15	7.94	7.95	8.05	7.86	7.91
German mark	2.24	2.13	2.07	2.07	2.05	2.05
Greek drachma	88.34	137.42	167.58	178.84	201.41	225.22
Portuguese escudo	115.68	147.09	170.06	173.41	181.11	178.61
French franc	6.87	6.80	7.04	7.02	6.91	6.97
Netherlands guilder	2.52	2.40	2.33	2.33	2.31	2.31
Irish punt	0.73	0.73	0.78	0.78	0.77	0.77
Luxembourg franc	45.44	43.80	43.43	43.38	42.43	42.22
Italian lira	1,381.38	1,461.87	1,537.33	1,510.47	1,521.94	1,533.23
Spanish peseta	126.57	137.46	137.60	130.41	129.32	128.47
Pound sterling	0.59	0.67	0.66	0.67	0.71	0.70

Currency	1992	1993	1994	1995
Belgian franc	41.59	40.40	40.40	38.63
Danish krone	7.81	7.61	7.60	7.28
German mark	2.02	1.97	1.96	1.88
Greek drachma	246.98	265.31	277.36	310.52
Portuguese escudo	174.70	175.10	175.06	197.08
French franc	6.85	6.66	6.66	6.47
Netherlands guilder	2.27	2.21	2.21	2.10
Irish punt	0.76	0.75	0.75	0.82
Luxembourg franc	41.59	40.40	40.40	38.63
Italian lira	1,595.29	1,701.30	1,701.40	2,079.58
Spanish peseta	132.51	141.52	141.43	159.88
Pound sterling	0.74	0.81	0.81	0.85

Source: Eurostat.

Table C.2.   Trend in consumer prices (1985 = 100)

Member State	1985	1989	1990	1991	1992	1993	1994	1995
Belgium	100	107.3	111.0	114.6	117.3	120.6	122.9	124.7
Denmark	100	118.1	121.2	124.1	126.7	128.3	131.2	133.9
Germany	100	104.2	107.0	110.7	115.1	119.9	123.1	125.3
Greece	100	184.8	222.6	265.9	308.1	352.5	390.6	426.9
Spain	100	128.2	136.8	144.9	153.5	160.5	167.4	179.8
France	100	112.7	116.5	120.2	123.1	125.6	127.6	129.7
Ireland	100	113.8	117.6	121.4	125.1	126.9	129.8	133.0
Italy	100	123.8	131.8	140.1	147.2	153.8	160.1	168.7
Luxembourg	100	105.1	109.0	112.4	115.9	120.1	122.5	124.8
Netherlands	100	101.2	103.7	107.7	110.9	113.8	116.8	119.0
Portugal	100	151.0	171.1	190.6	207.6	221.1	229.9	229.9
UK	100	121.8	133.4	141.2	146.4	148.7	153.0	153.0

Source: CEA.

Table C.3.   Significance of life assurance: gross direct premiums/GDP in the national economies of the Member States (percentages)

Member State	1984	1986	1988	1989	1990	1991	1992	1993	1994	V[1] 94/84
Belgium	1.25	1.36	1.60	1.63	1.61	1.68	1.72	1.86	2.10	0.85
Denmark	1.51	1.74	1.86	1.74	1.87	2.09	2.24	2.67	3.14	1.63
Germany	2.03	2.15	2.28	2.31	2.28	2.35	2.63	2.58	2.70	0.67
Greece	n.a.	0.35	0.48	0.57	0.67	0.77	0.88	0.96	0.82	0.47
Spain	0.24	1.30	3.83	1.89	1.09	1.40	1.38	1.68	2.45	2.21
France	1.27	1.82	2.70	3.17	3.09	3.40	3.77	4.59	5.24	3.97
Ireland	6.19	4.75	5.64	6.39	5.54	5.40	4.53	5.04	5.11	-1.08
Italy	0.27	0.40	0.58	0.61	0.66	0.74	0.83	0.97	1.13	0.86
Luxembourg	0.77	0.86	1.04	1.27	1.57	1.85	1.71	1.35	1.49	0.72
Netherlands	2.46	2.62	3.19	3.38	3.97	4.17	4.28	4.03	4.13	1.67
Portugal	0.22	0.25	0.53	0.64	0.82	0.95	1.10	1.20	1.44	1.22
UK	4.15	4.82	4.81	5.89	6.22	7.07	7.35	7.58	6.64	2.49

[1] Percentage variation.
Source: OECD.

Table C.4. **Significance of non-life insurance: gross direct premiums/GDP in the national economies of the Member States (percentages)**

Member State	1984	1986	1988	1989	1990	1991	1992	1993	1994	V[1] 94/84
Belgium	3.11	3.11	3.11	3.06	3.12	3.19	3.32	3.36	3.17	0.06
Denmark	2.33	2.49	2.77	2.76	2.69	2.48	2.58	2.61	2.59	0.26
Germany	3.45	3.46	3.63	3.63	3.44	3.69	3.82	3.73	3.82	0.37
Greece	n.a.	0.84	0.91	0.87	0.93	0.90	0.95	1.04	0.85	0.01
Spain	1.83	1.92	2.13	2.33	2.44	2.55	2.73	2.86	2.89	1.06
France	2.95	2.86	2.85	2.80	2.81	2.83	2.92	3.04	3.05	0.10
Ireland	3.79	4.44	3.88	3.58	3.82	4.17	4.23	4.04	4.26	0.47
Italy	1.70	1.78	1.81	1.88	1.94	2.04	2.18	2.25	2.24	0.54
Luxembourg	2.47	3.03	3.07	2.95	3.36	3.54	3.61	2.87	2.97	0.50
Netherlands	2.96	3.12	3.39	3.40	3.28	2.90	3.31	3.58	3.78	0.82
Portugal	2.44	2.36	2.38	2.46	2.60	2.63	2.70	2.62	2.69	0.25
UK	4.11	4.41	4.32	4.32	4.19	4.49	5.29	5.34	4.88	0.77

[1] Percentage variation.
Source: OECD.

Table C.5. **Gross premiums written in life assurance (million ECU)**

Member State	1984	1986	1988	1989	1990	1991	1992	1993	1994
Belgium	1,240	1,583	2,086	2,300	2,467	2,706	2,944	3,390	4,032
Denmark	1,115	1,520	1,795	1,741	1,919	2,209	2,473	3,101	3,858
Germany	16,990	20,790	25,154	26,749	29,451	33,125	39,888	44,983	49,929
Greece[1]	n.a.	138	216	280	350	439	531	512	655
Spain	489	3,087	11,234	6,568	4,275	6,005	6,164	7,263	9,883
France	8,790	14,258	22,885	28,670	30,252	34,085	39,912	50,371	59,588
Ireland	1,392	1,234	1,587	2,003	1,877	1,896	2,011	2,415	2,220
Italy	1,887	3,132	5,056	5,992	6,993	8,408	9,604	10,476	10,827
Luxembourg[2]	33	44	60	83	111	140	140	144	174
Netherlands	4,126	5,058	6,600	7,364	9,279	10,235	11,150	11,558	12,676
Portugal	55	76	186	263	382	527	717	947	1,043
UK[1]	22,814	27,607	34,203	45,230	48,142	57,733	59,068	58,664	56,388
Total EUR-12	**58,930**	**78,526**	**111,062**	**127,241**	**135,499**	**157,507**	**174,601**	**193,822**	**211,271**

[1] Net premiums written.
[2] Gross direct premiums written.
Source: OECD, figures in national currency converted using Table C.1.

Table C.6. Gross premiums written in non-life insurance (million ECU)

Member State	1984	1986	1988	1989	1990	1991	1992	1993	1994
Belgium	3,467	3,930	4,329	4,588	5,169	5,550	6,017	6,339	6,259
Denmark	1,765	2,249	3,079	3,208	3,482	3,489	3,957	3,806	4,274
Germany	29,431	32,791	38,400	40,729	42,431	49,236	71,942	81,869	90,408
Greece[1]	n.a.	336	409	428	488	511	571	520	725
Spain	3,785	4,806	6,610	8,524	10,025	11,544	12,902	13,208	12,408
France	23,398	25,964	28,112	29,003	31,529	33,377	36,944	40,859	39,788
Ireland	881	1,195	1,154	1,194	1,340	1 526	1,657	1,853	1,932
Italy	10,683	12,681	14,840	16,933	19,076	21,772	23,933	23,797	21,619
Luxembourg[2]	105	155	177	193	238	267	295	307	347
Netherlands	5,619	6,697	7,780	8,255	8,624	8,095	9,603	10,835	12,247
Portugal	638	732	868	1,034	1,251	1,487	1,784	2,101	1,984
UK[1]	22,568	25,243	30,753	33,113	32,420	36,713	42,524	41,349	41,419
Total EUR-12	102,340	116,778	136,512	147,203	156,074	173,566	212,129	226,844	233,410

[1] Net premiums written.
[2] Gross direct premiums written.
Source: OECD.

Table C.7. Population of the Member States ('000 inhabitants)

Member State	1989	1990	1991	1992	1993	1994
Belgium	9,938	9,967	10,005	10,045	10,010	10,116
Denmark	5,133	5,141	5,154	5,171	5,190	5,206
Germany	78,677	79,365	79,984	80,595	81,180	81,407
Greece	10,038	10,089	10,200	10,300	10,350	10,426
Spain	38,888	38,959	39,025	39,085	39,140	39,150
France	56,423	56,735	57,055	57,374	57,667	57,960
Ireland	3,515	3,503	3,524	3,547	3,560	3,571
Italy	56,705	56,737	56,760	56,859	57,070	57,190
Luxembourg	377	380	386	390	385	398
Netherlands	14,849	14,951	15,070	15,184	15,300	15,382
Portugal	9,891	9,877	9,862	9,858	9,860	9,900
UK	57,236	57,411	57,801	57,998	57,830	58,375
Total EUR-12	341,670	343,115	344,826	346,406	347,542	349,081

Source: National accounts, Vol 1. 1960–93, OECD.

Table C.8.   Expenditure on life assurance per inhabitant, 1989–94 (ECU)

Member State	1989	1990	1991	1992	1993	1994
Belgium	231	248	270	293	339	393
Denmark	339	373	429	478	597	738
Germany	340	371	414	495	554	565
Greece	28	35	43	52	50	63
Spain	169	110	154	158	186	252
France	508	533	597	696	873	1,001
Ireland	570	536	538	567	678	621
Italy	106	123	148	169	184	168
Luxembourg	219	293	362	358	374	438
Netherlands	496	621	679	734	755	748
Portugal	27	39	53	73	96	105
UK	790	839	999	1,018	1,014	966
EUR-12 average	**372**	**395**	**457**	**504**	**558**	**605**

Source: OECD.

Table C.9.   Expenditure on non-life insurance per inhabitant, 1989–94 (ECU)

Member State	1989	1990	1991	1992	1993	1994
Belgium	462	519	555	599	633	595
Denmark	625	677	677	765	733	609
Germany	518	535	616	893	1,008	800
Greece	43	48	50	55	50	65
Spain	219	257	296	330	337	297
France	514	556	585	644	709	583
Ireland	340	383	433	467	521	518
Italy	299	336	384	421	417	333
Luxembourg	511	626	692	756	797	871
Netherlands	556	577	537	632	708	685
Portugal	105	127	151	181	213	197
UK	579	565	635	733	715	709
EUR-12 average	**431**	**455**	**503**	**612**	**653**	**669**

Source: OECD.

Table C.10. Total expenditure on insurance (life + non-life) per inhabitant, 1990–94 (ECU)

Member State	1990	1991	1992	1993	1994	1994/90 (%)
Austria	798	849	943	1,074	1,127	41.2
Belgium	736	795	874	944	1,040	41.2
Denmark	893	940	1,039	1,172	1,213	35.8
Germany	1,061	954	1,078	1,198	1,329	25.3
Greece	78	91	102	117	125	60.7
Spain	335	414	444	429	531	58.8
Finland	1,393	1,263	989	1,002	1,162	-16.6
France	1,035	1,133	1,311	1,536	1,744	68.5
Ireland	886	925	907	993	1,062	20.0
Italy	391	457	461	461	486	24.1
Luxembourg	911	989	2,162	9,926	3,707	307.0
Netherlands	1,183	1,282	1,410	1,493	1,630	37.8
Portugal	161	199	250	271	324	100.8
UK	1,387	1,568	1,597	1,801	1,655	19.4
Sweden	997	988	1,008	1,19	950	-4.7
EUR-15 average	**816**	**856**	**972**	**1,096**	**1,206**	**47.8**

Source: CEA.

Table C.11.a. Number of insurance company employees per 1000 of the working population

Member State	1990	1991	1992	1993	1994	1994/90
Austria	8.0	8.0	8.0	8.9	8.7	8.1
Belgium	7.1	6.9	6.6	6.3	6.1	-14.9
Denmark	5.0	5.1	4.9	4.9	4.8	-2.9
Germany	7.7	8.2	8.4	8.3	8.1	5.5
Greece	n.a.	n.a.	2.5	2.5	2.5	2.3 (94/92)
Spain	2.8	2.9	3.0	3.0	3.0	7.2
Finland	4.9	4.9	4.8	4.7	4.5	-8.4
France	5.0	5.0	4.9	4.8	4.8	-8.4
Ireland	7.4	7.3	7.4	7.3	7.2	-3.7
Italy	1.9	1.9	2.0	2.1	2.1	9.9
Luxembourg	5.5	6.7	6.2	6.8	7.3	32.6
Netherlands	5.7	5.6	6.3	6.7	6.6	16.2
Portugal	3.1	2.9	3.1	3.0	2.9	-6.0
UK	9.2	9.5	9.4	9.4	9.6	4.6
Sweden	4.6	4.7	4.9	4.7	4.5	-4.1
EUR-15 average	**5.2**	**5.3**	**5.5**	**5.6**	**5.5**	**n.a.**

Source: CEA.

Table C.11.b. Employment in European insurance (by number of employees)

Member State	1990	1995	1995/90
Austria	28,234	32,346	14.6%
Belgium	29.818	25,501	-14.5%
Denmark	14,115	15,000	6.3%
Germany	233,200	145,600	6.3%
Greece[1]	10,000	9,600	-4.0%
Finland	12,700	10,770	-15.2%
France	123,400	121,800	-1.3%
Ireland	9,705	10,386	7.0%
Italy	46,558	48,616	-0.1%
Luxembourg	1,051	1,349	28.4%
Netherlands	38,900	40,000	2.8%
UK[1]	263,800	209,400	-20.8%
Spain	42,895	47,760	11.3%
Sweden	21,262	18,800	-11.6%
EUR-15	**875,638**	**834,828**	**-4.7%**

Source: CEA.

Table C.12. Productivity: total gross direct premiums per employee (ECU)

Member State	1989	1990	1991	1992	1993	1994
Belgium	227,456	256,115	283,533	320,975	360,266	385,131
Denmark	361,219	391,360	398,478	449,675	471,070	467,470
Germany	319,651	328,869	324,377	438,292	498,465	439,038
Greece[1]	76,205	88,224	102,135	110,181	51,608	138,562
Spain	387,283	333,377	379,074	407,349	459,307	467,633
France	468,886	500,656	544,927	620,812	747,786	752,087
Ireland	350,340	347,471	348,551	362,434	423,203	390,735
Italy	498,358	562,709	637,377	695,031	712,294	611,366
Luxembourg	272,540	317,635	350,871	364,887	373,439	407,574
Netherlands	290,314	327,287	326,736	354,750	n.a.	n.a.
Portugal	91,133	110,946	142,064	167,443	208,894	213,703
UK[1]	301,552	305,970	388,826	390,738	373,464	442,500
EUR-12	**338,687**	**352,398**	**380,118**	**444,020**	**476,395**	**541,615**

[1] On the basis of net premiums.
Source: OECD.

Table C.13. Number of insurance undertakings

Member State	Life assurance undertakings		Non-life insurance undertakings		Composite insurance undertakings		Specialist reinsurance undertakings	
	Total...	...of which branches of third countries	Total...	...of which branches of third countries	Total...	...of which branches of third countries	Total...	...of which branches of third countries
Austria	6	1	22	3	34	0	62	4
Belgium	32	1	96	9	47	3	175	12
Denmark	85	1	165	12	–	–	250	6
Germany	120	4	334	10	–	–	454	32
Greece[1]	20	2	102	45	26	1	148	0
Finland	12	0	148	2	–	–	160	12
France	138	6	356	23	–	–	494	20
Ireland	22	2	53	1	–	–	75	n.a.
Italy	72	2	128	6	24	0	224	8
Luxembourg	36	2	23	3	1	0	60	213
Netherlands[2]	95	5	290	29	–	–	385	8
Portugal	16	2	23	1	8	0	47	1
Spain[3]	507	3	264	3	76	1	847	5
Sweden[4]	29	0	109	2	–	–	138	6
UK[1]	191	18	573	125	57	7	764	47
EUR 15	1,381	49	2,686	274	273	12	4,283	374

[1] The number of branches also includes branches of undertakings with head offices in the EEA.
[2] Excluding about 270 local mutuals.
[3] Including about 440 social benefit institutions, non-profit-making accounting for about 15% of the life assurance market.
[4] Excluding 330 local non-life insurance undertakings.
Source: CEA.

Table C.14. Number of insurance undertakings with a distinction between life and non-life

Member State	1989			1994			Variation 94/89		
	Life	Composite	Non-life	Life	Composite	Non-life	Life	Composite	Non-life
Belgium	33	59	175	31	47	93	-2	-12	-82
Denmark	26	0	181	85	0	159	59	0	-22
Germany	354	0	404	319	0	334	-35	0	-70
Greece	10	35	105	20	26	102	10	-9	-3
Spain	62	61	382	508	75	278	446	14	-104
France	137	0	450	138	0	356	1	0	-94
Ireland	29	0	43	34	0	82	5	0	39
Italy	51	27	164	76	24	155	25	-3	-9
Luxembourg	24	5	26	39	3	34	15	-2	8
Netherlands	93	0	700	94	0	654	1	0	-46
Portugal	13	14	37	29	10	55	16	-4	18
UK	206	64	563	191	57	574	-15	-7	11

Source: OECD.

Table C.15. Gross direct premiums by origin of issuing undertaking (million ECU)

Member State	Life					Non-life				
	89	91	93	94	V[1]	89	91	93	94	V[1]
Belgium										
National undertakings	2,119	2,472	3,071	3,627	71.2	3,770	4,564	5,597	5,777	53.2
Undertakings of another Member State	24	25	45	n.a.	n.a.	266	260	242	n.a.	n.a.
Other	137	172	236	328	139.5	212	229	166	176	-17.2
Total premiums issued within territory	2,279	2,669	3,353	3,955	73.5	4,248	5,054	6,004	5,953	40.1
Premiums issued abroad	18	41	66	58	222.2	671	947	1,249	1,261	87.9
Denmark										
National undertakings	1,615	2,147	3,040	3,830	137	2,494	2,566	2,812	3,067	22.9
Undertakings of another Member State	n.a.	n.a.	n.a.	n.a.	n.a.	n.a.	n.a.	n.a.	n.a.	n.a.
Other	n.a.	n.a.	n.a.	n.a.	n.a.	n.a.	n.a.	n.a.	n.a.	n.a.
Total premiums issued within territory	1,655	2,200	3,093	3,856	132.9	2,630	2,617	3,023	3,185	21.1
Premiums issued abroad	0	0	0	0	n.a.	32	48	47	49	53.1
France										
National undertakings	27,303	32,188	48,013	57,403	110.2	23,438	26,409	31,336	33,250	41.8
Undertakings of another Member State	n.a.	n.a.	n.a.	n.a.	n.a.	n.a.	n.a.	n.a.	n.a.	n.a.
Other	n.a.	n.a.	n.a.	n.a.	n.a.	n.a.	n.a.	n.a.	n.a.	n.a.
Total premiums issued within territory	27,850	32,870	48,813	58,009	108.2	24,548	27,383	32,396	33,778	37.6
Premiums issued abroad	119	138	101	84	-29.4	15,470[2]	12,985	16,704	12,193	-21.1
Germany										
National undertakings	20,413	26,183	33,802	37,981	86	32,084	41,303	49,686	58,582	82.6
Undertakings of another Member State	1,617	1,908	2,395	2,565	58.6	4,264	2,207	4,595	4 242	-0.5
Other	1,591	2,240	2,703	2,298	44.4	2,011	4,308	5,549	2,789	38.68
Total premiums issued within territory	23,620	30,331	38,091	42,844	81.3	38,359	47,818	59,830	65,613	71
Premiums issued abroad	24	39	53	n.a.	121	456	469	519	n.a.	13.8
Greece										
National undertakings	n.a.	n.a.	465	519	n.a.	n.a.	n.a.	577	631	n.a.
Undertakings of another Member State	n.a.	n.a.	n.a.	n.a.	n.a.	n.a.	n.a.	n.a.	n.a.	n.a.
Other	n.a.	n.a.	n.a.	n.a.	n.a.	n.a.	n.a.	n.a.	n.a.	n.a.
Total premiums issued within territory	n.a.	n.a.	609	685	n.a.	n.a.	n.a.	656	707	n.a.

Table C.15. Gross direct premiums by origin of issuing undertaking (million ECU) *(continued)*

Member State	Life					Non-life				
	89	91	93	94	V[1]	89	91	93	94	V[1]
Ireland										
National undertakings	*1,435*	*1,275*	*1,659*	*1,812*	*26*	*686*	*927*	*1,243*	1,469	*114.1*
Undertakings of another Member State	n.a.	n.a.	n.a.	n.a.	n.a.	n.a.	n.a.	n.a.	n.a.	n.a.
Other	n.a.	n.a.	n.a.	n.a.	n.a.	n.a.	n.a.	n.a.	n.a.	n.a.
Total premiums issued within territory	*2,000*	*1,895*	*2,188*	*2376*	*18.8*	*1,122*	*1,464*	*1,753*	1,981	*76.5*
Premiums issued abroad	*101*	*142*	*181*	*152*	*50.5*	*56*	*52*	*91*	86	*53.6*
Italy										
National undertakings	4,755	6,792	8,737	10,727	125.6	14,111	18,164	19,771	20,782	47.3
Undertakings of another Member State	24	16	38	n.a.	n.a.	284	437	444	n.a.	n.a.
Other	75	104	126	163	117.6	416	416	421	397	-4.7
Total premiums issued within territory	4,854	6,912	8,901	10,890	124.3	14,811	19,017	20,637	21,178	43.0
Premiums issued abroad	163	232	194	92	-43.6	471	646	963	900	91.1
Luxembourg										
National undertakings	*40*	*114*	125.8	155.7	289.2	*135*	*211*	267.1	277.5	105
Undertakings of another Member State	n.a.	n.a.	12.0	9.9	n.a.	n.a.	n.a.	33.7	27.3	n.a.
Other	n.a.	n.a.	6.3	7.3	n.a.	n.a.	n.a.	34.3	39.6	n.a.
Total premiums issued within territory	*83*	*140*	144.1	172.9	109.2	*193*	*267*	335.2	344.4	78.4
Netherlands										
National undertakings	*6,694*	*9,584*	*10,805*	*11,815*	*76.5*	*7,677*[2]	*7,286*	*9,870*	11,117	*44.8*
Undertakings of another Member State	n.a.	n.a.	n.a.	n.a.	n.a.	n.a.	n.a.	n.a.	n.a.	n.a.
Other	n.a.	n.a.	n.a.	n.a.	n.a.	n.a.	n.a.	n.a.	n.a.	n.a.
Total premiums issued within territory	*7,364*	*10,235*	*11,558*	*12,526*	*70*	*8,590*[2]	*7,760*	*1,0458*	11,916	*38.7*
Premiums issued abroad	*2,189*	*3,575*	*6,497*	n.a.	*196.8*	*3,219*	*6,520*	*6,696*	n.a.	*108.0*
Portugal										
National undertakings	161	395	824	1,116	591.7	922	1,353	1,912	2,140	132.2
Undertakings of another Member State	87	111	73	27	-68.8	79	97	138	62	-21.1
Other	15	21	48	42	190.4	8	10	12	15	96.7
Total premiums issued within territory	263	527	946	1,186	350.9	1,008	1,460	2,063	2,217	120.0
Premiums issued abroad	13	0	0	0	-100	8	8	11	13	62.5

Table C.15. Gross direct premiums by origin of issuing undertaking (million ECU)
(continued)

Member State	Life					Non-life				
	89	91	93	94	V[1]	89	91	93	94	V[1]
Spain										
National undertakings	6,148	5,625	5,865	9,461	53.9	7,347	10,066	11,519	12,249	66.7
Undertakings of another Member State	92	139	163	204	120.7	258	290	224	231	-10.5
Other	286	206	178	526	83.7	433	531	567	656	51.5
Total premiums issued within territory	6,526	5,970	6,206	10,190	56.1	8,038	10,887	12,310	13,136	63.4
Premiums issued abroad	26	10	22	32	23.1	119	43	40	82	-31.1
UK										
National undertakings	*42,490*	*55,016*	*57,375*	*58,830*	*38.4*	*31,745*	*35,267*	*39,360*	41,106	*29.4*
Undertakings of another Member State	n.a.	n.a.	n.a.	n.a.	n.a.	n.a.	n.a.	n.a.	n.a.	n.a.
Other	n.a.	n.a.	n.a.	n.a.	n.a.	n.a.	n.a.	n.a.	n.a.	n.a.
Total premiums issued within territory	*45,230*	*57,733*	*58,664*	*60,105*	*32.8*	*33,113*	*36,713*	*41,349*	44,008	*32.9*
Premiums issued abroad	*9,433*	*10,711*	*11,609*	14,243	*50.9*	*17,524*	*12,731*	*14,714*	n.a.	*-16.0*
Total EU										
Total[3] national undertakings	113,173	141,791	173,317	197,276	74.3	124,409	148,116	173,373	19,0447	53.1
Total[3] premiums issued within territory	121,724	151,482	181,957	206,794	69.8	136,660	160,440	190,158	20,3796	49.1
Total[4] premiums issued abroad	12,086	14,888	18,723	n.a.	54.9	38,026	34,449	41,034	n.a.	7.9

[1] Percentage variation 94–89 (where 1994 data not available, 93–89).
[2] 1990 figures.
[3] Except Greece.
[4] Except Luxembourg and Greece.
Source: figures in roman: supervisory authorities; *figures in italic: OECD.*

Table C.16. Turnover of ten leading European insurance undertakings in 1994: non-life insurance (million ECU)

Undertaking	Country	Turnover
Allianz	Germany	5,042
UAP	France	4,511
AXA	France	3,387
Groupama	France	3,296
AGF	France	3,144
Sun Alliance	UK	2,698
Commercial Union	UK	2,399
DKV	Germany	2,310
General Accident	UK	2,194
Royal	UK	2,184

Source: CEA.

Table C.17.   Turnover of the leading ten European insurance undertakings in 1994: life assurance (million ECU)

Undertaking	Country	Turnover
CNP	France	10,557
Predica	France	7,033
Allianz	Germany	5,659
UAP	France	4,815
Standard Life	UK	4,460
Prudential	UK	4,314
GAN	France	3,266
AGF	France	3,175
Sun Life	UK	2,812
Hamburg-Mannh.	Germany	2,494

Source: CEA.

Table C.18.   Trend in consumer prices for EUR-15 and the USA (1989=100)

	1989	1990	1991	1992	1993	1994	1995
EUR-15	100	104.8	110.66	115.64	120.15	124	127.72
USA	100	105	109	112	114.7	117.5	120.3

Source: CEA.

APPENDIX D

Questionnaire submitted to the undertakings interviewed

	The scale of their development during the reference period (conduct, strategies, results)	The explanations for these developments
Changes in market access (Chapter 3)	• How many subsidiaries did your undertaking (group) own in the EU in 1989, then in 1995? • How many branches did your undertaking own in the EU in 1989, then in 1995? What was the turnover of these branches in 1989, then in 1994? • In which countries does your undertaking currently operate under the freedom to provide services? What was the turnover in 1989 and in 1995? • In which countries did your undertaking engage in co-insurance in 1989, then in 1995? What turnover was recorded? • Ditto for fronting operations?	• What are the reasons behind your undertaking not being present in (at least) one other European country? • What are the reasons behind your undertaking opting for subsidiaries rather than branches? • Do you think that your undertaking will change its strategy in the next three years (1996-99) and will develop more branches in the EU? • If so, or if not, for which reasons? • Why does your undertaking not use the freedom to provide services (or not use it more)? • Among the following reasons, which, in your opinion, explain why your undertaking does not use the freedom to provide services more to develop in the EU? • Do you think that your undertaking's strategy in relation to the freedom to provide services will change in the coming years? • Why? • Does your undertaking currently sell insurance products in other EU countries through national independent intermediaries (brokers or agents)? If so, which products are involved? If not, why not?
The development of partnership (Chapter 4)	To analyse the existence or the development of this trend among European insurers, the 100 undertakings of the sample group were asked the following questions: • did such agreements exist in their undertaking in 1989, then in 1995? • which types of agreement were involved? • with which other EU country?	• For those which have concluded partnership agreements in the EU: did you already have an establishment in the target country? • What led to you concluding these agreements? • Can you describe the partnership agreements you set up?

	The scale of their development during the reference period (conduct, strategies, results)	The explanations for these developments
Changes in the pattern of investments (Chapter 5)	European undertakings were asked the following questions to measure any change in their conduct in the investment field: What proportion of their technical reserves did they invest in 1989, then in 1995 • in their home country • in another Member State of the EU? • elsewhere in the world? In the case of investments in Europe, in which Member State were these reserves invested? Which type of investments were involved (first in 1989, then in 1995)? What were the reasons for a change in strategy (if any)? The questions asked only concerned the technical reserves.	• Has your undertaking changed the type of its investments (asset categories) over the past five years? (Yes/No) • Which of the following reasons had an influence on these changes? • Why, in your opinion, does your undertaking not currently invest more of its technical reserves in other EU countries? • Do you think that this strategy adopted by your undertaking may change in the near future? Why would this be?
Changes in concentration and competition (Chapter 6)	To measure the perception which the undertakings could have of the development of the market and its degree of competition, they were asked to indicate, on a scale of 0 to 3, whether or not they agreed with the following propositions (0 indicating that they did not agree at all, 3 indicating on the contrary total agreement). **Propositions** • Owing to insufficient size or performance, the number of insurance undertakings closing down has increased; • New entrants have appeared on my national market; • There have been changes in foreign investment, fewer mergers/acquisitions, more new undertakings set up; • Undertakings have endeavoured to cut their general operating expenses in order to improve their competitiveness; • Undertakings' results have improved in terms of profitability; • In my country, the degree of concentration of the undertakings in the insurance business has increased; • There has been concentration in the insurance business at European level; • There has been concentration at world level; • Some Member States adopt protectionist attitudes, especially by granting government aid to their national undertakings; • The insurers' federations and associations have developed protectionist behaviour.	No specific questions

	The scale of their development during the reference period (conduct, strategies, results)	The explanations for these developments
Trend in productivity of undertakings (Chapter 7)	To conduct the analysis for this chapter, the undertakings interviewed were asked to indicate the following figures for 1989, and then for 1995: • the total volume of premium income; • the number of employees; • the volume of capital; • the net profit of their undertaking (the average premiums per employee and profit to own capital ratios were then derived).	Since 1989, the 'net profit/capital' ratio of your undertaking has improved/remained stable/deteriorated (depending on the case); in your opinion, what is the main reason for this trend? Since 1989, the 'premium income per employee' ratio of your undertaking has improved/remained stable/deteriorated (depending on the case); what in your opinion is the main reason for this trend?
The international competitiveness of European insurance undertakings (Chapter 8)	To analyse this subject, the following questions were put to the undertakings interviewed: • how many subsidiaries did their group own outside Europe first in 1989, then in 1995? • what was the trend in their turnover? • how many branches did their group have outside Europe, first in 1989, then in 1995? • what was the trend in their turnover? • in how many different (non-European) countries did they sell their products, first in 1989, then in 1995?	What, in your opinion, explains the fact that your group has recently developed abroad outside the EU? What, in your opinion, explains the fact that your group has not recently developed abroad outside the EU?
Price movements (Chapter 9)	The interviewees were asked the following questions to measure and understand the price changes: • were efforts made in their group, in 1989 (then in 1995) to sell identical insurance products in several EU countries? • if there was a change (between 1989 and 1995) what were the reasons for this? • in 1989 (then in 1995) was the group concerned to unify the scales and conditions of similar products in Europe? • if so why, if not why not?	Since 1989, what has been the change in your prices (in %) for the basic contract for the following products: • personal motor vehicle • homeowner's comprehensive policy • personal life assurance
Contribution to reasonable development (Chapter 10)	To measure whether a development in demand had been felt by European insurers in the field of environmental risks, they were asked: • whether they had developed insurance products covering environmental risks? • if so, why?	Among the reasons for your undertaking developing such products, could you tell me whether the following reasons apply to your undertaking: • no demand on the part of policyholders; • no regulations in this country; • regulations too stringent ('claims made'); • difficulty in finding the financial capacity or partners (pools); • potential profit insufficient; • lack of expertise in the company in this type of risk; • not concerned (does not cover large risks in non-life).

	The scale of their development during the reference period (conduct, strategies, results)	The explanations for these developments
Impact of the single market on insurers' costs (Chapter 11)	To establish a quantitative assessment of the trend in costs of undertakings during the past five years, the undertakings interviewed were asked to indicate: • their general operating expenses ratio in 1989 • how this ratio had changed in 1995? • which business functions were the subject of the greatest productivity gains over the past five years and why? • whether they had made any efforts over the past five years to regroup any of their functions at European level. Which and why?	No specific questions
Impact of the single market on the strategies of the undertakings (Chapter 12)	The 100 undertakings were asked about the extent to which, in 1989, then in 1995, the following factors influenced their strategy: • the strength of their competitors; • the fear of possible new entrants on the market; • the possible appearance of substitute products or services; • the volume of the investments necessary to become competitive; • the pressure of certain major customers or suppliers.	No specific questions
The types of strategic responses (Chapter 13)	The 100 undertakings were asked whether in 1989, then in 1995, their undertaking's strategy had been affected by the following decisions: • internationalization of business activities within the EU; • internationalization of business activities outside the EU; • cost-cutting measures; • redefinitions of the supply of products/services; • reorganization of the management; • innovative measures; • efforts to ward off competition; • cross-border partnerships; • decision concerning the location of business activities; (by allocating a score of 0 to 3, 0 indicating that this priority had not been important, 3 on the contrary meaning considerable importance).	No specific questions

Bibliography

(a)   European Community publications

European Commission (1985), 'Completing the Internal Market', COM (85) 310 final, Luxembourg, Office for Official Publications of the EC.

European Commission (1988), *The cost of non-Europe in financial services*, Luxembourg, Office for Official Publications of the EC.

European Commission (1993), 'Market services and European integration: the challenges for the 1990s', *European Economy/Social Europe,* Reports and studies No. 3, Luxembourg, Office for Official Publications of the EC.

European Commission (1994), *The Community internal market,* 1993 report (2 vols), Luxembourg, Office for Official Publications of the EC.

European Commission (1994), *Panorama of EU industry 94*, Luxembourg, Office for Official Publications of the EC.

European Commission (1994), *Internal market: Current status 1 July 1994,* Vol. 1: 'A common market for services', Vol. 2: The elimination of frontier controls', Vol. 3: 'Conditions for business cooperation', Vol. 4: 'A new Community standards policy', Luxembourg, Office for Official Publications of the EC.

European Commission (1994), *XXIIIrd Annual Report on Competition Policy 1993,* Luxembourg, Office for Official Publications of the EC.

(b)   Publications of enforcement authorities

Belgium

Office de contrôle des assurances (1995), *Rapport annuel 1993-1994*; (1995), *Rapport annuel 1993-1994, Statistiques et Annexes.*

Denmark

Finanstilsynet (1994), 'Livforsikringsselskaber m.v.', *Statistisk Materiale 1993*; (1994) 'Skadesforsikringsselskaber', *Statistisk Materiale 1993.*

France

Commission de contrôle des assurances (1994), *Résultats comptables des entreprises d'assurance et de capitalisation, exercice 1993*; (1994), *Tableaux de synthèse, exercice 1993.*

Germany

Bundesaufsichtsamt für das Versicherungswesen (1994), *Geschäftsbericht 1993.*

Ireland

Department of Enterprise and Employment (1994), *Insurance Annual Report 1993.*

Italy

Rapporto sull'attività dell'Istituto nell'anno 1993 (1994), ISVAP, Vols. 1 and 2.

Luxembourg

Commissariat aux assurances (1994), *Rapport annuel pour l'année 1993.*

Netherlands

Verzekeringskamer (1994), *Financiële gegevens levensverzekeraars 1993.*

Portugal

Instituto de Seguros de Portugal (1994), *Actividade Seguradora em Portugal 1992,* Vol. 2;
(1995), *Actividade Seguradora em Portugal 1993,* Vol. 1.

Spain

Ministerio de Economía y Hacienda (1995), *Memoria Estadística 1993*; (1994), *Información Trimestral 1-1-94 a 31-12-94,* Boletín 4/1994; (1995), *Información Trimestral 1-1-95 a 31-3-95,* Boletín 1/1995.

UK

Department of Trade and Industry (1994), *Insurance Annual Report 1993.*

(c)   Publications of the European Insurance Association

Codification CEA des directives européennes sur l'assurance, France, 1994;
L'assurance européenne en chiffres 1993, France, 1994.

(d)   Publications of professional associations

Belgium

Union professionnelle des entreprises d'assurances (1995), *L'assurance en Belgique: rapport d'activité 1994.*

Denmark

Assurandoer-Societetet (1995), *Arsberetning 1994–95.*
Danish Insurance Information Service (1995), *The Danish Insurance Industry in figures and graph.*

France

Fédération française des sociétés d'assurances (1994), *L'assurance française en 1993*; (1995), *L'assurance française en 1994.*

Germany

Gesamtverband der Deutschen Versicherungswirtschaft (1995), *Die deutsche Versicherungswirtschaft Jahrbuch 1994*; (1995), *German Insurance Indicators 1994.*

Greece

Association of Insurance Companies (1995), *Private Insurance in Greece during 1993.*

Ireland

Irish Insurance Federation (1994), *Irish Insurance Federation FactFile*.

Italy

Associazione nazionale fra le imprese assicuratrici (1994), *L'assicurazione italiana nel 1993*.

Luxembourg

Association des compagnies d'assurances agréées au Grand-Duché de Luxembourg (1994), *Chiffres clés sur l'Assurance 1994*.

Netherlands

Verbond van Verzekeraars (1995), *Verzekerd van Cijfers 1995* (Dutch Insurance Industry in figures 1995); (1995), *Verbond van Verzekeraars Jaaroverzicht 1993*.

Spain

Unión Española de Entidades Aseguradoras y Reaseguradoras (1994), *Estadística de Seguros Privados: Información estadística del Seguro Privado*.

United Kingdom

Association of British Insurers, *Insurance Statistics Year Book 1983–1993*; *Insurance Review Statistics 1989–1993*.

(e)   Other sources

La distribution de l'assurance en Europe, CAPA, 1993.

'Insurance in the EU and Switzerland, the completion of the single insurance market?', *Financial Times* (1994), London.

Turner, David (1995), *Direct Insurance in Europe, The Ongoing Revolution,* Data Monitor, London.

Publications SIGMA, Zürich, 1994 and 1995.

Publications du Journal de l'Assurance, France, 1989 to 1994.

Publications de l'Argus, France, 1989 to 1995.

Europe Insurance Market, Lloyds of London Press Ltd, London, 1992 to 1995.

'L'heure de l'Europe', *Les cahiers de l'assurance,* 1991, No. 8, Revue Risques, France.

'L'assurance dans le monde', *Les cahiers de l'assurance,* 1995, No. 22, Revue Risques, France.